RURAL INDUSTRIALISATION IN KERALA

Rural Industrialisation in Kerala

Its dynamics and local linkages

MRIDUL EAPEN

MANOHAR
2001

First published in India 2001

ISBN 81-7304-359-0

Published by
Ajay Kumar Jain for
Manohar Publishers & Distributors
4753/23 Ansari Road, Daryaganj
New Delhi 110002

Printed at
Nice Printing Press
3-B, Rashid Market Extn.
Delhi 110051

Acknowledgments

I would like to acknowledge my deep gratitude to Prof. J. G. Waardenburg and the late Dr. T. N. Krishnan who took the initiative and gave me sufficient encouragement to pursue this area of Rural Industrialisation for my doctoral thesis. Later, Prof. Chandan Mukerjee's support and guidance were very valuable.

My own colleagues in the Centre were very helpful, being always willing to discuss parts of my work, among whom Dr. D. Narayana, Dr. Omkarnath, Dr. K. K. Subramanian, Dr. Michael Tharakan and Dr. Achin Chakravarty need special mention. Prof. K. Nagaraj of the Madras Institute of Development Studies who's own interest in the area, provided me with very critical inputs in the early stages of my writing. At the Centre for Development Planning, Erasmus University, Rotterdam, I had very fruitful discussions with Dr. Pete Terhal, Dr. Servaas Storm And Dr. Ro Naastepad.

G. L. Deepa assisted me with great patience in the enormous data work which had to be done and helped me in its processing too;in the later stages Mr. S. Suresh also helped out. Some of my younger colleagues, in particular Mr. M. Suresh Babu and Mr. Hari Kurup, rendered me great help with the data. Ms. Anita E. John of the Process House undertook the management of the field data, its programming and presentation in tabular form.

Among the officials, I receieved tremendous cooperation from the Director of Industries and the Directorate, Manager of the District Industries Centre, Trivandrum and Palakkad, Manager and senior officers at the National Bank for Agriculture and Rural Development (NABARD), Trivandrum. Two officials who helped and guided me very much with my field work were Mr. Sayeed Ali of the NABARD office in Palakkad and Mr. Sunil, who was the Development Officer in Kollengode Block. They spent a lot of time in helping out with my survey work. I would like to thank all the entrepreneurs who co-operated with me in providing the information I needed. The friendly and helpful atmosphere during the survey in the two blocks made the whole exercise very fruitful and pleasant.

In the Centre for Development Studies, I would like to thank all the support staff in the library and office who facilitated my work. Similarly I received tremendous help at the office and library of the Centre for Development Planning in Rotterdam, which made my working there very cordial. Ms. Christine Brittijn's help in the last year proved very valuable in running this long- distance project smoothly.

I would like to thank in particular the Erasmus University, Rotterdam which made it possible for me to do my Ph.D and the Ministry of Foreign Affairs, Directorate General for International Cooperation, without whose financial assistance via the Foundation WOTRO, this would not have been possible.

My whole family – parents, sisters, brother and their spouses, husband and two daughters – provided me with all the support I needed.

Mridul Eapen

IN MEMORY OF
DR. T N KRISHNAN

Contents

List of Tables

List of Figures

1
Introduction

1.1 The Background

The issue of rural industrialisation (hereafter RI) based on small-scale manufacturing activity, has drawn considerable attention as an instrument for spatial deconcentration of industrial activity in developing economies. However, given its potential developmental linkages with the rural sector, more recently it has assumed importance as a dimension of the larger process of rural transformation in these economies. Empirical evidence on considerable dynamism within certain segments of the rural industrial sector in developing economies has also raised the question of its possible contribution to the advance of "modern" industry. It is with the latter two perspectives on RI that we are concerned with in this study.

The importance of linkages, particularly the agriculture-industry linkages, in the process of rural transformation of the developed capitalist economies was well demonstrated in the English case. While agriculture provided food, labour, raw materials and capital to industry, the latter in turn provided the input requirements of agriculture and more importantly, the industrial consumer goods demanded by the agricultural population. The agricultural sector provided a vast "home market" for industrial goods. It was largely based on the assumption of some of these linkages, in particular the flow of rural labour and agricultural surplus into industry, that models of industrialisation were derived for late coming nations seeking to industrialise quickly.

A striking feature of these models was that the shift towards industry in the process of development was expected to be spatially urban oriented as was assumed to be the case in respect of early Europe. The latter has recently been modified chiefly through the efforts of Mendels, whose concept of proto-industrialisation, (despite its limitations), opened up a new perspective on industrial development in early modern Europe. However, the rural small-scale industrial sector in most developing economies, which was certainly large in quantitative terms, was apparently not potentially dynamic after years of colonial rule. It did not have any role to play in the industrialisation strategies of the fifties (India's case being an exception).[1] The industrialisation led development strategies failed to absorb "surplus" rural labour into urban large-scale industry. High proportions of the population in most developing economies in Latin America, large parts of Africa and South Asia, continued to depend on agriculture as a means of precarious livelihood. Rural poverty and underemployment persisted.

In this context there was a felt need for restructuring the development strategies of the fifties, the benefits of which had failed to "trickle down" to the rural poor households. One of the major restructuring exercises (especially in the context of large agrarian economies) entailed a re-examination of the role of agriculture and rural small-scale industries in long-term economic development. The agricultural (or more broadly rural) sector was to be regarded as a sector which had considerable flexibilty to generate employment and incomes rather than as one "passively" supplying labour to an urban based industrial sector. While the labour absorptive capacity of agriculture appeared to be limited in the aggregate, it was the generation of rural non-agricultural employment opportunities that was more crucial. A major role in this process was ascribed to (rural) small-scale manufacturing enterprises, the potential dynamism of which was being realised, despite their earlier neglect, in the context of new paradigms of industrial development like "flexible specialisation". Also, while the possibiliy of the rural small-scale sector in contemporary developing economies, graduating to large-scale modern enterprises(as envisaged under proto-industrialisation) appeared to be limited, there were other ways in which it could contribute to the advance of modern industry.

The emphasis in the restructured strategy was on manufacturing activity to meet the rural demand for industrial goods. And "small-scale" was stressed since the strategy envisaged involving the rural people not only as labourers but also as entrepreneurs in the process of rural employment and income generation. Other advantages of rural small-scale units in terms of use of dispersed unemployed/underemployed labour and natural resources available, also tilted the balnce in its favour. The growth of rural small-scale enterprises (RSSEs) was to be induced primarily through backward and forward production and consumption linkages[2] within the rural space itself minimising the need for a rural-urban migration of labour. This did not imply viewing villages as closed or isolated economies but as having greater autotomy in generating productive employment opportunities in the context of their own development priorities.

[1]A strategic role was attributed to the village industries in India since it was acknowledged that the capital goods strategy underlying India's development model would be unable to generate employment at an acceptable rate.

[2]These were basically agriculture-industry linkages mentioned earlier. Production linkages were in terms of intermediate goods required by agriculture or agricultural raw materials used by industry. Consumption linkages were the consumption demand for industrial consumer goods of the agricultural population. The need to broaden the focus to rural rather than only agricultural was also recognised.

The reason of course, why linkages were expected to operate in the context of the restructured strategy was due to the more direct intervention in the rural economy that it envisaged.

The above is of course a rather "centrist" version of what the restructuring exercise implied. There was a very sharp division in the whole approach to restructuring reflected in the question of what would induce the growth of linkages for a self-sustaining process of rural industrialisation.

1.2 The Stimuli

What could induce such a process of rural industrialisation was a highly controversial issue. On the one hand was the view that it was primarily agriculture induced and its proponents argued for a complete change in the development strategy from an industry-led to an agriculture-led one. A more moderate view in the same genre while upholding the dominance of linkages running from agriculture to non-agriculture also stressed the need to consider the impact of non- agriculture on agriculture. On the other hand were those who perceived it as being largely generated by the extant process of industrialisation albeit of a modified type. Agriculture did play a role; however, non-agricultural or rather urban linkages played a relatively more important role in rural diversification including rural industrialisation. The modification of the industrial process lay in taking account of the industrial goods needs of the agricultural sector which had been virtually detached from the earlier strategy of industrialistion. In policy terms this approach also implied some increase in government expenditure allocation to the rural sector, though not to the same degree nor necessarily concentrated on agriculture.

What did get excluded in the discussion on linkages, particularly the agriculture led "rural growth linkages", was the labour supply side factors in stimulating rural non-agricultural employment. The increasing demographic pressure on land resulting in uneconomic holdings tends to "push" rural work seekers into petty non-agricultural activity which may carry a wage lower than the agricultural wage. Increasing levels of literacy also generates a situation of surplus labour since educated work seekers desire to work outside agriculture. Evidence on distress induced diversification or setting up an enterprise as a survival strategy was not conclusive in terms of its relative importance. In case of female workers, however, that it was realtively more important could be said with greater certainty. It has been argued, however, that in a situation with limited options, the wage is set by the rural subsistence economy which offers only a precarious alternative. The distress and dynamic activities need not be mutually exclusive.

This aspect of diversification introduced a duality in the structure of the rural industrial sector:

- On the one hand are enterprises tiny in nature, mostly organised as household units using minimal capital equipment and where the skill level of workers is low or widely available. The product is very often agro-based. Entry is easy and targeted customers are generally the lower income groups in the rural economy.
- On the other hand are somewhat larger units, more highly capitalised and hiring in labour, with skill levels of workers dependent on the nature of the product. More of these units belong to the non-agricultural product groups. Considerable empirical evidence indicated that the latter tended to be more profitable and dynamic vis-a-vis the former.

1.3 Purpose of Our Study

It is against this background of a felt need for greater autonomy to the rural sector in evolving its own development priorities that we undertook this study. We regard rural industrialisation as a constituent of an industrialisation strategy placing particular emphasis on rural linkages for the generation of rural employment and incomes. Despite an impressive amount of literature on RI relating to a wide range of developing economies we are of the view that certain aspects of rural linkages have been relatively neglected or under-emphasised. For instance:

- An excessive concentration on agriculture induced linkages has resulted in an underestimation of the potential of rural linkages. This is especially so in respect of rurally manufactured goods. We would like to emphasise the role of the fast growing service sector whose demand for simple intermediate goods could offer a vast potential for the growth of RSSEs.
- At the same time the relative importance of agricultural linkages very often tends to be swamped out by urban related indicators of rural diversification. The former could play a more dominant role in generating non-agricultural employment in relatively isolated rural areas. This implies that linkages that promote occupational diversification vary across villages.
- Insofar as the rural industrial sector is to be included in the national economic and industrial trends, there is need to go beyond the narrow set of activities in which the rural activities have some advantage. It is in this context that local capital linkage or indigenous entrepreneurship, a relatively underemphasised linkage, assumes importance. There is a real (psychic) advantage for local entrepreneurs operating in a local environment which redresses to some extent the relative place-specific disadvantages of rural locations. The goal of rural industrialisation can be realised through the stimulation of local initiative.[3]

[3](See Bar-el and Felsenstein 1990).

1.4 The Research Questions Addressed

Within this broader perspective on rural linkages which we develop later into a framework of analysis, the following research questions have been formulated:

- What are the different paths by which rural households diversify into manufacturing activity? More explicitly, does the socio-economic background of the entrepreneur in terms of father's occupation impact on the decision to set up an enterprise and choice of activity?
- What are the implications of location for the patterns of rural industries? More specifically do SSES in relatively isolated rural areas display higher local-rural linkages?
- How strong are the rural links of the SSEs in terms of labour, capital, production and consumption linkages? More explicitly is agriculture the most important source of linkages?
- Is it necessary for all the rural linkages to be strong? More explicitly, which of these linkages has the strongest developmental links with the rural sector?
- What is the nature of RSSEs as they have emerged in the region of study? More explicitly are they largely a strategy of survival or do these enterprises generate adequate earnings for further growth? If the latter are they proto-industrial in nature to be transformed into large modern urban based industrial firms; or is it possible for such a sector to be a viable stage in itself contributing to the growth of modern industrialisation in the state?
- Does a high level of literacy, help in the process of diversification, given the availability of a pool of literate workers? Does it also help in raising the skill level of entrepreneurs and hence the promotion of relatively more modern industries?

1.5 Region of Study

Our study is on Kerala, a small state on the south-west coast of India which is unique in many respects among the states of India. Its history and specificities, particularly a broad-based rural socio-economic structure, make it especially amenable to a process of rural industrialisation. The agrarian structure has undergone a radical change given its fairly successful land reform policy implemented in the late sixties. It has a dispersed settlement pattern which makes it difficult to distinguish rural from urban. Villages are as large as towns in terms of population size and density. There is a much more even spread of achievements between rural and urban areas, including basic infrastructure, in which its unique settlement pattern has played a facilitating role.

Historically, it has been characterised by a high incidence of rural industries given its rich natural resource base, the products of which could be processed into industrial goods. It is interesting to note that the two major rural industries – coir and cashew– were also (like the proto-industries in England) historically, export-oriented. The state's industrial structure is characterised by a dispersed pattern of small-scale manufacturing activity. However, an area of major concern in its transformation process in the contemporary period, has been the declining fortunes of the traditional industrial production base in rural areas and the inability of the state to develop and "modernise" its industrial sector.[4] Since the second half of the eighties however, there has been a fairly rapid growth of the non-factory, "modern", small-scale industrial sector in the state, located largely in the rural areas.[5] The purpose of our research was to examine:

- The nature and growth of the rural small-scale industrial sector in the state during the period 1971–91;
- The effect of location on the structure of the rural industrial sector and its linkages in terms of labour, capital, production and consumption, with the different components of the rural economy or nearby urban areas; and
- In what ways could this sector contribute to the growth of modern industry in the state whose benefits should reach the rural poor.

Such an analysis would enable us to answer the research questions posed above.

1.6 Research Methodology

The methodology is based on a historical and contemporaneous-empirical approach. At an aggregate level secondary sources of information were used to study the extent and nature of economic diversification in Kerala, in particular manufacturing, in a historical perspective. Changes in its spatial spread and size structure were examined for the more recent period, 1971 to 1991. The spatial dimension was studied in terms of rural areas and size class of towns using the

[4]By "modernisation" we mean (a) gradual transformation of the traditional industries; and (b) establishment and growth of new, modern types of industries (Staley and Morse 1965).

[5]While this was so for most states in India, its incidence in rural locations was higher in Kerala.

continuous method.[6] This procedure was also used to understand the process of diversification in terms of certain socio-economic characteristics by studying villages which became urban between 1971–91. The characteristics could be used as proxies for some of the linkages under study. A correlation analysis was done to examine the strength of the relationship between rural non-agricultural employment and each of these characteristics at a point of time. The limitations of a cross-section analysis to understand a dynamic relationship have been frequently discussed. Nevertheless, it does enable us to gain some insight into the bahaviour pattern being studied. An analysis of the size structure of manufacturing activity over time focussing on the small-scale manufacturing sector, was undertaken using secondary data sources. The various data sources used and their limitations are discussed in chapters dealing with them.

The second and more insightful method adopted in studying the major issue of linkages and the degree of "localness", was the use of a field survey of a stratified random sample of RSSEs in a district of north Kerala. Palakkad, the district selected, is predominantly rural but has drawn and generated considerable industrial investments in rural areas in the recent period. A major reason for selecting the district was the possibility of capturing the tendencies, still taking shape, of the nature of linkages of rural industries. Our sample was drawn from the population of newly established (between 1990–5) units. Data on these units was generated through a structured questionnaire, relating to the socio-economic characteristics of the entrepreneurs and linkages of the RSSEs with the rural economy. A set of contingency tables were used to understand the relationships and the significance of local-rural linkages. Two different blocks[7] in the district were selected (the reasons for the choice of which would become clearer from our findings) and totally 130 units constituted the sample, 62 units from one block and 68 from the other of which 10 were located in an industrial development area.

1.7 Definitional Issues

Rural industries are to be defined not in terms of location in rural areas but whether they generate developmental links with the rural sector. Such linkages could be in terms of utilising local capital, drawing in rural labour, processing locally available raw materials and responding to rural market demand. While there is some ambiguity in delimiting "rural", most studies now recognise the need to adopt a broader concept than what is officially designated as rural. "Rural" is

[6] A settlement is classified according to size of population at a point of time and the same set of units belonging to each class of locality are compared over time.

[7] A block is the second tier of local development administration with the village panchayat below it and the district panchayat above it. A panchayat is a group of villages constituted to form a viable unit of administration. However, given the large size of a village on average, many panchayats are are single village panchayats.

defined more broadly including small towns and at times medium towns (Bagachwa and Stewart 1990; Papola 1992); others go even further focussing on the generation of non-agricultural employment opportunities for the rural resident population irrespective of its location (Saith 1992). However, that the reach should not extend to too large an urban settlement was also recognised since there was a danger of the latter sucking in most of the financial resources allocated for development of "micro" regions.

The difficulty in delimiting rural and urban is brought out sharply in the context of Kerala with its densely populated villages, dispersed urban pattern and a historically well developed transport system rendering every village accessible by road. In terms of population size and density an overwhelming proportion of the villages would be urban. Even in terms of the third critical criterion for defining urban areas, viz. the male occupational structure,[8] a number of villages are in fact urban. These semi-urban villages have linkages which spread beyond their rural confines given the ease of commutation between contiguous regions. However the nature and scale of operation of non-agricultural activities does vary between rural and larger urban settlements and hence analytically makes the distinction meaningful.

In our study "rural" is defined as including small towns. "Local" covers the rural area so defined and in the context of our field survey includes a block which is constituted of a few panchayats and a small town or two, given Kerala's dispersed urban pattern.

Despite the variety of ways in which "small" is defined in the vast empirical literature on the subject, general opinion has been converging towards defining it as upto 50 workers. With the extreme concentration of units at the lower end and the existence of units not hiring any outside labour (household units or "family enterprises") there is a further categorisation within the small into micro or tiny enterprises (upto 10 workers) and household units using primarily family labour. "Small" is defined in two ways in this study as is the official practice in India:

- in terms of workers, viz. units employing upto 50 workers and using power or upto 100 workers and not using power; and
- in terms of investment in plant and machinery at original cost. (This limit has been revised upwards very often).

Our major concern is with modern small-scale units to be distinguished from the traditional industrial sector characterised by a historical existence, low capital-use and older techniques of production. Its products may or may not cater to "modern" demands. "Modern" small

[8] At least 75 percent of the male workers should follow non-agricultural livelihoods(all categories of occupations excluding cultivators, agricultural labourers, livestock, fishing etc.)

industry on the other hand is more in keeping with emerging demands and its adaptability to changing conditions is greater. It uses relatively more of modern capital equipment, systematic organisation and management. However, some "modernised"[9] traditional industry units are included in our sample survey of rural small-scale enterprises.

Manufacturing activity includes processing of materials, repair and related service activity.

1.8 Structure of the Study

In order to place the study within a wider context, we begin in Chapter 2 with a theoretical discussion on rural transformation as embedded in the issue of agriculture-industry linkages. Its re-orientation in a strategy of rural industrialisation is then examined focussing on the "rural growth linkage controversy". The chapter concludes with an attempt to sketch a framework of analysis which places greater stress on certain neglected or under-emphasised aspects of linkages. In Chapter 3 we present certain macro-economic and structural characteristics of Kerala state, which serve as a backdrop to the study. The dispersed nature of its industrial process and emerging entrepreneurship is highlighted in a historical perspective, emphasising a certain continuity in its traditional product structure. Despite a high degree of commercialistion in rural areas and large remittance inflows, the state remains industrially backward. However, growth of manufacturing activity has been uneven across the state. In Chapter 4, the spatial dimension of the growth of the work force and its structural transformation during the period 1971 to 1991, is investigated using three different concepts of space: the rural-urban (by size class of towns) divide; the rural settlements that became urban in these two decades and the three regions, north, central and south Kerala (broadly corresponding to its earlier political constituents). The evidence reveals considerable diversification of the rural economy and the emergence of two distinct spatial formations implying two possible paths to generation of rural industrial activity. An attempt is made to examine this for the rural settlements of 1971 in which the scale of transformation was large enough to make them urban by 1991. North Kerala is identified as the region which has experienced a relatively high growth of employment in rural manufacturing. Palakkad district in the north is selected for the field survey to be carried out in two blocks, one relatively rural and the other very close to the city of the same name in the district. From space we then move to the size structure of manufacturing activity in the state in Chapter 5. The focus is on the small-scale sector, its relative significance, growth and changes in structure. The virtual absence of change in its agro-natural resource based product structure

[9]See footnote 5. While traditional units are administered by their respective official boards or agencies, those units which organise themselves into co-operatives can register with Small Industries Development Organisation which covers the "modern" small-scale units.

is emphasised. Chapters 6 and 7 present our findings from the field survey. The early part of Chapter 6 gives a brief socio-economic profile of the district and the two blocks under study. Some basic information on the population of small-scale units in the two blocks is given and a first attempt is made to examine their linkages with agriculture on the basis of secondary data. The Chapter then goes on to discuss the sampling methodology and procedure. It analyses certain characteristics of the entrepreneurs and the sample enterprises, focussing on the rural origins of capital and labour. The significant relationship between non-local entrepreneurs and non-local labour is highlighted. Backward and forward production and consumption linkages and their degree of localness, is examined in Chapter 7. The main objective is not only to analyse the relative importance of these two types of linkages in generating non-agricultural activity but also the differences between the two blocks to gain further insight into the impact of location on the type of activity and nature of linkages. A broad performance evaluation of the RSSEs and the evidence on wages and earnings is presented to assess the nature of these enterprises. The impact of literacy on wage earnings and choice of activity undertaken by an entrepreneur is aslo examined. Finally, in Chapter 8 a summary of the main findings and the major conclusions is presented with some policy recommendations emerging from our study.

2
Rural Industrialisation and its Linkages: Review of Literature

2.1 Introduction

A substantial part of rural activity in most developing economies consists of small manufacturing industry and processing. However, development theory of the fifties, rooted firmly in the seminal work of Arthur Lewis (1954), did not envisage a dynamic role for the rural industrial sector in the process of growth.[1] Its contribution was primarily seen in terms of providing another source of "unlimited supply" of rural labour for urban industry as a consequence of its ruin, resulting from growth in incomes and competition from modern industry.

The development experience in practice has not fully conformed to the path envisaged. Enough evidence has been thrown up in the course of a number of country studies to counter the "inferior goods" argument while at the same time highlighting the growth potential of rural industries (RI). The debate has therefore shifted from establishing its quantitative magnitude to identifying conditions within which rural industry can perform its role of generating employment and incomes to allieviate rural poverty (Saith 1992). We view this diversification of activity into manufacturing by rural households as a part of the wider process of rural transformation in which the issue of agriculture-industry linkages assumes significance[2] though somewhat differently than in the classic English industrialisation experience.

This chapter is structured in four sections. In Section 2.2 we situate our problem in the context of the interlinkages between agriculture and industry as they evolved in the case of developed economies and their limited role in the development process of developing economies.

[1] While it is true that the traditional rural industrial sector, particularly handloom weaving, did have a significant role to play in India's heavy industrialisation strategy underlying the Second Five-Year Plan, it was viewed purely in instrumental terms rather than in terms of wider societal change (Saith 1992). The failure of the policy is well-known (Eapen 1976).

[2] Agriculture-industry linkages can be defined keeping either agriculture or industry as the sector of origin. In the "rural growth linkages" literature the linkages flow from agriculture (Mellor 1976).

The twentieth century debate on the agriculture-industry linkages in the context of Soviet industrialisation, is also addressed. Section 2.3 focusses on the need to re-evaluate the role of agriculture as also that of small-scale industries in long run economic development. This section delineates the search for modified or alternative paths of development which centre primarily on rural non-farm employment, in particular rural small-scale manufacturing within the context of greater intra-spatial capital, labour, production and consumption linkages. In Section 2.4 we examine at some length the linkages literature, focussing on the "rural growth linkages" controversy and draw up a broad framework of analysis. While there is a strong view regarding the primacy of agriculture as the mainspring of such linkages, there are equally vehement proponents who perceive the possibilities within the extant process of industrialisation, albeit of a modified type. Available evidence based on a number of country studies is rather mixed regarding the strength of local rural linkages in the non-traditional rural industrial sector. However, we argue that a critical local linkage on the supply side, viz. local capital and entrepreneurship which has a potential for generating developmental links with the rural sector, has often been dismissed or underemphasised in disçussions of RI since it had weak links with agricultural surpluses. The linkages of rural small-scale units need not be primarily with agriculture. For instance there could be strong forward production linkages with the rural tertiary sector, a potential source of demand for simple industrial intermediate goods. Our emphasis on the local capital linkage has, needless to add, important policy implications, that is, designing a strategy of rural industrial development based on mobilising indigenous capital further strengthened by a decentralised planning set up. The latter does not imply viewing villages as closed or isolated economies but to regard them as having greater flexibilty in generating productive employment opportunities in the context of their own development priorities. It is possible that our approach has been influenced by the specificities of the region under study; however it throws up processes and factors which may have wider relevance.

2.2 Agriculture-Industry Linkages at the Aggregate Level

The three main agriculture-industry linkages identified, viz. the "financing" of industry, the transfer of rural labour into industry and the creation of a home market for industrial goods, historically played a dynamic role in the process of industrialisation of the developed economies (Bharadwaj 1987). However, industrialisation led development strategies in the context of present day developing economies which relied explicitly or, mostly implicitly, on the existence of such linkages failed to work in practice (Chakravarty 1987; Saith 1990; Bhaduri 1992). It is pertinent to point out that the agriculture-industry linkages discussed here subsume also a symbiotic relation between "rural" (corresponding to agriculture) and "urban" (corresponding to industry) and is conceived at the aggregate economy level. The discussion becomes relevant to our study on RI, since the latter is an attempt to, (a) establish similar linkages in developing economies within the rural space itself; and (b) break out of the conventional mould which equates industrialisation with urbanisation, historical support for which even in the context of developed economies in their early phase of industrialisation, is now questioned.

The nature of the agriculture-industry linkage or the way in which agriculture relates to the needs of industry and its historical evolution, based on the industrialisation experience of Western Europe, in particular England, has been well documented. The issue came in for heated controversy later in the context of the heavy industrialisation strategy of the erstwhile Soviet Union in the twenties and then more recently with the failure of the assumed linkages to operate in respect of the developing economies. Without going into details we present the essence of the relationship which has been discussed and debated at length elsewhere (Bharadwaj 1987; Storm 1992; Bhaduri 1992).

2.2.1 *Historical Evolution of the Agriculture-Industry Linkages: the English Experience*

The agriculture-industry linkage has been articulated most lucidly within the classical political economy framework (Bharadwaj 1987) covering the period from the Physiocrats to Marx (that is, the 18th to late 19th century). We outline it in brief below.

The expansion of non-agricultural activities has been viewed primarily in terms of the changing relationship between agriculture and industry. Agriculture, initially, is the mainspring of all economic activities, including within its fold very simple and primitive forms of industry viz. processing of raw materials within the household or artisan production which may sometimes be a supplement to peasant agriculture. Industry at this stage, is considered more an appendage of agriculture, in which situation one can hardly speak of interlinkages viz. of separate activities. However, with the growing division of labour and increasing specialisation in the process of capitalist development, industry separates spatially and organisationally from agriculture and the sectoral distinction becomes clearer. Over time the interlinkages between agriculture and industry grow through the progress of technology and diversification of production in terms of inputs and outputs.

This agriculture industry relation is viewed as a symbiotic one, spatially too, since the "country" (or rural) signifies agriculture and "town" (or urban) stands for manufacturing activities. While agriculture plays a critical role in providing a major element of subsistence viz. food, besides raw materials for manufacture to the town, the latter repays this by supplying the necessary industrial goods to the country people. In terms of the investible surplus for capitalist accumulation in industry, the process of "primitive" or "primary" accumulation was critical, which occurred with the break up of the feudal system and the development of capitalism in agriculture. It resulted in the displacement of small land holders and craft producers in the process of concentration of capital in the countryside by landlords, which constituted a major contribution to the needs of industrial capital. However, with productivity gains advancing more rapidly in industry the share of industrial surplus increased, finally dominating and moulding the accumulation process. At the same time, these very changing agrarian conditions constituting the expropriation of the peasantry and small craftsmen, created for the town industries the necessary supply of "free" labour and furthered its symbiotic relation with industry creating demand mutually for each others' product and hence the home market.

Some striking features to note in this transition of an agrarian, feudal economy to a capitalist, industrialised one are:

- the interlinkages between agriculture and industry evolve in a mutually interdependent manner. While agriculture provides food, raw materials and labour to the town industries, the latter in turn supply consumer and producer goods (tools and other inputs necessary for agricultural production) to the countryside;
- agriculture dominates initially as a critically essential source of investible resources, however the forces of industrialisation have enough vitality (given the tremendous scope for increasing division of labour), to subsume agriculture and render it slowly "a branch of industry";
- however agriculture retains its significance as a crucial provider of wage goods and as providing a market for industrial goods;
- rural industry does not appear to play much of a role in the process of growth since industry locates itself in towns in the post-feudal period. Marx (1938) did discuss rural small industry in terms of the "petty mode of production" which existed for a very long period of time and out of which capitalism originated but which was glossed over in the seemingly settled belief that capitalism arose out of feudalism (Habib 1995). The existence of rural industries was implicitly assumed to reflect the incomplete transition to a full blown industrial economy where the rural sector sheds all its non-farming activities (Saith 1992).

It was largely based on this historical experience of developed economies, that models of industrialisation were derived for late coming nations seeking to industrialise quickly: the Soviet heavy industrialisation strategy in the twenties in the course of its First Five Year Plan, and the Lewisian industrialisation led development strategy in the post-Second World War period which had a much wider impact on the newly independent developing economies. We take up the latter first.

2.2.2 *Industrialisation Led Development Strategies*

One of the critical problems in the development of the late developing economies has been the absorption of surplus rural labour; the shortage of capital stock in relation to available labour was widely perceived to be the major constraint to growth (Nurkse 1953; Lewis 1954). Most of these countries embarked on an industrialisation led path of development which appeared to be imperative if the basic needs of their people, long deprived under the colonial regimes, had to be fulfilled (Saith 1990). Such a strategy which dominated economic thinking in the fifties, drew its rationale from the simple, intellectually appealing Lewis' model, broadly based on the historical experience of the developed countries. This model viewed the problem of surplus labour absorption as essentially one of intersectoral labour transfer through industrialisation which would build up the necessary capital base and also raise per capita output in the economy since industry, typically, was more productive than agriculture. The steady expansion of the capitalist industrial sector would draw upon the "unlimited supply" of rural labour from a low productivity agricultural sector at a constant real wage to the point labour was no longer infinitely elastic (Lewis 1954). From this "turning point" which would suggest a tight labour market situation, the benefits of industrial expansion would trickle down to workers and the rural population through higher wage rates. The process of industrialisation, therefore was expected to remove underdevelopment and rural poverty.

The Soviet model of heavy industrialsation which was articulated intellectually by Preobrazhensky and developed as the Soviet planning model by Feldman (Chakravarty 1987) was a precursor of Lewis' model, though conceptualised more along Marxian lines. It varied from the latter in its two sector disaggregation of the modern industrial sector. Adopting the Marxian two department schema of a capital goods sector (Department 1) and a consumption goods sector (Department 2), the model focussed on the critical importance of the proportion of investment going into Department 1, machines to produce machines, which then determined the pace of growth of the economy. However, such a rapid growth of heavy industries raised the controversial issue of "financing" of industrial growth. This was a major issue in the early debates on Soviet industrialisation, Preobrazhensky arguing for extracting the surplus from agriculture to finance industrial growth, his famous law of "primitive socialist" accumulation. This could be done either by administratively holding down agricultural prices or by imposing heavy indirect taxes on industrial goods generally consumed by the agriculturists so as to force the peasants to part with the necessary agricultural surplus. Others, dominated by Bukharin, argued for a more "voluntary exchange" which would also be politically more feasible (Bhaduri 1992). However the issue of the mode of extracting the agricultural surplus was settled along the option mooted by Preobrazhensky and the model itself did not even incorporate explicitly the role of the agricultural sector which was expected to adjust by providing an adequate surplus.

The model of industrialisation, underlying the Indian Second Five Year Plan, influenced heavily by the work of Mahalanobis was viewed as a variant of Feldman's Soviet planning model. Basically these were of the same genre as the Lewis "dual economy model" differing in the nature of constraints envisaged. While in Lewis' own model, it was the supply of labour at a constant real wage and hence the ability of agriculture to adjust in terms of the marketed surplus, in the Feldman-Mahalanobis (F-M) model it was the limited capacity of the capital goods sector, that is the ability to physically transform savings in terms of the agricultural surplus into mother machines (Bhaduri 1992). Also, given the greater emphasis on heavy industries in the F-M model, in which the capitalist entrepreneurs may not be induced to invest, this model allotted an active role to the State in the industrialisation process (Chakravarty 1987).

It may be noted that in both its variants, Lewis' and Feldman-Mahalanobis', the industrialisation led development strategies did not envisage any role for a vibrant rural industrial sector. The shift towards industry was expected to be spatially urban oriented, as had been the experience of the developed economies. However in the Indian context the Mahalanobis model did create a space for the small-scale industrial sector (Saith 1992). It was recognised that a heavy industry based development strategy would not be able to generate employment at an acceptable rate and if permitted unrestrained growth in the modern consumer goods sector would, in addition, displace labour from the large traditional sector. Hence the plan model allowed for major non-food consumer good items like textiles, to be supplied by the small-scale, labour intensive handloom sector. It was recognised that such industries were largely located in rural areas; however the spatial dimension of this sector was not given any undue emphasis in terms of its links with wider societal change. This policy of trying to combine high employment growth in the traditional sector(s) with building up a modern capital goods industrial base was akin to what later came to be described as Mao's strategy of "walking on two legs" (Chakravarty 1987; Saith 1990). However, while the Indian policy on rural industrialisation met with very little success, China has been able to do much better.

That these industrialisation led development models based on certain assumptions regarding the agriculture-industry linkages, failed to work in practice and why, is now well documented (Chakravarty 1984; Saith 1990; Bhaduri 1992). Not only did the pace of accumulation slow down in most countries (with exceptions like Korea and Taiwan) or was retarded very soon, the strategy failed to "trickle down" to the agricultural-rural sector[3]. This was most starkly manifested in the persistence of rural poverty with the continued dependence of a high percentage of the population on agriculture as a means of precarious livelihood, and extremely concentrated patterns of industrialisation and urbanisation (Bharadwaj 1989). Nor did growth in manufacturing manifest itself as a unilinear tendency towards large scale industry; smaller as also traditional forms of organisation appeared to persist. Doubts were therefore raised regarding the assumed role of agriculture and thereby of the agriculture industry linkages, as also the size structure of manufacturing industry in the process of development of late developing economies.

2.2.3 Agriculture-Industry Linkages Underlying Industrialisation Led Development Strategies

A striking feature of the industrialisation led development strategies was the largely "passive" role assigned to agriculture viz. that the agricultural sector would adjust "endogenously"[4] to the requirements of industrialisation (Bhaduri 1992). In a sense the strategies were grossly over-optimistic regarding the performance of traditional agriculture in most developing economies, characterised by a limited technical base and highly stratified agrarian structure, in response to the needs of industrialisation. A number of assumptions regarding rural-urban migration of workers, agricultural investment and output as also investment in the modern industrial sector, had been made without an adequate appreciation of the structural and organisational conditions existing within the sectors (Saith 1990). That such responses were closely linked to the nature of agrarian systems in the economies being studied was hardly considered (Mundle 1985).

The Feldman-Mahalanobis model did not even incorporate the role of the traditional agricultural sector explicitly on the assumption that the necessary agricultural surpluses to be transformed into capital goods would be forthcoming from agriculture. Industrial development was viewed as virtually independent of the conditions in agriculture. On the other hand, while the Lewisian model did incorporate explicitly the contribution of agriculture to the industrial process, it was essentially in terms of rural labour supplies. That this labour had to be supplied at a constant real wage, however, implicitly assumed an endogenous role for the agricultural sector which would adjust in terms of making available adequate market surpluses. After all, at the relevant level of income the expenditure basket consisted mainly of food. If agriculture failed to adjust, the consequent shortage of food and shift in terms of trade in its favour would

[3]The process has to be seen in the context of the total rural economy which is constituted not only of agriculture but other sectors (Ranis 1990).

[4]The agricultural sector adjusting endogenously implies that the performance of industry is not constrained by agricultural performance.

thwart the process of industrialisation due to increasing wage costs and hence declining profitabiltiy (Kalecki 1972). The latter in fact turned out to be a critical constraint on the process of development. Though this was a possibility argued by Lewis it was not integrated into his characterisation of the growth model. It was only later that he emphasised the rate of growth of agricultural productivity as the major constraint on the long term development process (Lewis 1978).

The controversial and awkward issue had been who bears the burden of "financing" industrialisation: agriculture or industry. Should the real wage of industrial workers in the process of heavy industrialisation, be maintained through forced extraction of marketed surplus from agriculture at an increasing rate or can this wage be treated as flexible and allowed to fall, hence making the industrial sector bear part of the burden of industrialisation (Chakravarty 1987; Bhaduri 1992). Increasing empirical evidence from cross-country studies revealed that there was no unique pattern of net resource transfer between agriculture and industry. That in its early stages industrialisation requires substantial net finance contribution from agriculture (Fei and Ranis 1964) was not borne out; in the context of a number of countries it was in fact negative over much of the observation period (Karshenas 1992). Indeed even in the case of Soviet industrialisation, the urban industrial sector itself bore part of the burden of financing the cost of industrialisation (Mundle 1985; Bhaduri 1992).

It appeared therefore that assumptions regarding agriculture-industry linkages in terms of net intersectoral resource transfer did not in practice turn out to be realistic. And, to the extent that the agricultural sector failed to provide an adequate surplus, it would result in a slower growth in industrial accumulation or a downward pressure on the industrial wage rate (Bhaduri 1992). Again, the demand for rural labour which would induce the inter-sectoral transfer, was dependent on the output elasticity of employment in the urban industrial sector. A capital intensive type of industrial development, which is what occurred in the case of most late developing economies, since they could draw upon an enormous stock of (primarily Western) available technology, proved very inadequate to reduce the burden of rural underemployment (Johnston and Kilby 1975; Saith 1990). In fact the very changes generated in the agrarian sector as a response to the increasing industrial demand for agricultural goods, in terms of technical change, greater commercialisation and perhaps further differentiation, which "freed" labour for industry (to some extent)[5], added to the stock of underemployed labour (Saith 1990). Moreover, a very important linkage with agriculture in terms of the provision of a home market for industrial goods, was hardly emphasised in these development strategies. That there may be a

[5]We have stated to some extent since the type of polarisation that occurred between the landlords and the landless under capitalist development in the context of England did not occur for most of the large agrarian developing economies. See Bharadwaj (1989).

demand constraint for industrial goods resulting in a weak inducement to invest in industry was not recognised at all forcing a reliance over time on "foreign" as opposed to "home" demand (Chakravarty 1987; Bhaduri 1992).

Hence based on the actual development experience of many developing economies, serious doubts were raised on the assumption that agriculture adjusts passively to the requirements of industry in terms of the marketed surplus and labour supply. The strategy failed to trickle down to the rural poor even in countries which witnessed a fairly successful period of industrialisation, like for instance India. It came to be generally agreed, as reflected in the development dialogue since the 70's, that agriculture or more broadly the rural sector had been relatively neglected in the industrialisation led development strategies of the fifties both in terms of its supply side and especially demand side conditions. That the rural sector could play an active role by providing an inducement to economic activity through its demand for industrial goods came to be increasingly emphasised. Hence it was felt necessary to re-examine the role of the agricultural-rural sector in the process of economic growth viewing the agriculture-industry linkages in a spatially more organic way (Mellor 1976; Ranis 1990; Saith 1990; Singh and Tabatabai 1992; Bhaduri 1992).

2.3 Re-evaluation of the Role of Agriculture in Economic Development

There were some scholars who while upholding the primacy of an industry-led growth strategy had advocated a more balanced sectoral approach especially in the context of the Feldman-Mahalanobis heavy industrialisation model. The need to explicitly recognise the wage goods constraint on the development process was emphasised and hence the plea for "removal of obstacles to the expansion of agriculture" (Kalecki 1972; Kaldor 1960; Lewis 1978). Kalecki identified the obstacles as feudal land relations and dominance of merchant capital over the peasants. In fact even earlier, Mao had argued in the Chinese context, that "the production of the means of production must be given priority... it definitely does not follow that the production of the means of subsistence, especially grain, can be neglected..." (as cited in Singh and Tabatabai 1992). Growth would be counterproductive unless agriculture was put on a secure foundation and the consumption levels of the peasantry improved.

An extreme response to the failure of the industrialisation led strategies of growth (taking India as a case study) was the view that Lewis-type growth strategies had resulted in a complete neglect of the agricultural sector which was in fact a dynamic sector. Its potential had been constrained by the "urban bias" of such strategies which needed to be changed in favour of an "agriculture first" or agriculture-led strategy of growth (Lipton 1968; Mellor 1976). The latter must give priority to increasing agricultural production through investment in new technology, the ensuing incomes from which would generate indirect responses in the rural non-farm economy through backward and forward production and consumption linkages, viz.the "downstream effects".[6] A vast amount of literature appeared on "agricultural growth linkages" in an attempt to examine the experience of a number of developing regions undertaking large agricultural development projects.

More recently as a critique of the agricultural growth linkages strategy, attempts have been made to combine the advantages of industrialisation whose pace and content needs to be modified with extensive growth of the rural sector (Bhaduri 1992). The importance of rural economic diversification and rural industrialisation based on small-scale industries is recognised. As in Mellor's schema (1976) a powerful linkage identified in the process is the active role played by the agricultural-rural sector in providing a market for industrial goods, not necessarily separated by space. However it is not perceived to be primarily agriculture induced. Coinciding as this did with a widespread rethinking on the role of small-scale industries in economic development, particularly the rural small-scale sector in the historical experience of the develoed economies, rural industrialisation appeared to hold a significant potential for rural employment and income creation in developing economies.

It may be noted that these responses did not address the issue of a redistributive land reform for achieving a satisfactory level of rural development. An agrarian reform which was necessary prior to (or concomitant with) the growth of industry as occurred in the case of England, was not seriously envisaged in the agenda even while there was evidence of a close relationship between the nature of agrarian systems and the positive impact on the agriculture-industry relationship (Kalecki 1972; Mundle 1985; Bagachwa and Stewart 1990). It was acknowledged that this was a politically unrealistic option, given the configuration of class forces, even in those developing economies which aimed at a socialistic pattern of society. However very recent thinking in international organisations appears to be veering around to the need for land reforms, since lack of access to property is directly linked to rural poverty (Niloufer Cagatay 1997). But whether it would really be propagated as a critical policy measure in allieviating rural poverty remains to be seen.

2.3.1 The Relevance of the Rural Small-Scale Industrial Sector in Economic Development

It is evident from a number of developing country studies that the non-urban sector should be viewed not merely as agricultural, but more broadly, given the existence of a fairly large non-agricultural sector, composed of the services, manufacturing and construction sectors (Shand

[6]It refers to the difference between the total effect of a project and its direct effect alone. See Bell et al (1982).

1985; Mukhopadhyaya and Lim 1986; Islam 1987; Ranis 1990; Harris 1991). Though the share of manufacturing is relatively lower, a considerable part of the rural labour force in Asian countries, varying from 5 percent in Thailand to 14 percent in Nepal (in the eighties) made its living in primarily small-scale manufacturing activities (Islam 1987). In sub-Saharan Africa, the percentage of manufacturing employment ranged from a low of 13 in Chad to a high of 61 in Mali in the 60's and 70's (Haggblade *et al* 1989). The question is: how does one view this sector within the dual economy framework of the development strategies we discussed above?

The shift towards industry in the process of economic development of the developing economies, was expected to be spatially urban oriented as was the case in respect of England and other parts of Europe. Hence a dynamic rural small-scale industrial sector had apparently no role to play in the industrialisation of the now developed economies. However, the view on rural small-scale industries has recently been revised in the light of Mendels's "proto-industrialisation" phase which has opened up a new perspective on industrial development in early modern Europe (Hudson 1986). It is a phase of development in itself marked by a fairly long period of traditionally organised, market oriented, principally rural industry which preceded modern industrialisation (Mendels 1972). It was carried out in rural cottages by peasant families in the slack agricultural season thus utilising underemployed labour. The link between the peasant-producers and the market was the merchant who bought up the manufactured goods and supplied the raw materials. These cottage industries contained the conditions for the eventual development of factory-based industries. Other scholars such as Kriedte and Schlumbohm regarded proto-industrialisation as a distinct mode of production between feudalism and capitalism (Hudson 1986). Hence the role of rural small-scale industries has been reassessed in the historical process of economic transition of the now developed economies. Rural or proto-industrialisation can be regarded as a transition stage between peasant agriculture and modern industry. None of its proponents however, insisted that the passage from proto to factory industry was inevitable or automatic for all regions of household production.

However, the concept of proto-industry was criticised, especially its evolutionist aspect and the blanket nature of its conception of the emergence and dynamics of rural industry based as it was primarily on the textile industry. It excluded the more capital intensive types of enterprises such as iron smelting, paper making and milling as also the vast range of manufacturing occupations found in villages such as wood working, tailoring, shoe making, building etc. which cater to local demand (Clarkson 1985). Even within the textile industry it paid little attention to its very differentiated nature. Such a view masked the considerable differences in structure – organisational and financial – between rural industries and regions, with the independent artisan producer on the one hand and the wage worker of a putting out system on the other (Perlin 1983; Hudson 1986). And the diversity could not be incorporated into the model simply by assuming that each represented a different stage in some progressive and linear evolution towards capitalist industry which was not borne out by facts.[7] For instance the household unit of production did not disappear with the development of factories even in those branches of production most affected by the innovation of new machinery (Clarkson 1985).

Does the model of proto-industrialisation have any relevance for the developing economies? To the extent that it draws attention to the diversity of the rural industrial sector in its emergence and dynamics including its financing and the nature of its links with agriculture, the model is useful. However, historically, their own nascent rural industrial or proto-industrial sectors were destroyed under the colonial impact particularly in Asia (India and China), North Africa and Middle East though not perhaps in the case of Korea and Taiwan (Saith 1992). Some industries for instance did develop in India during the colonial period but were not located in the erstwhile artisan based centres (Banerjee and Ghosh 1988). There has been a recent interest in attempting to see whether the concept of "proto-industries" could be applied in the present-day context of developing economies. However, the limited evidence available on rural manufacturing in these economies, although limited, suggests that growth of such units into large modern firms was rare, the reasons for which could be many depending on the specificity of the country under study (Berry 1987). Nonetheless a factor which must have played an important role was the forced pace of industrialisation in most of these countries in the post-Independence period. Based as it was on urban large and medium-scale industries using mainly foreign technologies, there could perhaps be no link with the earlier "proto-industries". Whatever remained of the large rural industrial sector was perceived as essentially a traditional, pre-industrial form of production which would disappear over time. Hence, the rural industrial sector remained detached from the process of industrialisation.

However, as has been argued by some, even if the rural industries do not grow into factories in the developing economies, there are other ways in which this sector could contribute to the process of modern[8] industrialisation. This could be through the use of the same labour and capital for better organised, larger units which maybe located elsewhere, or through an inter-generational upgradation of the unit with better educated second generation entrepreneurs setting up medium-size units (Berry 1987; Grosh and Somolekae 1996). However, evidence on the operation of such mechanisms is also not encouraging. In our opinion the more important question in the light of the critique of "proto-industrialisation", appears to be whether the

[7]It was not necessarily the trades with a "more advanced" proto-industrial structure which graduated faster into factories due to the need for organisational economies. Other exogenous factors like nature of raw materials being used, the production process involved and technical possibilities open, affected the transition (Hudson 1986).

[8]While "modernisation" includes (a) a gradual transformation of the traditional small industries; and (b) the establishment and growth of new, modern types of small industries (Staley and Morse 1965), by modern we mean the latter.

rural industrial sector is necessarily transitional in nature. Small firms could adapt and adjust to changing economic conditions and need not be considered traditional or backward (Chandavarkar 1985). They could contribute to the advance of modern industry without necessarily becoming large. This of course implies a stratification of the rural industrial sector to identify segments with a growth potential. Usually a distinction is made between household activities and small-scale units hiring some labour and using more fixed capital, the former supposed to be tradition bound and primarily for subsistence while the latter is considered to be more dynamic (Berry 1987; Davies et al. 1992). However, here too studies have pointed to the adaptive role of the household sector in developing economies in providing earning opportunities to the rural households over long periods despite harsh conditions and low productivity (Anderson 1982). But, as pointed out by Schmitz (1990), this is the defensive response of the individual family or business and is different from adjustment aimed at growth. Recent literature on micro-enterprises has emphasised its growth potential and possibility of contributing to the process of industrialisation (Grosh and Somolekae 1996). However, more work has to be done in garnering information regarding the feasibility of the above and the constraints on the growth of this sector. Our own study also attempts to look into this question.

That there could exist a vibrant rural industrial sector leading to economic transformation, was borne out by the successful cases of (post Revolutionary) China, Japan and Taiwan (Saith 1992). Most studies on the successful East Asian cases emphasise the not inconsiderable role played by agrarian reforms in their process of rural industrialisation (Shand 1985; Mundle 1985; White 1986; Saith 1990). Although these cases are exceptional, there still exist a number of compelling reasons (explained below) why developing countries would strive for stimulating the growth of rural non-farm employment in general and small-scale rural industries in particular. It has assumed significance as a powerful policy instrument for generating rural employment and incomes.

2.3.2 *The Flexible Specialisation Paradigm*

The endeavour to encourage the growth of rural small-scale industries in the context of the development dilemma of developing economies, was further strengthened by the influential work of Piore and Sabel (1984) who evolved an alternative paradigm of industrial development – that of flexible specialisation. The latter refers to a major change in industrial organisation in advanced capitalist economies: a relative decline of Fordist mass production techniques and an expansion of activities based on less rigid and more adaptable structures. This new form of industrial organisation attributes to the small-scale sector the capacity for autonomous growth which was borne out by the adaptability of the craft sector in Europe. The economic organisation of industrial districts in 19th century Europe in which small firms often developed or exploited new technologies without becoming larger was well documented by the authors (Piore and Sabel 1984). Though evolved in the context of advanced countries, based on the success of agglomeration of small firms in Japan, Italy and Germany, attempts have been made to explore its relevance for developing economies (Schmitz 1990). Specific conditions are associated with its successful functioning. It refers to a cluster of small firms around a set of related activities and a more innovative and flexible system of multi-purpose machines and skilled workers, which seldom reflect the conditions of rural industry obtaining in developing economies. However, that in Italy for instance, it evolved from a typical sweatshop sector into an innovative network of small firms, the paradigm has strengthened the viability of the small-scale sector (Schmitz 1990). Flexible specialisation is certainly not confined to small-scale production; however it does imply a far greater role for these firms. Hence the role of small-scale industry, in particular rural small-scale industries, in the long term development process has assumed greater significance. As Schmitz observes, "Small has not become beautiful wherever it appears, but it commands more respect and attention than it has previously had." (Schmitz 1990 pg 280). We now review the major issue of agriculture-industry linkages as articulated in a process of rural industrialisation in the context of developing economies.

2.4 Rural Industrialisation and its Linkages

The strategy of rural industrialisation (RI) has come in different garbs given the assumptions regarding the nature of its major stimulant, its linkages and location. In this sub-section we do not intend to offer a comprehensive review of the literature on RI which has appeared in a number of other studies (Shand 1985; Mukhopadhyaya and Lim 1986; Islam 1987; Wickramanayake 1988; Weijland 1989; Harriss 1991; Uribe-Echevarria 1991; Tambunan 1994). Instead we concentrate on the major issue of linkages which assumes significance in our attempt to understand RI as a process induced primarily by extant conditions in the rural sector.

Recalling the discussion in the previous sections we note that the recent emphasis on rural industrialisation in the development literature stems largely from the following reasons:

- urban based industrialisation tends to be capital intensive and cannot be expected to siphon off the rural backlog of underemployed and unemployed labour; hence the need to preempt rural to urban migration;

- the overall labour absorptive capacity of agriculture is limited (though, in some local regions the scope for raising labour use in agriculture through additional irrigation facilities exists, a potential which should be explored);

- the agricultural-rural sector has to play a more active role in the generation of non-agricultural employment opportunities specifically in the small-scale industrial sector. While large and medium scale industries located in rural areas may also generate some local employment, so long as they do not have any other linkage with the rural area, they cannot be included as elements in the process of rural industrialisation (Islam 1987); and

- small-scale rural industries have a multiplicative impact on rural employment and incomes through the linkage effects, both production and consumption, labour and capital, with agriculture and the rest of the rural sector.

It may be noted that the emphasis on linkages is also to distinguish it from the locational approach to RI (Saith 1989).

2.4.1 Linkage versus Location

While the locatioanl approach is defined by virtue of the activity being located in a designated rural area with the objective of spatial planning or industrial deconcentration, the linkage approach views it from the rural end, that is, whether the activity generates any developmental links with the rurally resident population. Hence it implies a certain endogeniety in the process of growth of rural industries. The limitations of the locational approach in drawing in the rural sector into the process of industrialisation has been brought out sharply in a study by Uribe-Echevarria (1991). Such an approach was a strong policy instrument in the earlier attempts to deconcentrate industrial growth away from the larger urban centres through the "growth pole" strategy or industrial deconcentration policy. Both assigned a specific role to the small-scale sector: while in the growth pole strategy it was to play a complementary role to a "leading industry", in case of the industrial deconcentration policy, the small-scale sector of a "footloose" type had a relatively more autonomous role. However these attempts were met with very little success due primarily to the non-development of spread effects into rural areas through the linkages created. In fact the linkages were sometimes stronger with the metropolitan region rather than to the rural areas (Uribe-Echevarria 1991). The lack of impact of growth pole strategies on the rural hinterland in the Indian context by setting up large industrial complexes in peripheral rural areas, has been discussed in several studies (Kundu and Raza 1982; Harriss 1987a;

Kashyap 1988). The failure of such exogenously implanted RI strategies, focussed attention on the need to stimulate an endogenous process of industrial growth with strong rural linkages.

It needs to be noted that an important inference can be drawn from the distinction drawn above between location and linkage: RI which depends relatively more on external initiative with entrepreneurs almost always from outside the locality, fails to generate significant linkages with the local economy; what is necessary therefore in the context of reaching the rural poor is local initiative and capital which would have greater potential in utilising local rural resources and satisfying local demand. This observation which we will try to strengthen further constitutes an integral part of our own approach.

While a deep rural location is not necessary for the generation of rural linkages, we have used a mix of the two in our study, superimposing the locational criterion on the linkage one. Hence RI should be understood as that sub-sector of the mainstream industrial sector which is located in rural areas (as we have defined it) and displays considerable links with the rural sector. However given the nature of secondary information available, rural industry includes all such activity located in rural areas since it is not possible to precisely separate those with rural links.

2.4.2 *The Importance of Linkages*

While Hirschman (1958) had developed the concept of **production** linkages as inducement mechanisms for stimulating economic activity through backward and forward linkage effects, he had dismissed agriculture as a sector with very little linkage potential in developing economies primarily due to its backwardness. However, in the light of the emerging emphasis on a relatively endogenous process of rural industrialisation, attention was drawn to the potential linkages which could be generated by a fast growing agriculture. Of particular importance was the expenditure-linked multiplier effect of growing agricultural incomes, viz. **consumption** linkages, in generating rural based, small-scale, labour intensive industries, highlighted by Mellor (1976) in his "new strategy of agriculture-led growth" (see also Johnston and Kilby 1975; Ahluwalia 1978; Chadha 1986). In the context of the Soviet industrialisation debate,this was the linkage emphasised by Bukharin, the home market for industry in agriculture.While rural industrialisation has emerged as a powerful policy instrument, the tremendous amount of research which appeared on Mellor's "rural growth linkages" to quantify the links between increased agricultural production and rural based non-agricultural activities evoked considerable controversy. We examine the nature of the linkages first and the assumed mechanism which brings about Mellor's virtuous circle of growth, followed by some discussion on the rural growth linkages controversy[9] and findings from other major studies. This gives us greater insight into the issues critical for operationalising a process of RI in which the rural sector is attributed a certain autonomy.

2.4.3 Sources of Rural Linkages

Before we describe the linkages, it needs to be noted that while the linkages cited in Mellor's model flow from agriculture to non-agricultural activities, we present them as flowing from non-agricultural activities to agriculture. This is so, since in our study we have taken the rural small-scale manufacturing sector as the sector of origin of linkages.

Any industrial activity, whether related to agriculture or not, can be linked to the rural region through four types of linkages. These are:

- backward production linkage effects;
- forward production linkage effects
- consumption linkage effects; and
- capital and labour linkages.

(a) Backward Production Linkage Effects

These linkages focus on inputs, both intermediate and capital goods, required by the unit which may be in the nature of processing of a number of agricultural crops or intermediates from other rural industrial units. Very often a major advantage of rural small-scale industry is its use of locally available raw materials. However, here a range of technological options is available, some of which could be very capital intensive and urban oriented; the precise choice is affected by the nature of the raw material, whether it is perishable, is subject to economies of scale etc. and the macro policy environment. The local response in the setting up of processing units is generally high in case of foodgrain processing and a more egalitarian agrarian structure.

[9]The controversy has been reviewed in depth in Hart (1989), Dunham (1991) and Saith (1992)

(b) Forward Production Linkage Effects

These refer to output utilisation of the activity if it does not cater to a final demand. This could largely be in the nature of input requirements of agriculture. However this would depend on the nature of the agricultural practices in use, the overall macro policy environment and the prevailing agrarian structure. Use of fertilizers and other chemical inputs as also heavy labour saving machinery, result in poor local multiplier effects. The well-known distortion of relative factor prices through subsidisation of machinery, biases demand in favour of tractors vis-a-vis power tillers as also the choice of post-harvest technologies. This discourages local responses since such producer goods may be import intensive or produced in highly capital intensive urban large-scale units. However, increased irrigation facilities, including the use of engines and pumps for lifting water, new varieties of seeds, mechanical threshers, a wide range of farm implements and equipment, repair services and construction inputs, generate greater linkages for local industries. Forward production linkages exist also in the case of sub-contracting arrangements which large units located locally enter into with small units. Though hardly discussed in the literature, the tertiary sector offers considerable potential for the growth of small rural industries, through its demand for simple intermediate goods.

(c) Consumption Linkage Effects

This effect, viz. the demand for consumer goods from both agricultural as also non-agricultural households, has been stated to be quantitatively the most important. It is dependent on the level and distribution of rural incomes, since expenditure patterns vary across different income classes. In the lower deciles of the rural population an overwhelming share of consumer expenditure is on agricultural commodities. In successively higher income classes, the proportion of expenditure on foodgrains declines sharply. Demand for non-foodgrain agricultural commodities is highly income elastic and hence the linkage effect generated by such demand is particularly strong. In respect of non-agricultural goods and services, which is our main area of concern, the proportion of expenditure is much lower in the lower deciles compared to the higher income classes; however consumption patterns of the latter are generally more import and/or urban intensive. While the demand for services, which are primarily non-tradables, exerts a strong local linkage, that for manufactured commodities is governed by the distribution of the incomes. The strength of this linkage then lies in the pattern of demand that is thrown up with existing and changing incomes depending on whether it is biased in favour of the kinds of consumer goods typically produced by small-scale rural industries. That this linkage does have a great potential is due also to the possibilities of new consumer goods becoming available. At times of course this may generate a negative impact by a substitution away from an existing local industry as for instance plastic or metal products replacing mud pots and utensils.

(d) Capital and Labour Linkages

One of the important linkages in the context of RI is the utilization of local resources such as rural capital (which may otherwise be siphoned off through the financial institutions), and unemployed and underemployed labour from agricultural or other households. This generates a direct developmental impact on the rural population. The role of the local entrepreneur in the process of RI needs to be emphasised. Needless to state the rural sector would score less favourably than the urban sector in terms of locational factors for attracting industry (excluding of course agriculture related industry). As a result attracting outside initiative would imply substantial expenditure on inducements. The potential for initiating a process of RI based on mobilisation of local capital lies in the relative subjective advantage local entrepreneurs would have in a rural setting despite locational disadvantages (Bar-el et al 1990).

Given these possible linkages, what has been their empirical validity in inducing the growth of rural small-scale industries across developing economies? Mellor's (1976) is perhaps the most consistent model of rural industrialisation based on the linkages discussed above (which in his framework run from agriculture to non-agriculture) and needs to be briefly stated to understand the controversy evoked by the attempts to validate it empirically and quantitatively.

2.4.4 *Mellor's Rural Growth Linkage Strategy*

The underlying growth mechanism in Mellor's framework is the effect of an efficiency increasing technological change in agriculture (assumed to be exogenously given) which can lead to substantial indirect growth in non-farm employment and incomes. This occurs partly due to an increase in the use of farm inputs (backward production linkage)[10] as also processing, transportation and marketing of increased agricultural output (forward production linkage) but, most importantly, from increases in household expenditure on consumer goods and services as a result of growth in agricultural incomes (consumption linkage). This induces investment in other sectors of the rural economy, particularly rural manufacturing and services, mobilising underutilized labour resources which in turn generate a demand for agricultural output and so on, resulting in a virtuous circle of rural development. In the long run, purchases of consumer goods absorb most of the increased rural incomes, while the local supply response for intermediate goods may not be significant, depending as it does on the nature of agricultural and processing technology adopted. Given the extremely varying consumption patterns between the labouring classes and the dominant owner cultivator classes (the former spend almost three

[10]Backward production linkages of agriculture with industry would be forward production linkages of industry with agriculture. Similarly with respect to forward production linkages of agriculture.

fourths of the increment in expenditure or "marginal budget share"[11] on agricultural commodities while for the latter it is less than one fifth) it is clear that increasing foodgrain production in a manner which benefits the workers would be a "self balancing process". In contrast agricultural technology which distributes benefits to the dominant owner cultivator classes, provides more complex linkages leading to an endogenous demand led growth sustained by the higher levels of rural consumption expenditure. It was also argued that the consumer goods industries stimulated by increased rural incomes are likely to be small-scale and labour intensive (Mellor 1976).

An assumption critical to Mellor's argument was regarding the investment behaviour of these prosperous cultivators who would save additionally from the increased incomes. The increased demand for industrial goods and services acts as a strong incentive for these households to invest in local small-scale non-agricultural activities and diversify their interests. Mellor also stressed the need to back this strategy of rural led growth by an appropriate macro policy environment which would enable the right technological choices and a decentralised administrative framework given the dispersed nature of the growth process.

Considerable research was inspired by Mellor's work on rural growth linkages which appeared to offer a simple path to a dynamic process of rural industrialisation. Attempts were made to investigate the links between agriculture and non-farm activities by measuring the indirect impact of agricultural growth, induced by large agricultural development projects (mostly internationally funded). By examining consumption patterns and expected changes in consumer demand through changes in income and its distribution, the strength of the growth linkages was estimated (Bell et al 1982; Hazell and Roell 1983; Ahammed and Herdt 1984; Deb and Hossain 1984; Haggblade et al 1989; Hazell and Hojjati 1995).

Most of these modelling exercises based on household consumption surveys of large agricultural projects appeared, as Mellor wrote, "to confirm some of the key arguments in my book... The strength of the growth linkage multipliers and their concentration on labour intensive goods and services produced within the rural areas for local household consumption suggests that agricultural growth has the potential to significantly enhance rural non-farm employment..." (Mellor in Foreword to Hazell and Roell 1983). The regional growth multipliers estimated were very significant; for instance Bell et al (1982) found for the Muda Irrigation Project in Malaysia, that one dollar of value added generated directly by the project induced a downstream effect of 0.80 cents. However, the growth multipliers varied across different regions; they were higher in Asia (0.80) compared to 0.40 in Africa which, however it was pointed out were underestimated (Delgado et al 1994).

[11]It refers to the incremental expenditure on a commodity due to a unit increase in income or expenditure.

Supplementing these studies based on household consumption expenditures, large-scale field surveys of rural small-scale enterprises in a number of developing economies were undertaken since the latter half of the seventies in an attempt to understand their linkages, particularly with agriculture. These surveys were also a valuable contribution in filling up the data gap on small firms, particularly those at the lower end of the size spectrum. The evidence thrown up by these surveys though not very extensive, suggested considerable linkages between agriculture and small-scale rural enterprises, particularly consumption linkages and the main source of dynamism identified was agricultural growth (Ho 1980; Chuta and Liedholm 1985; Liedholm and Mead 1987; Bagachwa and Stewart 1990; Ranis 1990). However, some of these studies also emphasised the need to take a broader (than the rural growth linkage) view on the agriculture-non agriculture linkages (Ranis 1990; Bagachwa and Stewart 1990). Mellor's model drew considerable appeal since it appeared to bypass the need for a politically unpalatable land reforms policy. What needed to be done was somehow to increase agricultural productivity, which would result in larger agricultural incomes, leading to the virtuous circle of growth. However, its limitations were many and it evoked considerable controversy.

2.4.5 The Rural Growth Linkage Controversy

A major limitation of this approach was that it was too techno-centric subsuming the "efficient but poor" hypothesis. Peasant farmers are poor not because they allocate resources inefficiently but because of the restrictions on the kinds and quantum of resources they command. Implicit and explicit markets are believed to exist to ensure full employment of all resources and their efficient utilization leaving no room for surplus labour (cf. Storm 1992). Hence the only way that output can increase is through technical innovation. However, quite paradoxically, according to Mellor, the benefits of this will accrue more effectively to the rural poor through the "downstream effects" if concentrated on the larger cultivators. The possibility of the rural poor diversifying as a survival strategy in the face of increasing pressure on land, does not enter the perspective at all.

Again, while it could not be denied that growth in agricultural production and incomes does have an indirect impact on rural non-agricultural economic activity by raising the demand for goods and services, some elements of this strategy were highly controversial, such as:

- the **primacy** of agricultural growth in the inducement of local non-farm activity, in particular rural manufacturing;
- the need to concentrate the strategy on the larger cultivators based on their consumption and investment patterns supposedly most beneficial for the trickle down process;

- the location, scale and nature of non-farm activity generated through growth in agricultural incomes; and
- the relative importance of consumption vis-vis production linkages.

Needless to state these aspects are inter related and their critical examination also yields alternate views on the significance of rural linkages. We address each of these aspects below.

i. Distress Induced Diversification

The history of proto-industries shows that in its early phase it was in the nature of a supplementary activity for agricultural households at the bottom of the social scale who did not have enough land to eke out a living for their family. Engaging in some type of industrial activity was a supplementary source of income not necessarily induced by any perceived growth linkage. It also helped to improve the time pattern of rural employment given the seasonal rhythm of agricultural operations (Mendels 1972). Such secondary activity of those who were mainly agriculturists was in the nature of distress diversification. In the context of developing economies too, there has been considerable discussion on the dual nature of rural economic diversification in terms of the above type of labour-supply side factors or the survival strategies of households, and the more dynamic product-demand side stimuli. These are alternately referred to as the "push" and "pull" factors generating the growth of rural non-agricultural activities. An expansion in non-farm employment may either be a reflection of the spill over of rural workers who cannot be absorbed in agriculture or other productive work resulting in low paid, marginal activity acting as a sponge for the excess labour, or it could be a more dynamic process responding to increasing demand for certain types of commodities and higher returns. This also throws up broadly two categories of rural industries:

- Those products or activities in which the enterprises are run on a stable basis using relatively more of hired labour and capital, generating surpluses for further growth; and
- Those industries which operate, at times on a seasonal basis, using primarily family labour, minimal capital and respond to a very small, local markets with low returns.

The difference between the two is not so much in terms of broad product group categories as in the use of capital and labour (Mukhopadyay and Lim 1985). Attempts to assess the relative importance of the two categories of rural industries have been made in terms of labour productivity (that is, earnings per worker); those industries providing a wage below the agricultural wage are deemed to be residual in nature (Hossain et al 1994). However, as has been pointed out the floor for wages is set by the rural subsistence economy which mostly offers only a precarious alternative (Schmitz 1990). Also in situations in which workers of small-scale enterprises are members of a wider family set-up, wage claims are substantially moderated given the family support. This is especially the case with women, who have limited options for employment (Simmons et al 1994). In this sense earnings of such an activity do not really reflect its distress character. Other attempts have been made using some measure of excess labour, for instance the unemployment rate or the proportion of landless labour households or the land-man ratio to identify distress diversification (Vaidyanathan 1986; Unni 1990; Eapen 1994). However, given the nature of employment data generally available, with few correlates of employment besides the product group classification, it is not easy to precisely demarcate the two types of rural industries. Nonetheless,in the context of a slow growth of formal sector employment, the contribution of the distress type of activities despite their low returns should be recognised as forming a vital aspect of the livelihood of rural households (see .

ii. Primacy of Agricultural Growth

It has been argued that an agriculture-led strategy of growth is justified if we can assume that the performance of agriculture is not constrained by industrial performance which adjusts endogenously to agricultural performance (Bhaduri 1992). Agriculture as the prime source of dynamism emerges from most of the above mentioned rural growth linkage literature due to the manner in which the impact was measured viz. by excluding any other source of inducement. This was reflected in the selection of a region for study. For instance the large irrigation project in Muda is a geographically isolated area in which exogenous sources of demand would play a negligible role. However, for another region nearer to an urban centre an important component of increased aggregate demand could come from urban growth (Dunham 1991). Evidence for the East Asian success stories of rural industrialisation (which followed divergent paths) in Taiwan, Japan and China does suggest the existence of a fast growing agriculture characterised by extensive land reforms as a major source of demand for rural industrial products. However, there was at the same time a high sustained growth rate of industry which generated considerable impulses for the growth of rural small-scale industry through the device of ancillarisation. Also from a very early stage, except in the case of China, a rapid exploitation of export demand was a strong inducement for the growth of rural industry (Saith 1992). Even in the case of Taiwan, an example par excellence, of a dispersed pattern of RI located largely in rural areas, Ho (1979), while emphasising the stimulating role of a robust and diversified agriculture, acknowledged the critical roles played by a well developed infrastructure and high levels of rural literacy. In fact it must be remembered that the all important agricultural productivity change which was to initiate the process of growth and keep it going through the various kinds of linkages, was exogenously given. It should itself be seen as a significant function of the (spatial) proximity to non-agricultural activity (Ranis 1990).

In India too, studies differ in their understanding of the role of a technology induced agricultural growth in the diversification of the rural economy, particularly in terms of the spread of small-scale manufacturing. Rangarajan's study (1982) finds a link between agricultural performance and industrial growth, particularly of consumer goods industries at an aggregate level without focussing on location. However, micro level studies for some regions, which also attempt to trace the spatial location of the growth of industries, attribute only a partial role to agricultural growth in inducing the diversification of the rural economy. The study of Harriss and Harriss (1984) and Harriss (1987, 1991) based on village fieldwork in 1973–4 and again in 1983–4 and surveys of a market town in the district of North Arcot in Tamil Nadu which was a region of green revolution,[12] concluded that "the economic diversification that has occurred can only partially be explained in relation to agricultural growth...". (Harriss 1991 p 455). It was linked more to the growth of the public sector and of an urban industry which was independent of the growth of agriculture. On the other hand another research based on Mellor's approach in the same region of N.Arcot estimated a very high agricultural growth multiplier (Hazell, Ramaswamy and Rajagopalan cited in Haggblade et al 1989). Papola's (1987) detailed study on Uttar Pradesh (UP) included a field survey of two districts, one located in an agriculturally fast growing region of Western UP and the other in an agriculturally less developed and slow growing region of Eastern UP. It was found that there was hardly any relationship between agricultural development and rural industrial activity in terms of magnitude or composition. However, a high rate of agricultural growth appeared to improve the productivity of rural industries. Papola concluded that RI needs to be viewed not merely as an adjunct to agricultural growth but as an independent element of a strategy for generating non-agricultural employment and incomes in rural areas.

The primacy of agricultural growth or the priority of agriculture over other sectors in a process of sustained industrialisation has remained and will remain a controversial question since it is a political economy question subsuming an ideological perspective on the long term process of capitalist accumulation in the context of non-socialist societies.

---

[12]It was a region of green revolution since over 90 percent of gross cropped area was under high yielding varieties.There was a rapid increase in the use of chemical fertilizers and insecticides and a further expansion of groundwater irrigation from already existing high levels.

iii. Consumption Patterns of the Large Farmers

The size of the consumption linkage multiplier depended not only on how much agricultural income increased but also on its distribution and associated consumption pattern. Whether the large farmers have the most desired consumption patterns for growth of local non-agricultural activities was an empirical question, which could not be resolved conclusively even by the evidence provided by the studies on rural growth linkages. It is not clear why despite advocating the desirability of targeting the agricultural growth policy on the more prosperous farmers, Mellor focussed on the sixth, seventh and eighth deciles[13] which according to him, represented farmers producing a major portion of the national agricultural output. These were obviously not the largest cultivators who would have constituted the ninth and tenth deciles. However, the study by Hazell and Roell (1983) finds that the households operating the larger farms have the most desired expenditure behaviour in terms of locally produced, labour intensive goods while the one by Bell et al (1982) for the same region (Muda) finds that it is the low income households that have the more desired consumption patterns. Mellor qualified the Hazell and Roell finding by stating that the larger farms in Muda were in fact not large by most standards. Indeed, Hazell and Roell admitted that this finding went against the prevalent view that the labour intensity of goods and services consumed by households decreases as incomes increase and hence the poorer households should be the target of policies on agricultural growth. The question of which kinds of agricultural households have the most beneficial expenditure patterns to induce employment intensive growth in rural areas was not resolved satisfactorily. Perhaps for this reason it was concluded by the growth linkages research that it would be better to target agricultural technologies on a broad range of farm size groups (Hazell and Roell 1983).

This policy focus on large farmers as the most appropriate vehicle of delivering the strategy suggested a naive faith in the "trickle down" mechanism of the benefits of agricultural growth (Saith 1992). There was no doubt, given Engels' law[14], that the richer farmers would spend more on non-food consumer goods. However, the quantitative significance of this demand depended on the nature of the agrarian structure (Dunham 1991). Evidence from the green revolution region of Punjab based on a survey in the mid-seventies across three agro-climatic regions, revealed that the large and the largest farmers were not the dominant source of demand for non-food goods and services except in the region where large farms were very dominant. More importantly the existence of an "appropriate" pattern of demand did not automatically

[13]Mellor (1976) had used data from an All-India Consumer Expenditure Survey giving consumer expenditure patterns, food and non-food, by population deciles, conducted by the National Council of Applied Economic Research, New Delhi.

[14]Engel's law states that the share of food in total expenditure is inversely related to the household's income (or some other measure of its total resources).This implies that the income elasticity of food expenditure is less than one.

translate itself into the generation of local, small-scale, labour intensive enterprises (Hart 1989; Saith 1992). The desired results were derived from the way in which consumption patterns across different deciles were assessed (Harriss 1987b). Hazell and Roell (1983) compared actual and potential demand for locally produced goods and services with the demand for imports which then was taken to indicate the potential for relatively labour intensive, small-scale locally produced goods. While over 40 percent of expenditure on non-food goods and services in the four highest farm-size deciles was for imported goods, Hazell and Roell argued that it was the expenditure out of incremental incomes that mattered (Dunham 1991). That even this tended to be import intensive among the rich farmers in the region under study was pointed out by Hart (1989).

A question arises: Would the strategy have resulted in a self-sustaining growth of rural regions if it had been focussed on the small farmers?. Besides the non-feasibilty of such a policy given the political milieu in a wide range of developing economies, the possibility of a "trickle down" to the large proportion of rural landless still remains conjectural. Hence it would appear that an agricultural production based strategy in an inegalitarian agrarian structure need not produce the desired results.

iv. Location, Size and Nature of Non-agricultural Activity

The question was to what extent did the increase in demand lead to a generation of small-scale manufacturing activity located in the local rural areas? Here, both from the demand and supply side the evidence was weak. Evidence from the Muda region and Bangladesh suggested that a larger part of the incremental consumer expenditure was on imported industrial goods (Hart 1989; Hossain 1987). Most of the diversification that occurred in Muda was in terms of expansion of commerce and services, especially government services (Hart 1989). The "... important demand driven sectors that expanded to meet increased household demands were trade, entertainment, travel, residential construction and financial services" (Bell et al 1982). The Hazell and Roell study stated that "... the additional expenditure on nontradables goes mostly to non-food goods and services particularly those associated with housing, education, health, transport, personal services, entertainment, and social obligations and festivities". Harriss also found that while agricultural growth might have stimulated industrial expansion it was not always local industry or when it was local, it was not necessarily small-scale (Harriss 1987a). However, the argument that it was not local since it may have come up in the nearby market town was not convincing (Dunham 1991). This was so, since Mellor had emphasised the locational potential of market towns which as observation suggests, do appear to be typically an integral part of the rural community. Hence rural need not be defined rigidly in terms of designated rural areas.

What this implies clearly is that the definition of local is important to measure the strength of the linkages and the further upwards one moves from the village, the higher the possibilty of "local" linkages (Tambunan 1994). On the whole however, over time studies on household expenditure surveys appear to confirm that consumption linkages are stronger with rural services (Haggblade et al 1989) or the food sector itself, primarily livestock and horticulture products (Delgado et al 1994; Hazell and Hojjati 1995) rather than rurally manufactured goods.

It may be noted that the poor response in terms of growth of local small-scale industries implied that the investment pattern of the larger farmers also failed to conform to expectations. Mellor had argued that with increased earnings, large farmers would divert a part of their increased earnings into small-scale consumer goods industries as a response to the increased demand for non-food goods and services. However, even in the Muda region in which considerable rural incomes were generated, the study by Bell et al (1982) revealed that there was huge and increasing capital outflow in search of investments elsewhere. Most other studies in the rural growth linkage literature too, did not provide adequate evidence on the investment behaviour of surplus producing farmers. Dunham's study on Punjab suggested that growth of the small-scale industrial sector was very much a process of evolution and evidence suggested that it was not initiated by the green revolution induced increase in agricultural savings. There appeared to be an outflow of savings from the Punjab to other parts of the country, as in the Muda region (Dunham 1991). Similar conclusions, that growth of industry could not be linked to the savings of the agriculturists, were reached for North Arcot district (Harriss and Harriss 1984). However, some other studies found a close involvement of agricultural and secondary activities in South and Central Gujarat (Breman 1985; Streefkerk 1985; Rutten 1991) among larger farmers and artisan castes. Economic diversification among the rural elite suggested that capital flows in both directions, between agriculture and non-agricultural business as a result of which the categorisation of economic activities into "mercantile" versus "industrial" or "productive" versus "unproductive" is very arbitrary. Agriculture, trade and industry are very closely intertwined in these regions (Rutten 1991). The investment behaviour of large farmers is perhaps critical to the issue whether increased agricultural production can generate self-sustaining growth of rural regions by promoting small-scale local enterprises (Hart 1989).

It appears therefore, that while increased rural demand should provide an impetus to the growth of the rural non-agricultural sector, the evidence on its strength and nature in terms of small-scale manufacturing is mixed.

v. Consumption Vs Production Linkages

Almost all empirical research on the subject has found household expenditures for consumption purposes to have significantly stronger multiplier effects within the local economy. Local production linkages particularly the supply of industrial inputs to agriculture were found to be weak given the nature of farm technology which tended to use fertilizers, and capital equipment imported from outside. Linkages in terms of agro-processing and transportation as also distribution of agricultural products (forward production linkages in the rural growth linkage literature) were second in importance to consumption linkages. However, it was argued that the local linkage multiplier in terms of consumption of industrial goods was overstated in the rural growth linkages studies due to the way in which it was assessed. For instance in the Bell et al study (1982), the demand claimed to be for locally produced goods and services (consumption linkages) was in fact for local services of wholesalers and retailers of goods produced elsewhere. Also the assumption of perfectly elastic supplies of locally produced goods inflated the consumption multiplier (Harriss 1987b). Even if the model was made more elaborate to incorporate the impact of less than perfect supplies of local consumer goods, the question was more of the inducement to invest which the studies did not deal with in depth (Hart 1989).

2.4.6 A Broad Framework of Analysis

The preceding discussion on the approach to rural industrialisation and its linkages enables us to draw up a broad framework of analysis (See Chart 2.1). Diversification of the rural sector is to be perceived as a dimension of the broader process of rural transformation in developing economies with a more direct role to the sector in generating and responding to linkages. Any development strategy has to acknowledge the dominant influence of the agricultural-rural sector in large agrarian economies and should not regard industrialisation as an exogenous process. The dual economy models tended to detach the process of industrialisation from development of the agricultural-rural sector. There is need to view the latter as having greater autonomy in generating productive employment opportunities in the context of its own development priorities. It offers a vast potential market for industrial goods, both consumer and producer goods, which can be exploited through a more organic link between agriculture or more broadly the rural sector and industry within the rural space itself through capital, labour, production and consumption linkages. "Rural" needs to be defined less rigidly, including the contiguous small towns with which rural areas are functionally related. However, from the point of view of development of a micro region and the devolution of financial resources, there is a virtue in not

Chart 2.1

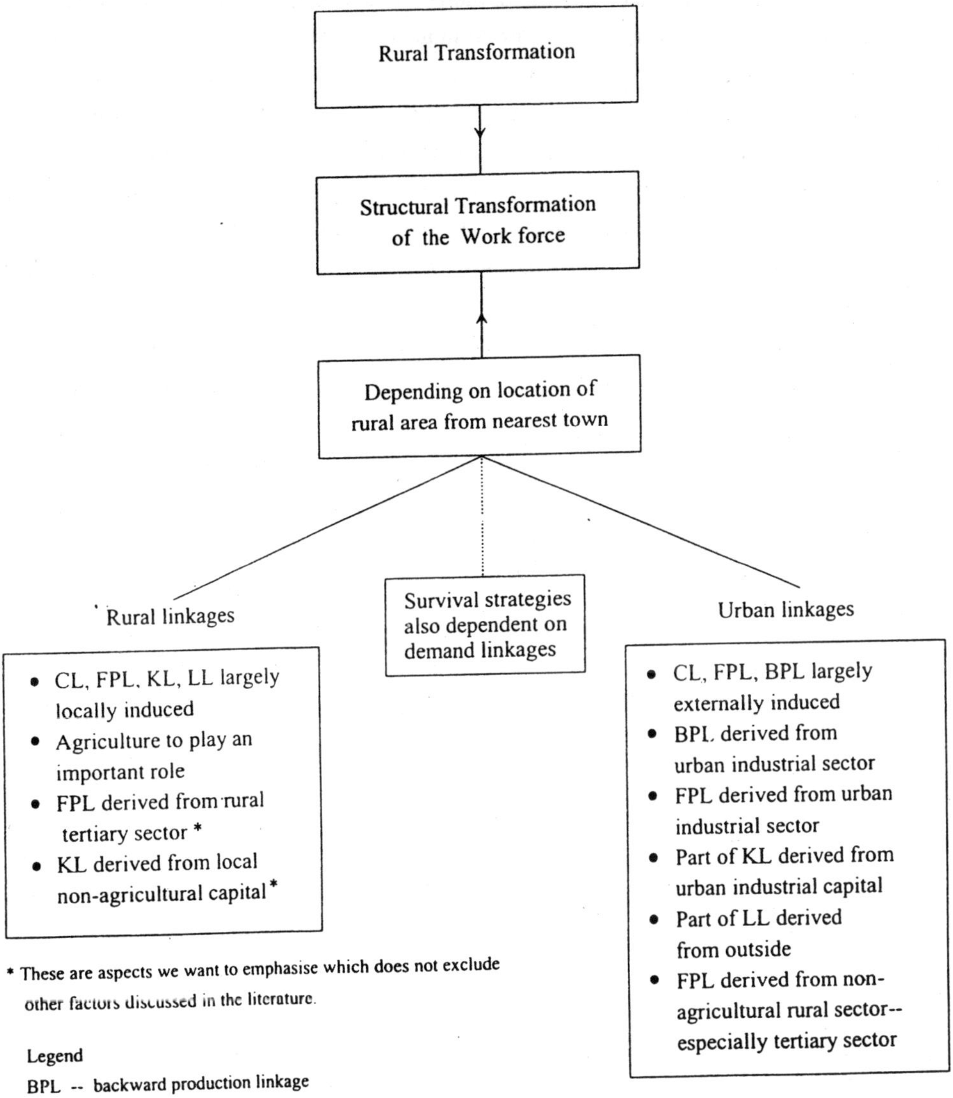

* These are aspects we want to emphasise which does not exclude other factors discussed in the literature.

Legend

BPL -- backward production linkage

FPL -- forward production linkage

CL -- consumption linkage

KL -- capital linkage

LL -- labour linkage

widening the definition too much. There could be a tendency otherwise for funds to flow to the larger urban centres.

A major role in the generation of productive employment opportunities within the rural areas, is ascribed to small-scale enterprises, the potential dynamism of which is increasingly being realised as recent discussions on "proto-industrialisation" and "flexible specialisation" reveal. However, rural small-scale industries need not be transitional in nature. While not growing into large-scale units, they could contribute to the growth of modern industry in other ways. There is certainly a potential for an endogenous process of rural industrialisation and in fact the rural sector in most developing economies has been diversifying, with both the labour supply side and product demand side stimuli operating, its pace and content determined by the region's specificities. Stimulating rural industries based on various linkages would strengthen the demand side stimuli.

In this context it needs to be emphasised that the survival strategies are not entirely detached from demand side linkages. These efforts should be seen as valuable economic endeavours undertaken after an initial preparation in terms of gaining experience in the type of activity to be undertaken. They are also in response to some perceived demand for their product. However, what happens perhaps is that given the poorer socio-economic background of such entrepreneurs, they tend to concentrate in activities which need very little initial capital and hence easy access. The resultant over-crowding in these sectors ensures low earnings.

However, these need not be primarily agriculture induced. Increasing agricultural incomes without considering the agrarian structure cannot induce the type of virtuous circle of growth discussed by Mellor. An agriculture-led strategy of rural growth which implies that agricultural performance is not constrained by the performance of industry is not very convincing. In fact it needs to be emphasised that the whole process has to be viewed in a broader rural rather than agricultural context and hence not merely as an adjunct to agricultural growth. While there is considerable evidence that external or urban factors may be more important in generating the desired linkages, rather than agriculture, particularly in rural areas contiguous to large urban settlements, the potential in terms of non-agricultural sectors of the rural economy providing developmental links with the small-scale manufacturing sector needs to be explored further. Most studies also reveal that linkages are stronger between growing rural incomes and demand for rural services rather than with rurally manufactured goods. However, the potential for locally produced goods is higher with a more egalitarian agrarian structure and in rural locations relatively distant from large urban settlements. In such locations agriculture would play a relatively more important role in inducing rural diversification. Factors that promote occupational diversification vary across villages.

While demand creates the necessary incentive to invest, to ensure that the gains are internalised, local capital has to play an important role. It is likely that local entrepreneurs investing locally would tend to generate higher developmental links with the rural sector particularly in terms of employment of local labour, and cognisance of local rural conditions in investment decision-making. The magnitude of local savings and its utilisation is rather critical to sustain the process, in particular for the setting up of non-agriculture related activities. Insofar as rural industrialisation is viewed as a constituent of the national economic and industrial trends, it has to extend beyond the narrow set of activities in which rural areas have an advantage. It is in this respect that indigenous entrepreneurship assumes importance. Local entrepreneurs attribute a real (subjective) value to the development and extension of local economic activity which reduces the place specific disadvantages. Mobilisation of local capital becomes even more important in the context of decentralised local-level planning.

Once again, agricultural surpluses may not be the most dominant source of investment, though as found in studies relating to Gujarat, this may be more apparent than real. Agricultural and non-agricultural activities are intertwined in ways which make it meaningless to categorise them into "mercantile" versus "industrial". It is possible that the larger farmers invest first in agriculture related business and then venture into industrial activity. The potential for greater utilization of agricultural surpluses for setting up small-scale manufacturing activity certainly exists. Savings are being generated also among the non-rich in rural regions and the better off non-agricultural households who invest in small-scale manufacturing activity. The question is one of channelling all savings into more productive income generating activities which keeps the process going.

It is also possible that **production** linkages with agriculture may increase in relative importance over time, as the extent of irrigated area grows and mechanisation is not too rapid. More importantly such linkages in terms of simple, intermediate goods required by the rapidly growing tertiary sector in most developing economies could also offer considerable potential for the setting up of rural small-scale enterprises. The question whether rurally linked small-scale enterprises would display adequate dynamism to sustain growth and provide adequate earnings for the rural work force is a controversial question. A judicious policy in terms of allocation of resources and development efforts is essential to maximise each without sacrificing too much of the other objective.

We now examine the specificities of the region under study which make it especially conducive to a process of rural industriialisation.

3

Industrialisation in Kerala: The Background

3.1 Introduction

In this chapter we present certain macro economic and structural characteristics of the Kerala economy which serve as a backdrop to the study. More importantly, our attempt is to highlight their role in generating an environment, especially conducive for rural industrialisation in the state, small in scale and linked to a broad-based rural market demand. Perhaps the most striking feature of the economy is the nature of its growth suggesting a widespread participation in the process and its benefits.

While education and the creation of human capital has been an important way in which broad-basing was attempted to be achieved, more direct redistributive methods were also used to lay its foundations. Equity considerations, tending to improve the lot of the broad majority of the population, have played a more important role in economic policy measures rather than aggregate economic growth considerations (Ratcliffe 1978). At the same time the state has remained more diversified with much lower (than all India) rural-urban differentials in socio-economic structures. While growth of manufacturing has indeed been dispersed, the state remains industrially backward in terms of the share of manufacturing in the state domestic product (SDP), its rate of growth and product structure.

To the extent our study relates not to a nation state but to a sub-national entity as the unit of analysis, there is need to consider those aspects of the national context, such as overall economic policy, which have an impact on regional growth. In India as is well known, the development of industry in the post Independence period occurred within a centralised planning framework. It was very uneven (Bharadwaj 1982) and regional disparities have widened in the recent period (Krishnaji 1993). Kerala was one of the states which received very little attention in the heavy industrialisation strategy pursued; its share in public sector investment remained low and in fact declined over time (Subrahmanian 1990).

In the Indian federal set up the states do not have complete control over the local resources and in shaping their own economic future. The pattern of financial devolution between the Centre and the states is weighed heavily in favour of the former. It has been noted, however, that over time region specific characteristics have assumed an important role in industrial development at the regional level, as for instance the nature of agricultural growth (Banerjee and Ghosh 1988) or of individual state policy (Subramanian 1994). Coupled with the regional differences in respect of historical evolution, resource base, industrial structure, labour organisation and nature of entrepreneurship, the states have attempted to carve out a sphere of relative autonomy enabling them to shape the process of industrialisation and hence of the level and nature of employment opportunities generated. There is a certain rationale therefore in studying RI at a regional level.

However with the adoption of the policy of stabilisation and structural adjustment since the early nineties, almost wholly a prerogative of the national Government, the manouverability of states is likely to have been eroded. And for a state like Kerala, highly dependent on primary resource exports, indiscriminate globalisation can impact adversely on the rural economy (Kurien 1994). On the other hand, the enactment of the 73rd and 74th Constitutional Amendments in the Indian Parliament in 1994, which endows "panchayats"[1] and urban local bodies with powers to function as institutions of self-government has enhanced the autonomy of such units vis-a-vis the states. A critical function of the panchayat is "the preparation of plans for economic development and social justice" (Bandyopadhyay 1997), which has been made possible with the follow-up state legislations in respect of powers and devolution of funds to the local bodies, as in Kerala. Its significance in the context of rural industrialisation will be discussed later.

This chapter is organised in 4 sections. We start in Section 3.2 with a brief discussion of some physical and macro economic features of the economy. In Section 3.3 we examine certain structural characteristics which have helped in broad-basing the rural economy as also making it relatively more diversified over the past few decades. The evolving industrial structure and emerging industrial entrepreneurship is analysed in Section 4.4 in a historical perspective. A natural question that arises and which we will touch upon is: why despite considerable industrial dynamism[2] in the period just prior to Independence, has the state responded so little in terms of industrial growth?

This chapter is largely descriptive, piecing together necessary information on various aspects of the Kerala economy from other studies. It relies heavily on an earlier study of the author on rural economic diversification in Kerala (Eapen 1994).

---

[1]A three-tier local administration system ("panchayati raj") in the rural areas, grama (village), block and district panchyats, came into existence in the state on 2nd October, 1995.

[2]Travancore, one of the erstwhile princely states and later part of Kerala, had ranked top among the princely states in industrial development in the decade prior to Independence (see Issac and Tharakan 1986).

3.2 Kerala: The Economy

3.2.1 Physical Aspects[3]

The state of Kerala is a small, narrow strip of land on the extreme south west coast of India. With a coastline of 590 kms it does not exceed 100 kms at its widest point (see Map 1). It has a total area of about 39,000 sq.kms. Constituted on November 1, 1956 it comprises of the Malabar district in the North (which was till then part of Madras state), the whole of the former Cochin part of Travancore-Cochin state in the Centre and the major part of Travancore state in the South. Among the three, Travancore is the largest accounting for more than half the area. While the first was directly administered by the British in the pre-Independence period, the last two had been princely states and hence under indirect colonial rule. The differential nature of colonial rule, for instance differences in state policy regarding land relations (Raj and Tharakan 1983), education and health (Kabir and Krishnan 1991), had its impact on subsequent development of the regions. Malabar inherited a relatively backward economy vis-a-vis the other two at the time of the state's formation (CDS 1975; Krishnan 1994). However, Malabar played a critical role in Kerala's development achievements through its numerous mass movements against economic and social oppression as also the freedom movement from which emerged the left movement. Lessons from these were drawn by the other two regions. State wide peoples' movements helped in a wider spread of the achievements (Ramachandran 1996). At present the state is administratively divided into 14 districts which in turn are divided into 152 blocks, 1384 villages, 990 grama (village) panchayats, 54 municipalities and 3 corporations. Many panchayats cover more than one revenue village.

In terms of its physical features, the land is divided into four distinct types: (i) the highlands touching the Western Ghats; (ii) the midlands; (iii) the lowland plain; and (iv) the coastal belt. It is fed by over 40 rivers. The undulating topography of the state, the tropical climate (high incidence of sunlight, rainfall and warm temperatures) as also the cool temperatures of the hills, generate a variety of agro-climatic conditions within a small spatial entity, conducive for the growth of a range of crop species (Shyamsundaran Nair 1994). The state has a fairly high proportion of area under spices, ginger, tea, coconut and rubber, the latter two being perennial in nature; the share of food crops in the total cultivated area, at about 30 percent, is one of the lowest in the country. With population growth rates higher than India's since early 20th century, Kerala, with its 29 million inhabitants in 1991, in a limited geographical area,has become one of the most densely populated regions in India (as also in the world), particularly in the lowland and midland regions (Krishnaji 1979; Krishnan 1994; Zachariah and Rajan 1997). The density

[3]Most of this information has been collated from the Gazetteer of India, Kerala, 1986 and 1989.

Map 1: Kerala

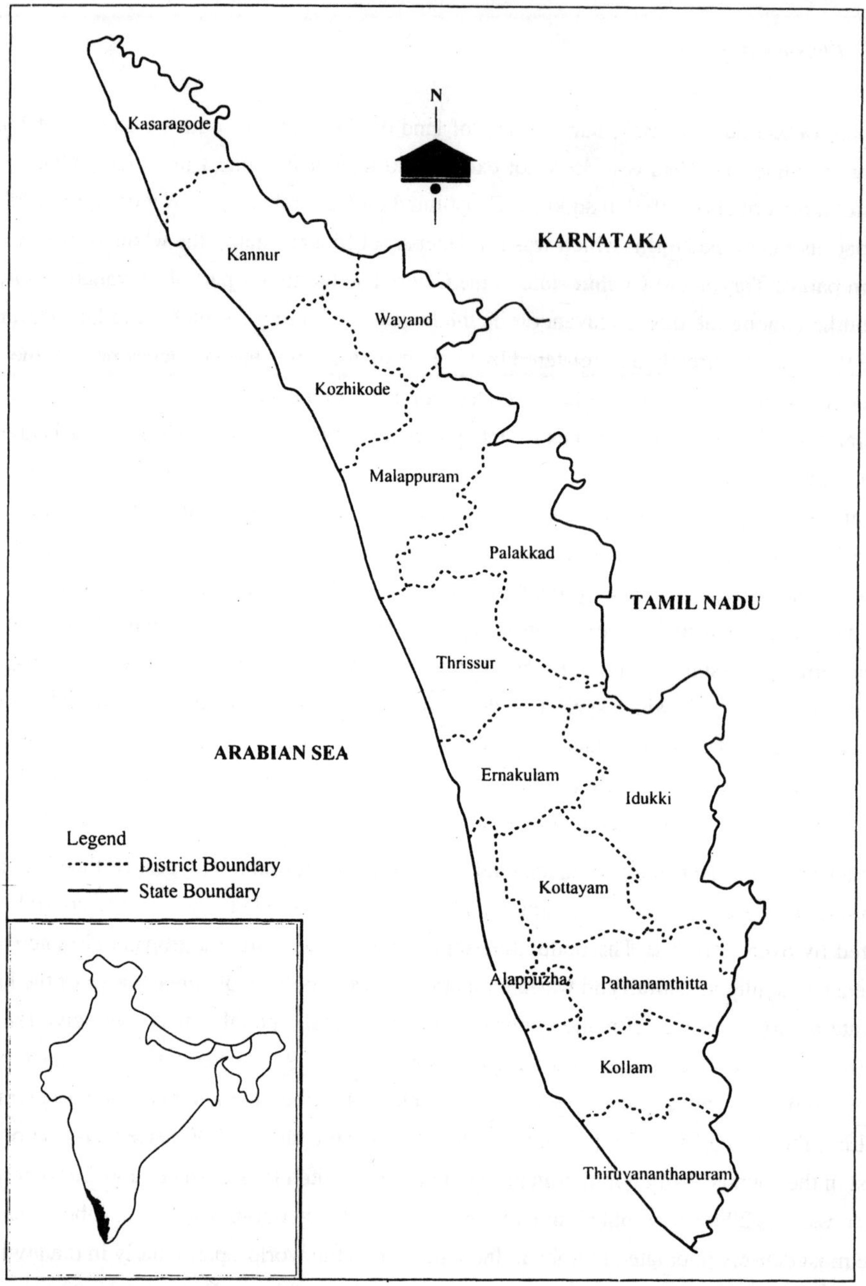
N
KARNATAKA
TAMIL NADU
ARABIAN SEA
Kasaragode
Kannur
Wayand
Kozhikode
Malappuram
Palakkad
Thrissur
Ernakulam
Idukki
Kottayam
Alappuzha
Pathanamthitta
Kollam
Thiruvananthapuram
Legend
District Boundary
State Boundary

of population as recorded in the latest Census of 1991 (749 persons per square kilometre) was nearly three times that of all India. This has had an impact on the size of Kerala's villages: at the 1991 Census, the average size of a village in the state was almost 16,000 persons compared to a little over 1,000 persons for all India.

3.2.2 Macro Economic Aspects

(a) The State Domestic Product

Kerala has performed rather poorly on the economic front when viewed in aggregate terms. However its pattern of development with strong government intervention in the social sectors, has been unique and has drawn considerable attention being popularly described as the "Kerala Model" of growth. Its basic characteristic is the paradox of high social development and economic stagnation. In terms of certain indicators of social development such as life expectancy, birth rates, infant mortality rates, sex ratio and literacy levels especially of the female population, its performance is rated very high. It is not only high in comparison with other states and developing economies but also developed countries (Krishnan 1994; Tharakan 1996) However, its per capita income is low and growth in State Domestic Product (SDP) has generally lagged behind the all-India average (Panikar and Soman 1985; Isaac 1993; George 1993; Ramachandran 1996).

Upto the mid-sixties the state failed to reflect the general buoyancy of the Indian economy with growth rate of the SDP lower than the all-India average. However in the post mid sixties period when the national growth rate stagnated, for Kerala it was significantly higher but per capita income still remained lower than India's due to the higher population growth rate. Since the mid-seventies, when the growth rate of the National Domestic Product (NDP) picked up, there was again a deceleration of the SDP growth rate, barely managing to grow faster than the rate of growth of population which had started declining (Subramanian and Pillai 1986; Isaac et al 1992). During the eighties, 1980–1 to 1989–90, SDP growth rate was hardly 2 percent for Kerala compared to 5.2 percent at the national level.[4] In this period growth in per capita income would have been negative but for the steep decline in rate of growth of population. The share of Kerala's SDP in the NDP declined from 3.5 percent to 2.8 percent between 1981–91. It is interesting to note that in the most recent quinquennium 1990–1 to 1994–5 the growth rate of SDP in Kerala was marginally higher at 5 percent compared to 4 percent at the national level. While per capita real income at Rs. 2246 still lags behind the national figure of Rs. 2449, the

[4]At the all India level, the growth rate corresponds to the period 1980–1 to 1990–1 (Bhattacharya and Mitra 1993).

gap has been narrowing over the last few years (GOK 1996). The disparate growth of the SDP in Kerala vis-a-vis the NDP, is argued to be largely on account of differences in the industrial structure between the nation and the region (Subramanian and Pillai 1986).

(b) Remittance Incomes and SDP

It has of course been pointed out that since income estimates refer to incomes originating in the region and do not take into account incomes accruing, Kerala SDP is underestimated due to the non-inclusion of remittances received from Keralites working abroad. This inflow started growing substantially since the mid-seventies in the wake of the large-scale migration of Kerala workers to the Gulf countries. That it made a quantum improvement to the standard of living in Kerala is evident from the anomalous situation of per capita consumption being higher than per capita income in certain years of the post-Gulf migration phase. For instance in 1986–7 while per capita income was Rs. 2371 at current prices, per capita consumption expenditure was Rs. 2436 (Krishnan 1991).

Attempts have been made to estimate the remittance incomes indirectly[5] since data on the actual inflows into Kerala are non-existent. In a pioneering attempt to estimate income from a consumption function, Krishnan found that the flow of remittance incomes varied between 15–22 percent of SDP during 1972–3 to 1989–90; it peaked to 30 percent in 1978–9 and there was another high of 26 percent in 1986–7 (Krishnan 1994). These remittances made possible a moderate increase in the rate of growth of per capita incomes in Kerala, from 0.45 percent to 0.90 percent between 1972–3 and 1989–90. Whatever be the growth rate in per capita incomes, it is significant to note that Kerala experienced a steady growth in per capita (real) consumption during this period, at 1.8 per cent per annum (Krishnan 1994).[6] A striking fact is that the remittances did not result in a greater inequality of per capita consumer expenditure within the state, rather, its growth was reasonably broad based (Issac 1997). Between 1977–8 and 1987–8 there was an increase in the share of the bottom 30 percent of the rural population in the per capita consumption of all items, food, non-foodgrains and industrial goods and services (Eapen 1994). In fact, the period witnessed a significant decline in the incidence of poverty in Kerala from its high level in the sixties (Krishnaji 1994).

[5]The method adopted for making these indirect estimates is based on taking the total flows of private remittances in the balance of payments accounts of the country and attributing a particular proportion of these as emanating from Kerala workers living in sizable numbers in certain regions. Gulati and Mody assumed the proportion to be 50 percent from the Gulf countries and 5 percent from the rest of the world; unofficial flows via informal channels are not considered. Estimates derived on this basis were lower than Krishnan's and the years in which they peaked were also different (Gulati and Mody 1983; Issac 1994).

[6]While there was some deceleration in remittance inflows in the mid eighties, the inflow picked up again since the early nineties despite the Kuwait crisis (Isaac 1997).

However, the relatively higher consumption expenditures in the post-migration period, did not seem to have had much impact on the commodity producing sectors of the economy which continued to grow much slower than the tertiary sector (Isaac 1993; Krishnan 1994). The economy was unable to take full advantage of the growth in consumption expenditures despite a potential increase in productive capacity by way of savings generated from the remittance inflows. Most of the increase in investment that occurred was in housing. While this did open up a major avenue of non-agricultural employment in rural areas in construction, it failed to generate adequate backward linkages in terms of manufacture of building materials. The above implied a growth in import dependence of the regional economy, the requirements being met almost entirely from other Indian states (Isaac et al 1992). While the state is a major exporter of its primary products,[7] interstate and international, studies have shown that the trade deficit, estimates for which are available since the mid-seventies, grew sharply from 16 percent of the SDP to 24 percent between 1975–6 and 1980–1. In the 80s it was expected to grow further.

Hence potential employment opportunities, which could have been generated through the "downstream effects" of the induction of remittance incomes, were largely lost and Kerala continues to be characterised by the highest open unemployment rates among the major states of India (Eapen 1994a). Almost 12.5 percent of rural males and 25 percent of rural females were "usually unemployed" in 1987–8 (that is for more than half the year) according to the 43rd Round of the National Sample Survey Organisation (NSSO). The corresponding proportions for all India were 2.8 percent (males) and 3.5 percent (females). Urban unemployment rates were higher.[8] While the latest viz. 50th Round of the NSSO for the year 1993–4, largely indicates an all-round decline in unemployment rates since 1987–8, the state continues to be characterised by the highest rates of unemployment (NSSO 1996).

Comparing the growth rate in SDP with the employment growth over the recent period 1981–91, it is interesting to note that growth has, in fact, been the most labour intensive in Kerala; employment elasticity of output at 0.93 is the highest among all states, compared to 0.45 for India (Bhattacharya and Mitra 1993). However the elasticity is high because of low growth of output rather than high growth in employment and it reflects low productivity growth.

---

[7]More than half the gross output of its primary and manufacturing- processing sector is exported to other states or abroad (Isaac et al 1992).

[8]In Kerala the usual status urban unemployment rate for males was 14.1 percent (6.1 percent for all India) and 33.8 percent for females (8.5 percent at the all India level) in 1987–8 (NSSO 1990). The NSSO provides three estimates of employment and unemployment to capture the irregular nature of work in large agrarian economies, varying with the reference period adopted: the usual status, current week and current day status. The former has the longest reference period.

3.2.3 *Summing Up*

From the above it appears that international labour migration and remittance inflows played a critical role in mitigating the poor economic performance of the state. There was a moderate increase in the growth rate of per capita income between 1972–3 to 1989–90 with the inclusion of remittance incomes. However, it masked the seriousness of the economic situation reflected in the low rate of growth of domestic industrial production and high unemployment rates. In fact the study on the basis of which (CDS 1975) the Kerala "model" was projected never intended it to be described as such, since the authors emphasised that development of the social sectors should also lead fairly rapidly to all round advances in agricultural production and manufacturing industry (Raj 1994). The limitations of this pattern of development biased heavily in favour of the non-commodity producing sectors both in terms of income and employment, have become very evident, manifested most vividly in the severe fiscal crisis in the state which is of an earlier origin and greater intensity compared to most other states. The state is unable to spend adequately not only on economic services but also on social services, to maintain and improve the social sectors which have historically accounted for the larger share of public expenditures. Its primacy in social services vis-a-vis the other states in India, is gradually being undermined (George 1993; Gulati and Narayanan 1994). It is also becoming increasingly clear that there are some sections of Kerala's population to whom the so called "model" does not extend since their status in terms of education and health is extremely poor (Kurien 1994; Ramachandran 1996).

The fairly high external orientation of the economy, with a growing trade deficit on account of the increased import intensity since the mid-seventies and the vagaries of employment in the Gulf countries, renders the state fairly vulnerable to exogenous events. This was dramatically brought out by the 1990 Kuwait crisis resulting in the return of a large number of migrants (Isaac 1993; Gopinathan Nair 1994). The impact of the more recent sharp fall in rubber prices from Rs. 60–65 to Rs. 27 per kg in 1997 due to import liberalisation has yet to be worked out.[9]

Hence it is evident that there is an urgent need to emphasise the development of domestic industrial production. And it has to be achieved within the low growth scenario sketched above, a situation not very different to Malaysia's in the latter half of the eighties (Saith 1989). However that a potential exists in terms of funds, a large part of which are flowing out of the state (Mohan and Raman 1990; Isaac et al 1992) and demand, generated by commercialised agriculture and international migration (Eapen 1994b) cannot be denied. This is evident from signs of change in certain pockets of the state even while the overall scenario is gloomy. Together with the new democratic initiatives in decentralised planning being attempted under the Ninth Five Year Plan

[9] Currently, the state government is attempting to stabilise it at Rs 34 per kg.

of the state (1997–2002), through empowering and mobilising people (as also resources) for local level development, the potential may even be greatly enhanced.

While in aggregate terms the economy appears to have grown slowly, structurally, significant changes have occurred. Our focus is of course on rural diversification, in particular, rural manufacturing and we now examine some of the specific features of the economy which have important implications for these changes.

3.3 Some Specific Characteristics of the Kerala Economy

There are at least five unique features of the Kerala economy which are relevant in the context of our study:

- the redistributive land reforms;
- the cropping pattern;
- demographic changes and migration;
- the wide spread of literacy; and
- the enigma of the "rurban" settlement pattern. We examine each of these below.

(a) Land Reforms

Kerala is often cited as an example of a state which has been relatively successful in implementing land reforms in terms of benefitting the landless and small holders. In the late sixties the land reform legislation abolished tenancy giving one and a half million tenants full title to either rice fields they cultivated, hutment land they dwelt in or both (Franke and Chassin 1991). However the impact was not entirely unmixed: to some extent it was made ineffective through prior evasive transfers of land by landlords who could anticipate such legislation in the prevailing political environment. At the same time, almost two thirds of the beneficiaries had very tiny holdings, one third of an acre on average and their gains could only be marginal. A large proportion of these were hutment dwellers (essentially landless agricultural labourers living on a small piece of the landlord's land) who now obtained ownership rights to their dwelling house and a few cents of adjoining land.[10] The land was generally good to grow a few coconut trees

[10]This right had to be achieved through a fierce struggle by the hutment dwellers in early 70s which came to be known as the "land grab" movement. The size of the homestead plot on which the occupants were to be given ownership rights varied from 0.03 acres in urban areas to 0.10 acres in a village. It could be purchased at 25 percent of the market rate and half that if the owner had land above the ceiling.

and other garden crops. More significant gainers were nearly half a million tenant households who had larger holdings of 1–5 acres. However, the real gainers were about 0.1 million households who had holdings above 5 acres, some of whom could increase it threefold by acquiring ownership over leased in land (Raj 1992). Hence by conferring ownership rights to some former tenants who cultivated fairly big holdings particularly in the erstwhile region of Malabar in the north and in the fertile region of Kuttanad in the south, tenancy abolition also paved the way for the emergence of a class of capitalist farmers. Together with the fact that there are a large number of "absentee" farmers in Kerala,[11] both on small and big plots, abolition of tenancy did not always mean "land to the tiller" (Oommen 1993).[12]

On the other hand, the land reform legislation in respect of ceiling on land was quite ineffective since very little land could finally be mobilised for redistribution due to bogus transfers made in anticipation of the legislation.[13] While it is true that a substantial part of the land over which ownership was transferred through the land reform was to households who already had more than 5 acres, nonetheless, the landless and small holders also benefitted from the reforms and its achievements are far from negligible. It abolished feudal landlordism and reduced concentration of ownership of landholdings with a substantial redistribution of landed assets. There was a drastic decline in the percentage of landless households, which came down from about 57 percent in 1966–7 to about 14 percent in 1982 (Radhakrishnan 1989).[14] The impact of this was larger in Travancore-Cochin where the incidence of such hutment dwellers was relatively higher (Radhakrishnan 1989). The qualitative change which this brought about in the distribution of economic and social power in a caste ridden countryside, especially in Malabar, was striking. The landless labour households were able to improve their bargaining power in the labour market and agricultural workers made the highest real wage gains after the Land Reforms Act. Compared to other states, real daily agricultural wage rates for men and women have increased faster in Kerala between 1970–1 and 1988–9 among all the states of India (Jose

[11]In Kerala one finds that a number of persons currently engaged in non-agricultural occupations, such as teachers, shopkeepers, lawyers, government employees, politicians etc continue to have farming links in terms of owning land but may not be involved in cultivation at all (Oommen 1993). This characteristic has had important implications for struggles by the agricultural workers on higher wages and land for redistribution (Krishnaji 1979).

[12]This slogan was raised by the Congress in the pre-Independence days to mobilise the peasantry and the agricultural workers for the anti-colonial struggle. It defined tiller as one who is engaged in "personal cultivation" which means putting in a "minimum amount of physical labour and participating in actual agricultural operations". However it was later considerably modified by including "supervision" in the definition of "personal cultivation" (Oommen 1993). In Kerala hiring of labour is common even on small plots of land.

[13]Only about 50,000 acres (out of over 167,500 acres which was finally identified as surplus land) could be distributed to 90,000 households (Radhakrishnan 1989).In fact the earliest estimate of potential surplus land was almost 18,00,000 acres; finally the extent ordered for redistribution was less than one tenth of this (Oommen 1993).

[14]Village level evidence from a survey in north Malabar, in the post-reforms period highlighted the striking difference in the land system after the reforms, which was no longer characterised by extreme concentration of land in a single group (Radhakrishnan 1989).

1994).[15] In 1988–9 the daily money wage rate paid to men was highest in Punjab (Rs. 28.90) followed by Kerala (Rs. 27.70).

On the whole therefore, the reforms did help in establishing a more egalitarian rural society; it "reduced both land and income inequality" (Franke 1993 p 148).[16] Coupled with measures to improve the supply of credit to rural areas, particularly to small and medium sized holdings, it was possible to bring about a significant transformation in the countryside in Kerala (Raj 1992). A more egalitarian agriculture broadens the rural economic base and increases the potential for rural linkages. If incomes are more evenly distributed, consumption of locally produced goods is higher and small farmers use more local inputs and undertake local processing (Bagachwa and Stewart 1990).

(b) Cropping Pattern

Both topographical and economic factors in terms of a favourable export market encouraged the growth of commercial crops in Kerala some of which were processed further, even while the state was deficit in food. Demand for food was met through imports. A study for the Travancore region showed that the area under commercial crops among which coconut and rubber were the more important ones, increased continually since at least the 1920s with some fluctuations given the relative price of the major competing food crop, paddy (Panikar et al 1977). There was a rapid expansion of the external trade of the region which increased nearly 10 fold between the latter half of the 19th century and 1938–9. While exports were made up of most of the agricultural produce, coconut, coffee, tea, rubber and various spices, food constituted the single largest item of imports followed by manufactured products like textiles and other necessities.

While this trend of a relative decline in paddy acreage continued in the post-Independence period, an absolute shift in its acreage had been halted between 1952–3 to 1974–5, a period which witnessed a sharp increase in paddy prices and state policy emphasised the need for some degree of self sufficiency in food (Panikar et al 1977). However a recent study on the performance of the agricultural sector in Kerala suggests that since 1975–6 there was again a sharp shift away from paddy, the latter losing acreage even in absolute terms. While area under

[15]It should be mentioned here that agricultural wage rates are high in Kerala primarily on account of the strong trade unionism among agricultural workers (Jose 1980). However the fact that these have been maintained at high levels is explained also in terms of the unwillingness of literate work seekers to engage in agricultural work (Shaji 1990; Sunny Jose 1991). This generates a situation of shortage of workers in agriculture despite high levels of unemployment.

[16]However more recent data on land holdings operated suggests an increase in inequality in land distribution, even while the proportion of, and area under, marginal holdings has increased; the proportion of area under the largest holdings (that is more than 25 acres) has increased but proportion of such holdings has declined (Padhi and Nair 1992).

paddy grew at an annual rate of 0.8 percent during 1962–3 to 1974–5, in the subsequent decade, the rate of growth, 2.1 percent per annum, was negative (Kannan and Pushpangadan 1988). Paddy acreage continued to decline and by the early nineties, almost 70 percent of the gross cropped area was under non-food crops in Kerala compared to about 30 percent for all India. The significance of cash crops for the Kerala economy is also brought out by the per hectare value of agricultural output which is Rs. 8953 in the triennium ending 1986–89, almost double that of India's at Rs. 4537. While the tendency all over the state is a shift away from paddy, it is uneven. There are districts in Kerala which are still predominantly paddy growing areas, like for instance Palakkad and Alleppey in which almost three fourths of the area is under food crops (CRD 1995).

However that commercialisation is extensive in Kerala, the pace of which accelerated since the mid-seventies cannot be denied. And what is rather unique in the spread of cash crops is that historically, such crops are grown even in very small holdings in Kerala; both poor and middle peasants are engaged to a large extent in their cultivation. In fact over 80 percent of the rubber is grown on small holdings (George and Joseph 1992). Hence the smaller land holders are involved in the market as sellers of their produce to a much greater extent than in India (Krishnaji 1979).

The major determinant of the shift away from paddy has been the disparate price movement between paddy and its alternate uses, which with the high and increasing money wage rates of agricultural labour, has rendered its cultivation uneconomic from the point of view of the cultivators. Not only have paddy fields been converted to other crops or uses in response to price changes, there has also been an increasing tendency to leave paddy land fallow. What has caused greater concern is the seemingly long term stagnation in agricultural output both of paddy and even the non-food crops like coconut and rubber since the mid-seventies despite the increase in acreage of the latter. In fact the rate of output growth was negative for both food and non food crops in the period 1975–6 to 1985–6 (Kannan and Pushpangadan 1988). However, it has been shown that since relative prices of cash crops, in particular rubber and coconut (the latter with greater fluctuations), registered dramatic increases since the mid-seventies, cultivator incomes certainly did not stagnate (Narayana 1990). Hence considerable surplus was being produced in the commercialised agricultural sector and given the high incidence of small and middle farmers growing cash crops in the state, its spread was wider.

More importantly, it has been argued that the post mid-seventies period of stagnancy of agricultural output could have in fact been one of intense investment activity in planting or replanting of tree crops, the fruits of which would become evident only later (Narayana 1990; Sathian 1994). It was the downswing phase of the production cycle of a tree crop agricultural economy. This hypothesis appears to be confirmed by the upturn in rate of growth of agricultural output since the late eighties; in the period 1987–8 to 1993–4 the growth rate was over 9 percent per annum. However it was largely on account of non-food crops (Sathian 1994; DES 1995) and hence the employment elasticity of agricultural output would have been low since per unit labour requirements of tree crops is lower than for paddy. While a commercialised agriculture does generate non-agricultural employment opportunities, the growth of rural employment has been lower than the growth in the rural labour force. Also per capita foodgrain production continues to be very low in Kerala,just 38 kg (average of the triennium 1989–92) compared to 203 kg for all India (Kurien 1994). The declining acreage under paddy has aroused considerable controversy in the state not merely from the viewpoint of declining employment opportunities but also from the point of view of food security(Krishnaji 1994).

(c) Demographic Changes and Migration

While the process of commercialisation did play a positive role in generating rural non-agricultural employment, the much higher than all-India rates of population growth in the first half of the century resulted in a rapid decline in land man ratios with a proliferation of small uneconomic holdings and high population densities. The declining land man ratios and the low labour intensity of commercial crops, acted as a powerful "push" factor out of agriculture resulting in widespread unemployment and making the population mobile both across space and occupations. As far back as 1931, unemployment rate was the highest in Travancore (TSM 1940). Hence the proletarianisation of the work force not totally dispossesed of land started much earlier in Kerala, at least from the beginning of this century, compared to all India. This generated a large supply of workers seeking wage employment outside agriculture (Krishnaji 1979) aggravated over time by a decline in the number of days of employment available in agriculture.[17]

The extreme pressure of population on land in the early decades is evident from the efforts of the state Government to settle people in sparse regions not only inside but also outside the state. Large scale migration occurred to sparsely populated regions in the highland division within Travancore in search of cultivable land which accelerated between 1921–31 (Velu Pillai 1940) and to Malabar which continued into the sixties (Tharakan 1976). As late as the early sixties, the state Government was requesting the Central Government to allot some lands for colonisation of Keralites in the newly developed areas alongside the Rajasthan canal, Nagarjunasagar and Dandakaranya in other states (GOK 1969). The more literate persons migrated to other parts of

[17]Data collected by the decennial Rural Labour Enquiries, indicate that the average number of days of employment for rural male agricultural workers declined from 198 days in 1964–5 to 169 days in 1974–5 and to 147 days in 1983–4. The corresponding decline for females was even larger (Krishnan 1991).

India into non-agricultural occupations, primarily in the service sector. Overseas migration did exist in the early period to neighbouring countries mostly as plantation workers but it was short lived and a new phase opened up of more educated, professional personnel migrating to the developed Western countries. However the numbers involved were small and did not provide much opportunity for the much larger number of low skilled, non-professional work seekers. Pressure on creation of employment opportunities was intensified further with the demographic changes since the early seventies.

There was a dramatic decline in fertility levels in the early seventies ushering in a demographic transition in Kerala which has drawn world wide attention. The earlier higher rates of population growth were reversed since the decade 1971–81. The birth rate which was above 40 until 1965 declined to about 35 by 1970; the pace of fertility decline accelerated in the seventies and by the end of the decade the birth rate had declined to 30. By the end of eighties it declined further to 20 (close to replacement level) and continued to decline further to 17 by 1993. At present the fertility rate in Kerala is significantly lower than the replacement level (Zachariah and Rajan 1997). This demographic change brought about a structural shift in Kerala's population towards the prime working age groups 15–29 years aggravating the problem of unemployment. The decline in fertility since the decade 1971–81 coupled with past reductions in mortality resulted in a much higher rate of growth of the adult population since the sixties. While the rate of growth of population declined significantly, the increase in population in the age group 15–29 was 8 percent in 1951–61, 37 percent in 1961–71 and 36 percent in 1971–81. It is projected to decline substantially between 1981–91. However, such large increments in the size of the population entering the labour force during the sixties and seventies was a major factor in the growth of unemployment in Kerala (Bhat and Rajan 1990).

Employment opportunities opened up by the development boom of the West Asian (Gulf) countries in the wake of the oil price hike of 1973, did contribute in relieving the pressure on the labour market. Unemployment rates had registered a sharp increase in the state since the early seventies, the daily unemployment rate being 25 percent for males and a little higher for females in 1977–8[18] (Eapen 1994a). Gulf migration assumed a significant proportion since the mid-seventies and marked a break from the earlier phases of international migration. This was not only in direction and numbers but also in the type of workers who were absorbed. The Gulf migrants were drawn from all strata of society with a more than proportionate share from the lower middle class. A larger proportion were unskilled and semi-skilled manual workers. They included a fair proportion from rural labour households (Gopinathan Nair 1986; Isaac 1997). Between 1977 and the early eighties there were almost 73,000 new migrants mostly to the Gulf countries constituting about 10 percent of the (usually) unemployed persons. The stock

[18]See NSSO, 32nd Round (1983)

of migrants totalled about 187,000 persons in the early eighties. By 1987 migrants to the Gulf increased by almost 114,000, that is 12 percent of the unemployed, resulting in a total stock of over 300,000 persons. Gulf migrants constitute over 90 percent of total overseas migrants from Kerala. In 1990 (before the Kuwait war), very rough estimates put the number of migrants in the Gulf at nearly 1 million (Saith 1992). Kerala, accounts for almost 40-50 percent of the Indian migrants to the Gulf.

(d) Increasing Literacy Levels

Kerala is well known for its historically high and expanding levels of literacy, in rural areas too, resulting in a much larger (than all-India) proportion of population reporting as students. While almost 31.6 percent of males and 26.5 percent of females were recorded as students in rural Kerala in 1987–8, the proportions were 19.2 and 10.8 respectively for the country as a whole (NSSO 1990). Male literacy by the latest Census (1991) is over 90 percent for Kerala (52 percent for all India) and 87 percent of the female population is literate (39 per cent for the country as a whole). Kerala is the only state where there is mass literacy; education is increasingly being perceived as a means of social and economic mobility. The relatively late entry into the labour market has depressed participation rates to some extent (CDS 1975). By raising income and status aspirations of the younger work seekers, it has altered their perceptions on types of work they would be willing to engage in.

Over the years an increasing proportion of the population has been entering the educational stream and when they come out of it, they do not want to work in agriculture, particularly as agricultural labourers. This is evident from some data on the educational level of the work force. While it would not be surprising to find the incidence of very high levels of education to be greater in non-agriculture, even at lower levels the data are revealing. Those with middle level of education (that is 7 years of schooling) constitute about 33 percent of casual non-agricultural workers which is more than double that in agriculture. An idea of the change that has occurred in the educational levels across activities is provided by a comparison between 1977–8 and 1987–8: the proportion of those with middle level more than doubled in non-agricultural work while it increased by only 5 percentage points in agriculture. The increase in the share of those with secondary level (that is 10 years of schooling) was also faster for non-agriculture and it may be noted that a small proportion of graduates too are engaged in casual work. A most striking feature of these data is the extremely low level of illiteracy among workers in Kerala. For instance, while almost 54 percent of the male workers in agriculture were illiterate for all-India in the late eighties, this proportion was less than 20 percent in Kerala (NSSO 1990).

The growing supply of literate and educated workers at a rate higher than the increase in demand for it has resulted, in the increasing contractualising or informalising of erstwhile regular work. This response to a "surplus labour" situation in non-manual types of occupations implies fairly low earnings in a broad range of non-agricultural activities (Eapen 1994). On the other hand there is a shortage of labour in manual, especially agricultural work despite a high daily wage rate for agricultural labour. Wage rates of agricultural workers in Kerala are high due to the unionised strength of the workers (see footnote 15) despite high rates of unemployment. However, they could be sustained at high levels due to the declining numbers, in particular of males, entering the agricultural work force.

Hence the role of sociological factors operating through the modernising influence of education, (which has also tended to concentrate less on technical and vocational training), has played an important role in shaping people's attitude towards work. This also accounts to some extent for the higher incidence of open unemployment especially of the educated (that is secondary level and above) in the state since the younger job seekers are not willing to engage in low status occupations, not even if the wage rate is high. Recent estimates show that almost 30 percent of male matriculates (57 percent for females) and 18 percent of male graduates (39 percent for females) were unemployed; these figures are three to five times higher than for all India (NSSO 1990). In the absence of an adequate growth in desired employment avenues there has also occurred a growing preference for some form of self-employment. Setting up of small-scale enterprises is one such form, just as migration is another.

(e) The Rural-Urban Continuum

The peculiar settlement pattern in the state with a diffused spatial ordering of houses confounds village or rural-urban boundaries. Coupled with the high population density, the average size of a village is much larger in Kerala (than for India), with a mix of agricultural and non-agricultural activities, adding to the difficulty of distinguishing between rural and urban (Sreekumar 1990). In fact the usual three fold criteria for defining "urban", viz. in terms of population size, density and proportion of the male work force engaged in non-agricultural activities, is not very meaningful in Kerala in terms of the first two, since over 80 percent of the villages fulfill the conditions and can be termed semi-urban. Even in terms of the third criterion, rural non-agricultural activities, the proportion of the male work force thus engaged is not very low (as we see later) resulting in not very dissimilar rural-urban occupational structures. A very important component of urbanisation in Kerala (unlike at the all-India level) has been the emergence of towns through an upgradation of such villages with a change in their occupational structure. While in the seventies almost 22 percent of the growth in urban population was on account of this "extensional" component, in the eighties it had increased to 32 percent. By 1991, almost 92 new small and medium towns had been added to the existing total of 106 towns in 1981 (Sreekumar 1993).

It is interesting to note that a study comparing the proportion of non-agricultural activity in the rural areas of the midland and coastal districts of Kerala with the rural areas adjacent to the six largest Indian cities[19] and the transport corridor stretching from Gandhinagar/Ahmedabad to the Bombay-Pune nexus, found the proportions to be significantly less in the last two. The rural-urban mix with its mix of agricultural-non-agricultural activities appears to be unique to Kerala (Casinader 1994).

Besides the occupational structure, in other respects too, there are no great disparities between rural and urban areas. Historically, there was a fair spread of educational and health facilities in rural regions[20] which has been kept up by public policy in spread of infrastructure too. With the rapid growth of commercial agriculture, there existed a well developed road transport system, further strengthened in the post Independence period, making almost every village in Kerala accessible (Sreekumar 1993; Ramachandran 1996). Kerala ranks first[21] in terms of percent of villages with select infrastructural and basic services (roads, post office, schools, ration shops, primary health centres, hospitals, banks etc) available within 2–5 kms, among all the states of India (Franke and Chasin 1991).

Even the facility of investing in shares is fairly widespread in rural areas and small towns. The phenomenal growth of the Cochin stock exchange in Kerala and trading in shares since the late seventies was not primarily an urban activity unlike other stock markets where investors are mostly urban based. Most of the (nearly) 450 strong nexus of authorised stock market assistants as also a large number of share brokers were located in rural areas and small towns. While their offices were in Cochin, their reach for share funds extended to their own villages and towns (Mohan and Raman 1990).

A striking way in which the rural-urban gap has narrowed in Kerala is the growing convergence of rural and urban per capita consumption expenditures as a consequence of the remittance incomes (Sunny 1988).[22] Even more interesting is the improvement in Kerala's per capita consumer expenditure compared to all India's since the early seventies, particularly in

[19]The cities are Bombay, Calcutta, Delhi, Madras, Hyderabad and Bangalore.

[20]This was not true of Malabar (Krishnan 1994).

[21]Kerala ranks first not merely in relation to other states; its performance in itself is very high. In respect of most of the educational, health, communication and transport services, between 90–95 percent of the villages have access to them (Franke and Chasin 1991).

[22]The narrowing of the rural-urban gap in real per capita consumer expenditure is not evident using a different set of price deflators (Ramachandran 1997).

rural areas. The rural per capita consumer expenditure surpassed the national average by the late seventies, and was 20–30 percent higher than the all India average during the 80s; the urban average for Kerala was only slightly above the all India average since the early eighties (Sunny 1988; Issac 1997). In 1987–8 rural per capita monthly expenditure in Kerala was Rs. 211.47; the average for the country was Rs. 158.10. The spatial settlement pattern has helped in minimising rural-urban differences.

3.3.1 Summing Up

Significant social and (to a limited extent) economic transformation could be achieved through the collective contribution of the specific characteristics of the Kerala economy (though listed one by one above). Strong public action responding to well articulated popular demands of deprived sections of the population, was a critical factor facilitating the process. As a consequence there was a broadening of the socio economic base of the economy, with no great disparities between rural and urban areas. Several scholars have drawn our attention to it (CDS 1975; Ratcliffe 1978; Franke and Chassin 1991; Krishnan 1994; Ramachandran 1996). Migration, in particular to the Gulf countries, was also broad based. While it mitigated to some extent, the pressure on employment particularly in the rural areas given the rapidly declining land-man ratios, the fact that a high proportion of migrants were from the lower income households and from rural areas implied that the flow of remittances had a wide spread. There was considerable broad basing of rural demand and its diversification into industrial goods and services.

3.3.2 Implications of the Growth Process on Surplus Formation

However, we would like to draw attention to the fact that this very process of broad basing would have had some impact on the nature of surplus formation in the state and the industrial structure. While the highly commercialised agricultural sector generated considerable surpluses in the rural economy, the abolition of feudal landlordism and a radical redistribution of land deterred large concentrations of capital. Of course the plantation sector was exempt from the purview of land reforms; however, the fairly high incidence of cash crop production on small holdings at least in the case of rubber, would have tended to narrow down the base for larger accumulation of capital. The early industrialisation process was largely determined by the plantation sector and development of the agro-processing industries. And the mutual interdependence between the nature of surplus generation and the industrial structure would have resulted in keeping the size of capital small and more dispersed. It needs to be mentioned however, that we do not argue that this was the only factor determining the nature and size of industrial activity. It has been shown that capitalists in Kerala had responded to militant trade union activities by fragmenting the units, as in the case of the two major traditional industries, coir and cashew (Issac 1984; Beevi 1978). However, the more dispersed nature of surplus generation must have impacted on the size of capital.

With respect to the Gulf remittances too, a household survey showed that, given its broad spread, almost 75 percent tended to get invested in purchase of land and construction of buildings or used for current household expenditure; only 25 percent of the remittances were in the form of financial savings. However, these savings were concentrated in the richest migrant households. The latter contributed almost 60 percent of the financial savings while their remittances constituted a little less than 50 percent of total remittances.[23]

While the above seeks to provide a rationale for a dispersed, small-scale industrial structure in Kerala which is an empirical reality (Kundu and Raza 1982), the question is why it displays a continued dominance of primary processing industries and a tardy growth of modern industry in the post-Independence period. In fact an issue raised much earlier in the context of Malabar (see Shea Jr. 1959) and debated later tirelessly in the context of Kerala is still very pertinent: Why did not an area exposed to continuing commercial influence with the world market, initiate a process of sustained industrialisation. Attempts have been made to answer this question by examining the historical roots of the industrial structure and industrial entrepreneurship both of which are intimately linked to the contemporary industrial backwardness of the state. We discuss below some of the hypotheses put forward to explain industrial backwardness in Kerala before we digress briefly into a study of the historical evolution of the state's industrial structure and emerging entrepreneurship.

3.4 Kerala's Industrial Backwardness

The sluggish growth of the manufacturing sector in Kerala in the post-Independence period when the country was embarked on a path of rapid industrialisation and the state was under severe pressure to generate productive employment opportunities, has drawn considerable attention in academic and official circles (Pillai (ed) 1961; Subrahmanian and Pillai 1986). While the explanation in terms of lack of minerals like coal and iron is recognised as inadequate (Rudra 1961), a number of other substantive explanations have been put forward. These are:

- the gross neglect of Kerala in the country's heavy industrialisation strategy in terms of allocation of central resources (Namboodiripad 1961);

[23]These are broad estimates derived from Table 15.7 in Issac (1997 p. 297), based on a sample survey in 1993.

- certain infrastructure bottlenecks such as railway transport and power and the absence of a concerted attempt to implement an attractive state industrial policy (Lokanathan 1961);

- the lack of an industrial entrepreneurship both due to the scale of capital required as also existence of other more attractive projects promising quick and easy returns (Raj 1961);

- the widely held notion of the absence of industrial peace in Kerala, with an active trade union movement tending to push up wage costs in organised industry (Rao 1961; Government of Kerala 1984); and

- the industrial structure hypothesis. It is argued that the industrial backwardness of Kerala is related to its industrial structure characterised by a concentration of agro-based and processing industries with weak inter-industry linkages. It results in a process of "cumulative causation"[24] that tends to keep the economy industrially backward (Subrahmanian and Pillai 1986). The same study also persuasively demonstrates the inefficacy of the hypothesis regarding militant unionism and high wage cost. It was found to be empirically unsubstantiated for the organised factory sector. However, that the relativly higher degree of political awareness and working class consciousness among the workers in Kerala has impacted adversely on the small sector and, more importantly, created a feeling among entrepreneurs of labour being difficult to manage, cannot be denied (Thampy 1990). Hence the "psychic" cost of industrial location would be high in Kerala (Subrahmanian 1990).

As is true of most social processes there is very rarely a single component explaining a phenomenon; rather "the answer lies in the cumulative interaction of a number of factors which acquire a collective force much greater than the mere sum of each taken separately" (Shea Jr, 1959 pg. 521). The same is true of the various hypotheses put forward to explain Kerala's industrial backwardness. However, this does not preclude the predominance of particular components. While our research suggests a possible explanation for the lack of growth of large-scale industries in terms of the dispersed nature of surplus generation, we also reiterate the need to probe further the issues of product structure and nature of entrepreneurship. Studies have attempted to trace the historical roots of the industrial structure in the state and its relation to the size and nature of capital. We draw some insights from these studies in the following sub- section.

[24]A term used by Myrdal to describe the cumulative advantages accruing from industrialisation based on ever increasing differentiation of processes (See Myrdal 1957). It has worked in a negative direction in the context of Kerala.

3.4.1 The Evolving Industrial Structure in Kerala: Historical Perspective

The unique cropping pattern in Kerala and its impact on the occupational structure through intense commercialisation of the economy, had been noted as far back as the beginning of this century (Aiya 1906; Velu Pillai 1940; Menon 1967). About 65 percent of the male work force in 1911 in Travancore-Cochin was recorded as engaged in agriculture, livestock, fishing etc compared to over 70 percent for India. Similar was the case in Malabar where the significance of commercial crops, in particular pepper and its links with the external markets is of even older origin (Shea Jr. 1959; Menon 1994). In the beginning of the century only about 62 percent of the population in Malabar was supported by agriculture (Innes 1951). This it was pointed out was not due to the infertility of the soil but to the exploitation of other natural resource endowments of the region.[25] Such economic activity was primarily for export purposes given the channelisation of private foreign (colonial) capital into plantations and agro-processing industries like coir. Initially it was coffee and tea plantations and later rubber, resulting in an industrial structure which, as it evolved, was very much determined by the initial intervention and dominance of European capital. It is interesting to note that the share of manufacturing in the male work force increased in Kerala from about 11.6 percent to over 15 percent in the period 1911 to 1951 while for India it remained constant at around 9.5 percent during the entire period (Krishnamurty 1971).

In terms of total invested capital too, the plantation sector accounted for more than half, as late as the mid forties and it is only since then that there occurred a significant change in the industrial structure as reflected in the composition of invested capital. By 1946–7, for the first time, the share of manufacturing in the total invested capital exceeded that of the plantation sector due to the setting up of three relatively capital intensive modern industrial units. Since then there was an increase in investment in modern industries, most of which came to be promoted by immigrant capital, as also a spurt in the plantation sector with the growing importance of rubber. Investment by local and other Indian capital was growing in the plantation sector particularly in rubber. Travancore emerged as the princely state with the highest total corporate paid up capital by 1947–8. However the average capital of a company was the smallest suggestive to some extent of the relatively small size of capital in the region (Mahadevan 1988). It is interesting to note that a number of traditional industries, like coir, oil milling, tile making and cashew were being organised on a joint stock basis displaying considerable dynamism.

[25]Other agriculture and natural resource related activities viz.livestock, fishing, forestry, logging etc. accounted for a much larger proportion of the work force in Kerala, about 12 percent, during the three decades 1911–31, compared to less than 5 percent for India. However, even including the latter, the share of agriculture in the male work force in Kerala was much below that of all India.

3.4.2 The Nature of Industrial Entrepreneurship[26]

A series of reforms in relation to land holdings to augment revenue were initiated by the Travancore governmnet under British paramountcy by the end of the eighteenth century. These measures created the necessary environment for investment in agriculture, enabling communities outside the Hindu caste hierarchy to acquire land and accumulate. This opened up opportunities for an indigenous entrepreneurial class to emerge by the 1920s. The communities were the Syrian Christians and backward castes like the Ezhavas in the south. However, given the fact that most cash crops like coconuts, pepper, ginger, arecanut and cardamom, unlike those grown largely on plantations like tea and coffee under European dominance, were to a significant extent raised on small holdings, the surpluses generated tended to be small (Shea Jr. 1959; Isaac and Tharakan 1986). Hence growth of indigenous capital was restrained by the initial narrower base for accumulation and the dominance of European capital in the plantation and agro-processing sector which constituted the first phase of industrial development in both the south and north of Kerala (Isaac and Tharaken 1986; Mahadevan 1988; Menon 1994). For instance, the capital structure of the early coir firms was rather small, ranging from Rs. 20,000-70,000 in the 1920s and 30s. Compared with Rs. 200,000-500,000 on average in industrial firms in neighbouring Madras, around the same period, firms in Travancore were indeed small (Mahadevan 1978). With the introduction of natural rubber, local capital entered more actively into the plantation sector and over time managed to consolidate its position. Most of these cash crops were exported and hence external trade expanded very rapidly while food, that is rice, and also other manufactured goods were imported into Travancore and Malabar. To facilitate trade, the infrastructure in terms of port facilities and roads were developed, connecting the highland to midlands and the coast. However trade in plantation crops in the colonial period was almost entirely appropriated by European firms; those indigenous traders who persisted were reduced to acting as brokers and wholesalers of the foreign firms. Some items like import of rice, textiles and yarn was retained by indigenous and non-local Indian traders but the former was most significant in coir mats, cashew kernels and spices.

With the increase in international demand for the commercial crops, local entrpreneurs invested further in cultivation. Even the cultivation of rice was highly commercialised. Two sectors of commercial agriculture required high capital investment - large scale paddy cultivtion on land reclaimed from the backwaters and plantation agriculture primarily in rubber in which indigenous capital got a foothold despite the dominance of European capital even as late as 1933 and managed to maitain its share of the area during the depression which affected the

[26]More intensive studies on industrial entrepreneurship relate primarily to Travancore (Issac and Tharakan 1986; Mahadevan 1988). which we have depended on heavily in this section. Some information on Malabar has been collated from Logan (1887, reprinted in 1989); Innes (1951); Shea (1959); Menon (1994).

larger foreign plantations more adversely. And by the early 40s some of the indigenous entrepreneurs were acquiring the holdings which were being abandoned by British capital. While rubber cultivation had its start on a plantation scale by British planters, the greater part of the increase in area is attributable to Indian capital, predominantly small holders who came into the field later. Some of the entrepreneurs were moving into agro-processing with surpluses earned in commercial agriculture–coir and coconut oil mills in the south and handloom weaving and coconut oil mills in the north (of Kerala). Two leading Syrian Christian business houses consolidated their gains from commercial agriculture by diversifying into banking and were able to make large profits which formed the basis of further diversification into insurance. Centres of commercial agriculture became centres of banking which expanded rapidly as a result of sharp increase in prices of commercial crops and the consequent increase in farmer's incomes.

The rapid growth of commercial agriculture and a boom in the demand for its processed products was an incentive for the growth of a number of agro-processing industries, the first phase of industrial development. The most important were tea and coir, tile and brick making. However, machinery, equipment and fuel required for these industries was imported. The tea industry was in the nature of enclave development, inputs were mostly imported and output almost entirely exported. Industries linked to coconuts had greater impact on the indigenous economy and capital. Copra making, oil milling and coir industry was dispersed through the coastal and midland regions, coconut being a small holder's produce; coir was spurred on by the trade boom in hard fibres in mid-19th century. Spinning was dispersed but coir weaving was more concentrated and primarily due to the large numbers employed in the former this industry employed the bulk of the manufacturing work force, mostly women. Cashew appeared as a major industry only around the 1920s and grew rapidly in the forties. What is interesting is the export orientation of these industries even though there was a potential internal demand. These industries involved elementary processing and had a low technological basis which meant very little linkage for the development of engineering industries; nor was there much interdependence between these industries.

The government also played a limited role in industrial development till about the mid-30s and in fact appeared to be apathetic towards the setting up of large scale industries in Travancore, perhaps because some early experiments had failed. Only since the mid 30s was there a change in government policy in terms of active encouragement and incentives being given. The government made direct investments too in industries in which private capital was not forthcoming or was inadequate. This change in policy did have an impact in terms of the emergence of a modern industrial sector, chemicals, rayon, aluminium and cement. There was a spurt of joint stock company activity in Travancore and its composition also changed. While the early phase of industrial development was characterised by a dominance of plantation and banking companies, the recent one was more in favour of manufacturing companies. Hence not only did the corporate sector expand rapidly in Travancore it also diversified towards modern industries by the late 40s. That it was not adequate to alter the employment structure which continued to be dominated by agro-processing industries, is seen in the following sub-section. Moreover indigenous capital did not play much of a role in the development of modern industry; most of it was initiated by capital from other states. While the plantation "boom" in the forties enabled considerable accretion of surplus with the indigenous Syrian Christain community, it is generally argued that its potential investment into industry was thwarted due to political reasons[27] (Issac and Tharakan 1986). However, this has been refuted on the basis of evidence which shows the rapid growth of profitability of investment in rubber plantations, with increase in its prices since the mid-1930s. The amount invested in rubber planting companies between 1941–2 to 1946–7 increased more than four fold since the latter half of the 1930s. Together with other factors like the absence in Travancore of institutional mechanisms for raising capital for industrial ventures and the uncertainty of the market for manufactured goods given the peculiar geographical location of the state, the response of indigenous capital to concentrate on plantations was in fact a rational one (Mahadevan 1988). Nonetheless, there could have been a 'psychic' cost in terms of the political factor which discouraged investment in industry by the Syrian Christians in Kerala.

There was some local capital investment in modern enterprises, primarily in the textile sector but the units were not very successful. However, the traditional industries showed considerable dynamism with a substantial growth in their numbers and capital invested. The cashew industry which began modestly in 1925 witnessed a spectacular growth in the 1940s; the later period saw the entry of a number of middlemen-traders. However, a few firms controlled the industry through a chain of factories. What is of significance in Travancore's modern industrial history is the role of immigrant capital during and after the second world war with the entry of Gujarati and particularly Tamil capital. The latter had already been associated with some industries in Travancore like paper and sugar which however had not met with much success. Some of the investments during the war were in rubber, plywood, and glass. Certain established business houses from Madras invested in fertilizers and chemicals, rayon and cement which formed the bulk of the capital in modern industries. The rayon unit's requirements of chemicals was met by the chemicals unit.

However, in the post-Independence period, there was another boom in plantation cultivation especially rubber during the Korean War and the withdrawal of European capital from the plantation sector also encouraged investment in plantations. Rubber plantations absorbed considerable investment funds of indigenous capitalists as also the entry of indigenous capital into trade,

[27]The Syrian Christians who formed part of a political alliance against the upper caste state administration, viewed several policy measures taken by the administration as directed against them.

opportunites for which opened up after the exit of foreign companies. During the Second Plan period of the state no significant emphasis was given to modern industries due to the emphasis on traditional industries in Kerala as part of the policy of "walking on two legs".[28] The possibility of state government's involvement in industrial development was severely constrained due to the loss of the elastic customs and excise revenue sources with its integration to the Indian union. The inflow of immigrant capital also appeared to stop in the post-Independence period.

From the above it appears that the following factors could possibly explain the tardy investment by indigenous capital into modern manufacturing in the post-Independence period:

- the agrarian roots of indigenous entrepreneurship in Kerala, which created a tendency to consolidate existing position in the plantation sector due to favourable conditions in the decade of the fifties;
- the existence therefore of a more familiar avenue of investment in which the gains would be procured with a smaller time lag. This was true of other alternatives, as for example trade and other service activities (Ram Mohan and Raman 1990);
- the small size of indigenous capital whose rate of expansion was influenced by the industrial structure; and
- the failure of the government to sustain its policy of active intervention and support to a process of industrial development of the state.

3.4.3 Structure of Manufacturing

That the growth of modern manufacturing in the forties was inadequate to alter the structure of manufacturing, despite an increasing share of manufacturing in the male work force, was highlighted by Krishnamurty's study (1971) cited earlier. It pointed to the near constancy of Kerala's industrial structure in terms of product group since the beginning of the century. Even upto the early 40s almost 75–77 percent of the male work force in manufacturing was in plantation industries, primarily tea and in coir. Other industries were cashew nut processing; tobacco, over 90 percent of which was in "bidi"; textiles, primarily handloom weaving; wood and wood products and non-metallic mineral products, primarily tile/brick making. The most phenomenal growth was in the coir industry in which the number of workers quadrupled in the decade of the thirties. The impact of large investments in modern industries since the mid-forties did not alter the dominance of natural resource based industries, except for a marginal increase in the share

[28]This was discussed in the preceding chapter in the context of the heavy industrialisation strategy underlying India's Second Five Year Plan.

of chemical and petroleum based industries. The share of metal and machinery based industries continued to be less than 20 percent of the male work force till 1951 (Krishnamurty 1971).

Hence, Kerala's large work force in manufacturing was engaged mainly in labour intensive, relatively simple processing industries, closely related to her natural resource endowment. A significant proportion of their production was linked to export demand. It is interesting to note that while in another state, West Bengal, the period of expansion of its most important agro-processing industry, jute, was over by 1911, in Kerala many of the processing industries underwent an expansion between 1911–51 (Krishnamurty 1971).

The value of output per capita of the manufacturing sector in 1950 in Travancore was Rs. 48 against an all India average of Rs. 37 and the state ranked top among the princely states in industrial development (Isaac and Tharakan 1986). However in the following decade itself that is, the fifties, the situation changed to one of industrial stagnation for the state. While the proportion of the male work force in manufacturing declined in Kerala from almost 16 percent in 1951 to about 14.6 percent in 1961, for all India the proportion increased, albeit marginally from 9.7 percent to 10.1 percent. The contribution of the manufacturing sector to the state's SDP was lower than its share in the work force. It is interesting to note that in this period, 1951–61, the share of agriculture in the state's income was higher than its share in the work force. Coupled with the high incidence of commercial cropping, this resulted in per capita agricultural productivity being higher than in the secondary (and tertiary) sectors.

This situation was reversed to some extent in the seventies with the growth rate in SDP originating in agriculture being negative while it was higher in the non-agricultural sectors. However, the gains were primarily taken up by the tertiary sector. The rate of growth of manufacturing has been generally lower than that of the tertiary sector and below the all-India level as also lower than the three neighbouring south Indian states in the post-Independence period. For instance betwen 1970–1 and 1986–7 the manufacturing sector in Kerala recorded a compound annual growth rate of a mere 2.8 percent (at 70–71 prices) compared to over 5 percent in both Tamil Nadu and Karnataka (Subramanian 1990). While the period since then and upto the early nineties shows a dramatic improvement in the growth rate per annum to 12 percent, in the first half of the nineties, 1990–1 to 1995–6, the rate of change was rather uneven varying from a low of 3 percent to a high of 8 percent, all at constant prices (GOK 1996). Other indicators like productive capital and gross output per capita in the factory sector is consistently lower in Kerala than in India and the neighbouring states of Tamil Nadu and Karnataka since the late sixties and upto early nineties.[29]

[29]Total productive capital per factory at constant 1970-1 prices was Rs. 124 in Kerala in the triennium 1969–72 and rose to Rs. 219 in 1988–91; in India the estimates were Rs. 205 and Rs. 370. Similarly gross output per factory at constant prices was Rs. 172 in 1969–72 and Rs. 418 in 1988–91 while at the all India level it was Rs. 240 and Rs. 586 respectively (Ramachandran 1996).

In terms of its product structure, the study by Subrahmanian and Pillai (1986) revealed that the situation did not alter very radically since the early decades of the century. Kerala's factory employment continued to be concentrated in resource based industries with only a small share of "footloose" type industries which has resulted in a fragile industrial base. Some diversification of the industrial base is necessary to ensure the required growth stimuli through inter-industry linkages and agglomeration economies (Subramanian and Pillai 1986).

Since an important question we raise in our thesis is the extent to which rural small-scale industries can contribute to the advance of modern industry, the performance of the factory sector alone does not present a complete picture. The large traditional household and non-factory, small-scale modern manufacturing sectors have also to be considered. However, other evidence suggests a state of crisis for the two large traditional industries, coir and cashew, since the seventies with very little attempt at rationalisation (until very recently).[30] That the modern small-scale, non-factory sector has not grown as rapidly in terms of output and employment as in terms of numbers also becomes clearer in a later chapter. Its product structure too continues to be dominated by low productivity, natural resource based industries. Hence the share of manufacturing in employment and value added continues to lag behind the growth of the tertiary sector in the state. In most other developing regions of the world too, it has been found that the tertiary sector takes up a large part of the decline in the share of agricultural employment and output (Syrquin 1988). However, in the context of Kerala, the continuing increase of its share in the state's work force not readily attributable to impulses generated by the commodity producing sectors, in particular manufacturing, makes the occupational structure rather lopsided.

3.4.4 Summing Up

In the preceding sections we have attempted to argue, against the backdrop of the state's historical specificities and characteristics, that the very process of broad basing of the development achievements of Kerala, had an impact on the size of capital in the region. It explains, perhaps the lack of growth of large-scale industries in the state. We have also tried to emphasise the conducive environment for small-scale industrialisation in the state in rural areas. The small-scale manufacturing sector as we discussed in the previous chapter, has a potentially more significant role to play in long-run economic development in the present day context. However, the question is: what is the nature of growth of the small-scale manufacturing sector in Kerala, located primarily in rural areas, in the recent period? Is it of a proto-industrial nature preparing the way for a higher stage of capitalist production located largely in urban centres? Or, can it be a stage

[30]There have been some attempts at mechanisation of the spinning sector with the setting up of a few mechanised spinning units in the state.

in itself generating self-sustaining growth? Or, is it likely to remain static and eventually die out? We now examine the structure of the manufacturing sector in terms of location and size in the following chapters.

4

Spatial Spread of Industrial Activity in Kerala: 1971–91

4.1 Introduction

In this chapter we explore in greater depth the spatial dimension of the diversification process in the state which has a relatively even mix of agricultural and non-agricultural activities across space. Our focus is of course on the manufacturing sector. While adequate evidence was presented to show its relative stagnancy in terms of employment (and value added) for the state as a whole, at a more disaggregate level, that is, in terms of its spatial spread and size structure, growth of manufacturing employment has been uneven (Eapen 1994; Subramanian and Pillai 1994).

To some extent this has resulted in a further levelling of rural-urban differences in occupational structure; however, there also appears to be a tendency emerging towards agglomeration. What are the implications of this for rural industrialisation? A spatial and size class wise analysis for the more recent period would enable us to identify areas and segments of growth despite an overall sluggish increase of employment in the manufacturing sector. While in this chapter we examine the spatial spread of manufacturing, an analysis of its size structure will be dealt with in the following chapter.

The spatial dimension of the growth of the work force in the state and its structural transformation during the period 1971-91 is investigated at three levels using three different concepts of space. We start, in Section 4.2 by defining space in terms of the rural-urban distinction. However, this is examined not merely in terms of rural and urban but in terms of rural and urban centres classified by size class of towns as well.[1] This is especially relevant in the Kerala context given the nature of its settlement pattern and urbanisation process; rural has to be viewed as an integral part of a spatial hierarchy. This exercise reveals that economic diversification has been particularly pronounced in certain rural settlements transforming them into towns by 1991. At

[1]Urban centres are classified into six size classes of towns on the basis of population:

the second level, space is defined in terms of the rural settlements of 1971 which became urban by 1991 for an analysis of changes in sectoral employment. This is done in Section 4.3. Probing further into where these rural settlements are located reveals that they are situated primarily in the northern and central regions of the state. In Section 4.5, the spatial dimension of changes in occupational structure is examined at the third level, viz. the three regions of Kerala, north, central and south. These three regions correspond broadly to the three erstwhile constituents of the state[2], Malabar, Cochin and Travancore and so the analysis would throw some light on the movement, over time, of economic disparities between Malabar and Travancore-Cochin. By highlighting the differentials in the growth of manufacturing across the state, it would also help us in identifying an area for our field study on rural small-scale enterprises. In an attempt to capture the process of diversification, albeit in a limited manner, in Section 4.5 we focus on certain socio-economic characteristics of the villages which became urban in 1991 to see the relation between some of the linkages discussed earlier and the growth of non-agricultural employment. As the linkages are not directly observable from the secondary data available, we attempt to approximate them by some of these village level characteristics given for 1971. The analysis is of course severely constrained by the limitations of secondary data.

	Population
Class I (Cities)	100,000 and >
Class II (Big Towns)	50,000–99,999
Class III (Med Towns)	20,000–49,999
Class IV	10,000–19,999
Class V	5,000–9,999
Class VI	less than 5,000

Class IV, V and VI constitute small towns. While the population size of the last size class of town is the same as that of rural areas, there are two additional criteria, on density of population and its occupational structure, that urban areas have to satisfy.

[2]The frequent changes in administrative divisions of the state constrains analysis at a more disaggregate level, viz. district, over time. While Kerala was divided into 9 districts in 1961, by 1971 there were 10 districts; 12 by 1981 and in 1991 there were 14 districts. Hence we divide the state into three regions broadly corresponding to the erstwhile constituents of Malabar, Cochin and Travancore (Gazetteer of India, Kerala 1986). That is, Northern Kerala, comprising of Kasargode, Kannur, Wyanad, Kozhikode, Palakkad and Malappuram; Central Kerala including Trichur and Ernakulam and Southern Kerala covering Kottayam, Alappuzha, Idukki, Pathanamditta, Kollam and Thiruvananthapuram.

4.2 Spatial Dimension of the Growth of the Work Force and its Changing Pattern: The Rural-Urban Divide

4.2.1 Data Base

The two major sources of data on workers and their industrial distribution in India, are the decennial Population Censuses and the various Rounds of the National Sample Survey Organisation (NSSO), neither of which is free from problems for an analysis of long term trends. In respect of the former, the problems of inter-censal comparability due to changes in the definition or concept of "worker", make a significant impact on the enumeration of female workers for whom work and non-work can be indistinguishable, especially in rural areas. The concept of secondary, subsidiary or marginal workers, as opposed to principal or main workers, was introduced in the 1981 Census[3] to take care of work which may be irregular, for less than half the year or interspersed with household work and hence draw in the workers, primarily women, who otherwise would be classified as non-workers. However full information, particularly the industrial distribution of such workers is usually published quite a few years after the census year. Hence a part of the work force, viz. the marginal workers, is left out of the analysis.

While it is generally accepted that the NSSO methodology and concepts ensure a better enumeration of the work force, especially the female workers, the estimates thrown up by these surveys are not without limitations, constraining long term comparisons. A major problem is the non-comparability for all states of the two surveys in the seventies (28th and 32nd Rounds)[4], nor is the industrial distribution of the work force available at the state level in the 28th Round relating to the year 1972–3. The non availability of the NSSO data at a disaggregated level, below that of a state, except for very broad regions[5] within a state, also limits its use.

Considerable research has gone into delineating comparable long term series for each of these sources as also the possibilities of combining the two.[6] As far as our own study is concerned, we

[3]There was a change in the definition of worker between the 1961 and 1971 Census. The 1971 Census adopted the concept of main activity that is, the activity in which he/she is mostly engaged. Those who had worked intermittently would have reported non-work as their main activity. This was a big shift from the 1961 Census where a person was deemed a worker if he/she had worked for the major part of the working season or fortnight, preceding the date of enumeration, resulting in a sharp fall in the worker participation rates in the country in the decade 1961–71. In order to capture irregular workers, the concept of marginal workers was introduced in 1981 (Krishnamurty 1984).

[4]This was due to a problem similar to the one noted in footnote 3. The 28th Round (for the year 1972–3) had used a relatively liberal definition of worker and the concept of subsidiary workers was introduced in the 32nd Round relating to the year 1977-8 to make the two sets of data comparable.

[5]The NSSO divides the 15 major states of India into 56 regions; Kerala is constituted of two regions, north and south.

[6]For instance attempts were made to combine 1961 census data with the 28th Round of the NSSO and the subsequent Rounds including main and subsidiary workers. Or the 1971 Census was combined with the 32nd and subsequent Rounds using only main workers (see Krishnamurty 1984; Bhalla 1985; Besant 1988; Chandrashekhar 1993).

have used the decennial Census as the basic source of information since it gives the spatial distribution of the work force, not only for broad rural-urban categories, but for urban centres disaggregated further by size class of towns. We use the latest Census of 1991 with which, however, the earliest Census that can be compared is the 1971 Census which defined a worker in terms of his/her main activity. Since the industrial breakup of marginal workers is, at the moment of this analysis, not available for 1991, we compare "main" workers in 1991 with the more restrictive[7] definition of workers in 1971. The underestimation of the female workers who constitute an important segment of the marginal workers, arising from this necessary procedure, is a serious limitation.[8]

4.2.2 Methodology for Studying Spatial Growth Rates

The relevance of stratifying urban centres further in the context of our study has to be understood against the state's mixed rural-urban settlement pattern. The latter had a considerable impact on the process of urbanisation in the state propelled largely by the diversification of densely populated rural settlements which resulted in the emergence of a number of "new" towns. A stratification of urban centres and the use of the "continuous method" to study spatial change would enable us to capture the process of rural diversification more vividly.

Spatial growth can be estimated either by the instantaneous or by the continuous method. In the first method the locality is classified as rural or as belonging to a particular town group according to the size of its population at the time of each census, and collections of centres of the same size category in different census years are compared. No allowance is made for the fact that the number of towns in each size class may change between censuses. In the latter method, rural areas and towns are classified according to size of population at one point of time and the same set of units belonging to a particular class of locality are compared over time. That the two methods can yield quite disparate results was brought out in the study by Suri (1968) on size and growth of towns. While the instantaneous method established a positive relationship between growth of urban population and size of locality, the continuous method showed that the smallest towns have grown the fastest in terms of population. We have adopted the continuous method since it would enable us to follow the structural transformation of the work force in rural settlements over time. In some rural settlements the transformation may occur without changing the agrarian character of the

[7]cf note 3.

[8]The proportion of marginal workers, both for males and females has declined in the decade 1981–1991 for the state as also for all-India. In 1991, 4.1 percent of the women and 3.6 percent of men were marginal workers in Kerala. However of all female workers, almost 23 percent were marginal workers; in the case of men it was about 7 percent (Census of India, Kerala, 1991).

settlements. However, in some it may be of a scale large enough to change the rural economy into an urban one resulting in the emergence of "new" towns (see Jayaraj 1996). We study first the rural, small towns and large urban units, including urban agglomerations (UAs)[9] as they were defined in 1971[10] and changes in their employment structures by 1991. Subsequently we focus on the "new" towns, some of which have become extensions to UAs while the rest are in the nature of independent towns, probing further into their occupational structure. If, as appears to be the case, the most rapid growth of manufacturing has occurred in the "new" towns, that is those which were rural in 1971, this suggests that manufacturing activity has tended to be relatively dispersed in Kerala. It can be argued that the potential for growth of rural industries is high.

4.2.3 Rural-urban Growth Rates by Industry Group

We now examine Table 4.1 which gives annual growth rates of employment for the period 1971–91 by industry groups across three spatial categories, rural, small towns and the larger urban units viz. medium, big towns and cities including urban agglomerations which were considered as one urban unit.[11]

From the table we observe that total employment grew by less than 2 percent per annum; growth of employment in rural areas was even lower and was slower than the rate of growth of population. Population growth was fastest for the small towns confirming Suri's findings (1968) based on the continuous method. Industry group wise rates of growth showed considerable variations which had significant implications for changes in the occupational structure.

The slow growth in rural employment is largely a reflection of the slow growth in agricultural employment which was less than 1 percent per annum due primarily to the declining acreage under paddy. Considerable employment was generated (particularly for females) in other agricultural activities like dairying, livestock, poultry production etc. (data not shown separately). The relative

---

[9]An urban agglomeration is a continuous urban spread consisting of a city/big/medium town (or contiguous towns) and its (their) adjoining urban outgrowths.

[10]There were no urban agglomerations in 1971 in Kerala. However, by 1981, 9 were formed which increased to 16 by 1991. Given the continuous methodology used, UAs were constituted for 1971 by taking the core cities and contiguous towns of 1991 UAs which existed as urban units in 1971. All extensions/outgrowths which were newly added during the period but which were rural in 1971 were treated as rural in 1991.

[11]Medium towns have been taken together with cities and big towns since their occupational structure in terms of the agriculture - non-agriculture mix between 1971 and 1991 moved very close to the structure of the latter. These three spatial categories have been defined in terms of their status in 1971. For instance all those settlements which were designated rural in 1971 are treated as rural in 1991 though some may have become small or medium towns in 1991. Similarly for small towns and the medium/big towns and cities.

Table 4.1 Annual Compound Growth Rate of Employment by Industry Group and Spatial Categories: 1971–91

Industry group	Spatial category									
	Rural		Small Towns		Cities/Big/ Medium Towns*		All urban		Total (Rural and urban)	
	P	M	P	M	P	M	P	M	P	M
Population	1.5	1.4	5.1	5.1	1.5	1.4	1.9	1.8	1.6	1.6
Main workers	1.3	1.4	5.4	6.4	1.6	1.6	2.1	2.0	1.5	1.6
I. Agriculture	0.5	0.6	8.1.	7.8	1.2	1.4	2.8	2.8	0.6	0.7
II: Non-agriculture	2.5	2.4	4.2	4.1	1.6	1.6	1.9	1.8	2.5	2.4
1. All manufacturing	0.9	0.7	3.2	2.6	0.5	0.5	0.8	0.7	0.8	0.7
i. Household Manufacturing	–1.2	–2.0	0.1	neg	–1.4	–1.6	–1.2	–1.3	–1.1	–1.9
ii. Non-Household Manufacturing	1.6	1.3	4.2	3.3	0.7	0.8	1.1	1.0	1.5	1.4
2. Construction	5.6	5.5	9.6	9.6	6.0	6.0	6.3	6.3	5.9	5.8
3. Trade & Commerce	3.3	3.1	4.6	4.5	2.6	2.4	2.8	2.6	3.3	3.1
4. Transport & Communication	4.3	4.4	5.1	5.1	2.1	2.0	2.3	2.3	3.9	3.9
5. Other services	2.3	1.8	3.5	3.4	0.9	0.4	1.1	0.6	2.1	1.7

Source: 1. Census of India, Series 9, Kerala 1971, Economic Tables BI-BIV and Census of India, 1971, Kerala, Town and Village Directory, Director of Census Operations, Thiruvananthapuram.

2. Census of India, Series 12, Kerala 1991, Economic Tables for District, Taluk, Block, Panchayat and Town for each district (not wholly published).

Notes: 1. As indicated in the text, growth rates have been estimated by using the continuous method.

2. Agriculture inlcudes Cultivators, Agricultural labour, and Livestock, Fishing etc.

P - person; M - male. *Cities, big and medium towns include urban agglomerations.

neg - negligible

increase in the consumption of non-grain food commodities with rising rural incomes appears to confirm Mellor's expectations and is supported by most studies on rural diversification (Hazell and Hojjati 1995). However, such employment has tended to grow much faster in small towns resulting in a "ruralisation" of small towns as we see later. Almost a quarter of the increase in workers in small towns over the period under study was in livestock, poultry, fishing and the like (see Appendix A which gives the distribution of the total increase in workers between 1971–91 in each spatial category by industry group). As pointed out elsewhere frequently small towns absorb ruralities from surrounding hinterlands (Lindert and Verkoren 1997).

Non-agricultural employment has grown at a higher rate (almost 2.5 percent per annum) than agricultural (0.5 percent) in rural areas. Growth rate of non-agricultural employment was highest in small towns (4.2 percent), however agricultural employment grew much faster (8.1 percent) swamping out its impact on the occupational structure. In the large urban units growth in non-agricultural employment was lower than in rural areas. Within non-agriculture, growth was highest in construction for all spatial categories. Growth of employment in the tertiary sector was much higher than in manufacturing for all locations. The uneven growth of manufacturing employment in terms of its spatial spread is indicated by the fact that while for the state as a whole it grew at about 0.8 percent per annum, it was as high as 3.2 percent in small towns and almost 1 percent in rural areas; growth of employment in manufacturing was as low as 0.5 percent in cities/big/medium towns. Even if household manufacturing is excluded, in which the absolute numbers have declined,[12] growth in non-household manufacturing employment was higher in rural areas and small towns. A large part of this growth was due to a much higher rate of growth of female employment in manufacturing (data not shown separately)[13] which suggests the increasing importance of labour intensive industries in these locations. Women are employed in such industries primarily on account of the lower wages that are paid to them (Saith 1989).

4.2.4 Emerging Spatial Pattern of Employment

We now examine the impact of these differential growth rates by industry and type of location on the occupational structure of the state. The significant expansion of non-agricultural activities in rural areas is confirmed by Table 4.2. From a little over one third of the work force in 1971, by

---

[12]This is true even if we include marginal workers whose incidence would be higher in household manufacturing (see Table 5.1 in Chapter 5).

[13]The ratio of female to male manufacturing workers in rural areas increased from 0.48 in 1971 to 0.58 in 1991; the increase in urban areas was marginal.

the early nineties, almost half the workers in rural areas were engaged in non-agricultural pursuits. On the other hand in the small towns there was a sharp increase in the share of employment particularly for females in non-crop related agricultural activities. This resulted in a significant decline in the proportion of the non-agricultural work force in small towns, despite high growth rates in manufacturing and other activities. The large urban settlements showed a more stable occupational structure; the shift towards non-agriculture was marginal, from 82 percent to 83 percent. However, there was some change in the composition of non-agricultural employment in large urban units in terms of a decline in the share of manufacturing while the service sector increased its share further. Almost one third of the increase in total employment over the period 1971–91 in cities/big/medium towns was in trade and commerce (Appendix A).

The share of manufacturing declined for all spatial categories especially for males, given the low growth rates of employment in manufacturing, aggravated by an absolute decline in household manufacturing. However, it may be noted that in rural areas the share of non-household manufacturing increased marginally for both men and women and for women in small towns. Of the total increase of about 226,000 persons employed in manufacturing between 1971–91, almost 778 percent of the increase was in rural areas. Women accounted for over 54 percent of the increase. This increase in the proportion of female workers in manufacturing is corroborated by the latest Round of the National Sample Survey Organisation (NSSO), the other source of data, which however is not strictly comparable.[14]

A striking feature of the above trends is that structural change was not accompanied by an increased concentration of non-agricultural employment in large urban settlements. The gap in the proportion of non-agricultural employment between rural areas and CBM is lower in 1991; however it is really between the small towns and rural areas that the distance has narrowed dramatically. Manufacturing activity in the state continues to be dispersed as was found in the study for the period 1961–71 by Raza and Kundu (1982). However, our data as we shall see, also show an emerging tendency towards agglomeration which may tend to sharpen rural-urban differences in the years to come.

Ho, in his study on Taiwan (1979), tracing the growth of non-agricultural activity by size of locality, finds a similar broad basing of the changes. In fact in Taiwan, not only was the rate of growth of employment in manufacturing the highest in rural locations, it was also higher than the growth rates in tertiary sector employment, which however was absent in Kerala. The study by

---

[14]The proportion of female workers in manufacturing increased from 23.5 percent in rural Kerala in 1987–8 (NSSO 43rd Round) to 24.5 percent in 1993 (NSSO 50th Round). Male workforce in manufacturing declined from 10.7 percent to 9.9 percent over the same period. These estimates are not strictly comparable since rural areas in this context are defined as per the instantaneous method.

Table 4.2: Spatial Pattern of Employment by Industry Group (in percent)

Industry group		Spatial Categories								
		Rural			Small Towns			Cities/Big/Med. Towns		
	Year	P	M	F	P	M	F	P	M	F
I Agriculture	71	61.9	61.1	64.6	29.6	28.8	32.6	17.6	17.4	18.5
	91	52.3	52.2	52.5	46.8	44.7	53.1	16.5	17.0	14.5
1. Cultivators	71	20.2	25.1	5.1	8.4	10.1	2.5	3.5	3.9	1.6
	91	13.9	16.4	6.2	9.8	11.5	4.6	2.7	2.9	1.7
2. Agricultural Labour	71	34.4	28.3	53.5	17.6	14.3	29.4	9.1	7.4	16.4
	91	28.7	25.2	40.2	20.2	19.5	22.5	7.9	7.2	11.2
3. Livestock Fishing etc.	71	7.4	7.8	6.1	3.6	4.4	0.7	5.1	6.1	0.6
	91	9.6	10.6	6.2	16.8	13.7	26.0	5.8	6.9	1.5
II. Non-Agriculture	71	38.0	38.9	35.4	70.4	71.2	67.5	2.4	82.6	81.5
	91	47.7	47.8	47.5	53.2	55.3	46.9	83.4	82.9	85.5
4. Mining and Quarrying	71	0.5	0.6	0.1	0.7	0.8	0.4	0.3	0.3	0.3
	91	1.1	1.2	0.8	0.7	0.8	0.4	0.3	0.4	0.2
5. All Manufacturing	71	14.5	12.8	20.1	22.2	21.6	24.5	22.5	22.4	23.1
	91	13.5	11.1	21.2	13.9	12.7	17.8	18.1	18.3	17.3
i. Household	71	4.4	3.2	8.3	7.2	5.5	13.5	3.4	2.6	6.7
Manufacturing	91	2.7	1.6	6.2	2.5	1.9	4.1	1.8	1.4	3.8
ii. Non Household	71	10.1	9.7	11.8	14.9	16.1	10.9	19.2	19.8	16.4
Manufacturing	91	10.8	9.5	14.9	11.5	10.8	13.7	16.3	16.9	13.5
6. Construction	71	1.6	2.0	0.2	1.8	2.2	0.6	2.5	2.9	0.8
	91	3.7	4.6	0.8	3.8	4.7	0.9	5.9	6.8	1.7
7. Trade and Commerce	71	7.4	9.3	1.5	16.9	20.4	4.2	18.8	21.8	6.0
	91	10.9	13.1	3.5	13.9	17.1	4.7	22.9	25.7	12.0
8. Transport and	71	2.8	3.5	0.8	6.9	8.5	1.5	10.2	12.0	2.4
Communication	91	5.0	6.3	1.3	6.2	7.9	1.0	11.4	13.3	3.5
9. Other Services	71	11.1	10.6	12.7	21.9	17.8	36.4	28.1	23.2	48.8
	91	13.5	11.6	19.9	14.6	12.0	22.2	24.7	18.5	50.8

Source: Same as Table 1

Notes : 1. The spatial categories have been defined by using the continuous method

P - person; M - Males; F - Females.

Haggblade et al (1989) which also looks at structural change by size of location in Sub-Saharan Africa, finds a much sharper increase in tertiary sector employment as one moves from rural settlements to small towns and above, the increase is much less pronounced in the case of manufacturing.

4.3 Pattern of Employment in the "New" Towns

Before we discuss the pattern of employment in the "new" towns it is essential to note that a number of these settlements which became urban in 1991 were in all senses of the term, "urban" in 1971 too.[15] Hence the speed of diversification of the rural economy is to some extent exaggerated. However, all these settlements registered a further increase in the proportion of male non-agricultural work force by 1991.

That the occupational change was rapid in rural areas primarily on account of the "new" towns, that is those rural settlements which became urban in 1991 either as extensions to urban agglomerations (UAS) or as independent/isolated towns,[16] is brought out strikingly in Table 4.3. This is a two way table, the underlying rationale of which is akin to that of the continuous method. With 1971 as the reference year, the rural of 1991 is split into those locations which remained rural in 1991 (cell 1) and those which became urban (cell 2). The latter constituted about 12 percent of the population of all rural locations in 1971 numbering roughly 128 villages.[17] A most striking feature of the second cell, that is, the rural settlements which became urban, is that the proportion of workers in non-agricultural activities and manufacturing in particular, 76.1 percent and 25 percent respectively, is almost double the proportion for villages in the first cell, that is, those that remained rural. This suggests that an overwhelmingly large proportion of the rural hinterland is still very rural in terms of its occupational structure. While the urban centres which remained urban in 1991, that is, the entry in the fourth cell, are characterised by a higher proportion of non-agricultural employment, the share of manufacturing is much lower (18 percent) than in the new towns (cell 2) in which almost a quarter of the workforce is in manufacturing as we noted above. Entries in cell 3 indicate urban settlements which were de-classified into villages between 1971-91.[18]

---

[15]"Urban" is generally defined in terms of a three fold criteria: a. Places with a minimum population of 5000 persons; b. Density not less than 400 persons per square kilometre, and c. At least 75 percent of male workers should follow non agricultural livelihoods (all categories, excluding cultivators, agricultural labourers and livestock, fishing forestry etc). The shift away from agriculture is the most important criterion of being designated as urban.

[16]The word "independent" is used to distinguish such towns from the extensions or those towns connected to UAS. These towns are also, on average, relatively isolated in terms of distance from the nearest town, compared to the extensions. However, this may not always be so.

[17]The equivalence between the village of 1971 and "new" town of 1991 may not always be exact due to change in area or name particularly if the village is bifurcated or combined with another village. Hence while new towns number 138, the equivalent villages were 128.

[18]This feature is a negative component of the process of urbanisation lending it considerable instability. It has played a significant role in Kerala's urban system just as the emergence of new towns has also played an important role. De-classification may occur due to fall in the proportion of employment in non-agricultural occupations, for instance as a result of the decline of traditional household industries or increase in population growth in an urban area without a commensurate growth in non-agricultural employment (Sreekumar 1990).

Table 4.3: Two-Way Table, 1971 and 1991

1971		1991					
		Rural		Urban		All	
		Propn. of workers in Non Agriculture (%)	Propn. of workers in Manufacturing (%)	Propn. of workers in Non Agriculture (%)	Propn. of workers in Manufacturing	Propn. of workers in Non Agriculture	Propn. of workers in Manufacturing
Rural	P	38.3	10.0	74.7	25.2	46.2	13.3
	M	38.2	7.8	77.7	22.1	46.2	11.0
	F	38.6	17.0	75.1	35.6	46.3	21.0
			(1384)		(128)		
Urban	P	46.2	14.0	85.1	18.7	81.8	18.3
	M	48.2	11.5	84.2	18.8	81.4	18.2
	F	41.4	21.4	87.2	18.4	82.9	18.8
			(13)		(75)		

Source: Same as Table 4.1

Note: 1. Figures in brackets refer to approximate numbers of settlements.

P - Persons; M - Males; F - Females; Propn - Proportion.

We split the "new" towns into extensions of urban agglomerations and isolated towns, and decompose growth of non-agricultural activities in UAs on account of the extensions and on account of the UAs as set up for 1971 (see Table 4.4). The decomposition exercise for city based agglomerations was done in the following way: If for instance we take population,

X_{71} = population in year 0

X_{91} = population in year t

X^1_{91} = population in year t of the UA as it existed in year 0 (intensive component)

X^2_{91} = population in year t of the extensions to the UA

Then,

$$X_t = X^1_t + X^2_t$$

Therefore we can decompose the growth rate in the following way:

$$\frac{X_t}{X_0} = \frac{X^1_t}{X_0} + \frac{X^2_t}{X_0}$$

The results show that almost two thirds of the increase in all non-agricultural activities in 1991 in the UAs was on account of extensions. Interestingly in respect of manufacturing, the extensions contributed over 88 percent of the increase. These data suggest that the tertiary sector has been

Table 4.4: Growth Rates in Urban Agglomerations and its Decomposition into Intensive and Extensive Components

		Total growth rate	Due to Intensive growth	Due to Extensive growth
I.	Population	1.01	0.32 (31.6)	0.69 (68.4)
II.	Workers	1.09	.37 (33.5)	0.72 (66.5)
1.	Agriculture	1.61	0.33 (20.4)	1.28 (79.6)
2.	Manufacturing	0.86	0.10 (11.6)	0.76 (88.4)
	i. Household Manufacturing	0.65	–0.27 (–40.9)	0.92 (140.9)
	ii. Non-household Manufacturing	0.88	0.14 (15.8)	0.74 (84.2)
3.	Construction	4.25	2.24 (52.9)	2.0 (47.1)
4.	Trade & Commerce	1.31	0.69 (52.8)	0.62 (47.2)
5.	Transport & Communication	1.14	0.51 (44.5)	0.63 (55.5)
6.	Other Services	0.63	0.36 (57.1)	0.27 (42.9)

Source: Same as Table 4.1

Notes :
1. The growth rate and its decomposition has been estimated as indicated in the text.
2. These figures relate only to city agglomeration, that is city plus its extensions.
3. Intensive growth indicates growth of the UA as defined in 1971.
4. Extensive growth indicates growth on account of the extensions.
5. Figures in brackets indicate percentage contribution to total growth.

growing relatively faster in the large urban settlements while manufacturing activity is being increasingly located to the extensions and outgrowths. As for the independent towns about 20 percent of them are medium size towns, some of which may become the nuclei of future agglomerations while the remaining small towns would constitute part of the rural-small town nexus.

4.3.1 *Summing Up*

It appears from the above spatial analysis at two levels that there has been considerable diversification of the rural economy during the period 1971–91 which has resulted in the emergence of a number of "new" towns in the state. Growth of agricultural employment has not been able to absorb the additions to the rural labour force. The Kerala phenomenon supports McGee's hypothesis that emerging urbanisation in parts of Asia with high rural population densities, is region based rather than city based. Besides drawing people from rural areas to the cities, this process largely utilizes an *in situ* population in the rural area itself (Casinader 1994). While the tertiary sector has made the major gain in increases in non-agricultural employment, manufacturing activity is tending to get increasingly located in the new towns which were erstwhile rural areas.

Even while there has been no increased concentration of non-agricultural employment in large urban centres the process of diversification in rural areas appears to have been fairly concentrated in a small number of villages, a large proportion of which are in fact getting absorbed into the growing number of UAs. It may be noted that in 1971 (cf. footnote 10) there were no UAs in Kerala. Our findings suggest that two distinct spatial formations may be emerging in the state: on the one hand is a rural-small town nexus apparent in the narrowing down of the occupational structures between the two, where possibly rural linkages will be more important. On the other hand is the urban agglomeration, including those parts of the erstwhile rural areas which have been absorbed as extensions. Linkages of rural small-scale enterprises in this case are more likely to flow from urban to rural areas. Needless to state that in Kerala no village is too distant from a town except in the highland regions, however, in relative terms some rural areas are more isolated and hence the degree of influence from urban settlements would be lower.

Keeping this emerging duality of the spatial structure in mind, our field survey of rural small-scale enterprises covers two rural locations; one is part of a big city urban agglomeration and the other is a relatively rural location in which small towns (though part of a medium-town UA) intermingle with rural settlements. Since much the larger number of villages in the state are not part of the UAs, the nature of rural linkages in the diversification process is of greater interest to us. This emerging duality appears to be a new trend in an economy characterised as yet by a relatively less differentiated spatial structure. In addition, the fact that almost 53 percent of the new towns are located in the northern and central regions of the state warrants an examination of the employment structure at a more disaggregated level using the third concept of space, viz. the three regions of Kerala, north, central and south.

4.4 Structure of Employment: By Regions

As noted earlier, due to frequent changes in administrative divisions with the formation of new districts, district wise comparability of employment structures over time is feasible only by merging some districts together. In fact in the north all the districts would have to be merged to make them comparable between 1971 and 1991. We have therefore disaggregated the state into three broad regions, northern, central and south Kerala corresponding approximately[19] to the erstwhile regions of Malabar, Cochin and Travancore. We examine the data on industrial employment focussing on manufacturing, in particular, its rural component.

4.4.1 Employment Structures at the Time of Integration

The first Census of the newly reorganised state in 1961 revealed that Malabar or the northern region was more agrarian in nature, with a much higher proportion of the work force in agriculture compared to the other two regions (Table 4.5). Almost 60 percent of those engaged in agriculture in the Malabar region were agricultural labourers; the average for the state was about half (data not shown separately).[20] In fact the percentage of agricultural labourers to total agricultural workers at 64 percent was the highest in one of the districts in the north, viz. Palakkad. With regard to females the proportion was as high as 76 percent, second only to a district in the south, Alleppey.

The proportion of the non-agricultural workforce was about 35 percent in the north while in the other two regions it varied between 41 to 44 percent. However, there were some interesting rural-urban variations.[21] In the north, manufacturing activity accounted for the lowest proportion of the rural work force. However, the proportion of employment in non-household manufacturing in urban areas was the highest in the north, 22 percent compared to around 15 percent for the other two regions. The north did have an earlier history of non-household manufacturing activity in the nature of factories ("karkhanas") engaged in handloom weaving under the aegis of the Basel Mission (Raghaviah 1990). Similarly, large factories existed also in the tile industry. Of course in the south too, cashew factories and coir weaving units were organised as non-household undertakings since the 1930s. However, the household form was overwhelmingly dominant in the major traditional industry viz. coir spinning in the south.

4.4.2 Structure of Employment, Region-wise: 1971–91

Since the three regions were unified in 1956, special policy initiatives, both social and economic, whose efficacy was enhanced by a literate, politically conscious people, helped to reduce disparities.

---

[19]Two northernmost "taluks" (sub-districts) of Travancore had been added to Cochin on integration with Travancore in 1949 and one portion of Cochin was added to Palakkad in Malabar in 1956.

[20]It may be noted that the estimate of agricultural labourers for the country was very high in 1961 due to the definitions used. A large number of general category workers, that is whose sectoral allocation was not very clear-cut were enumerated as agricultural labourers in 1961.

[21]It may be noted that rural and urban in 1961 are defined in terms of being designated as such in the 1961 Census.

Table 4.5: Industrial Distribution of the Work Force by Broad Industry Groups, Region-wise: 1961

Regions		Broad Industry groups					
		Agri-culture	Manufacturing Household	Manufacturing Non-household	All manufac-turing	Other Non-agri-culture	All Industry Groups
		P	P	P	P	P	P
North	T	65.3	6.6	8.1	14.8	20.8	100
	R	70.7	6.7	6.0	12.7	16.6	100
	U	28.8	6.0	22.2	28.2	43.2	100
Central	T	55.5	8.7	10.3	19.0	25.5	100
	R	60.9	9.6	9.3	18.9	20.1	100
	U	23.6	3.4	15.8	19.1	57.3	100
South	T	58.1	10.5	10.2	20.7	21.1	100
	R	62.2	10.9	9.4	20.4	17.3	100
	U	30.0	8.2	15.4	23.6	46.4	100

Source: Census of India, 1961, Kerala, Part II-B(i) General Economic Tables (BI-BIV), Suptd. of Census Operations, Thiruvananthapuram.

Notes: 1. In this table the spatial categories have been taken as defined in the 1961 census.
P - Persons (males and females)
T - Total; R - Rural; U - Urban

This was brought out sharply by the narrowing gap in respect of education and health between north, south and central Kerala (Krishnan 1994). With respect to industrial development some measures taken by the state government, like allotment of power for industrial purposes and rural electrification as also dispersal of certain public sector enterprises in the north,[22] appear to have resulted in a more rapid diversification of the rural economy in the north.

Some change was discernible in the regional employment structures between 1971–91. This is evident from an examination of growth rates of employment in the three regions, industry group wise across rural and size class of towns (Table 4.6). The tables in this section are constructed on the same basis as Tables 4.1 and 4.2 using the continuous method to study spatial change in respect of each region, northern, central and south.

[22]For instance the Second Plan states, "With the reorganisation of States it has become necessary to recast the original plan sanctioned for the residuary Travancore-Cochin State with a view to meet the power requirements of the Malabar area which lags considerably behind the residuary Travancore-Cochin State in the matter of power development.... Under the circumstances it is considered necessary to make adequate provision in the Kerala plan for meeting the entire power demand for Malabar area from the Travancore-Cochin grid." Similarly provision was made for rural electrification to being it on par with the T-C region. Of the total plan provision for power development in Kerala, almost a quarter was for the Malabar area (GOK 1958).

Table 4.6: Growth Rates of Population and Workers by Select Industry Group: Region-wise, 1971–91

	Industry group		Region					
			North		Central		South	
			P	M	P	M	P	M
I.	Population	R	2.1	2.1	1.0	1.0	1.3	1.3
		ST	5.2	5.2	2.3	2.4	4.8	4.8
		CBM	3.8	3.8	1.3	1.2	1.0	1.9
II.	Workers	R	1.4	1.6	1.2	1.3	1.5	1.4
		ST	4.7	4.9	2.8	3.0	6.0	5.4
		CBM	3.4	3.5	1.8	1.7	1.2	1.3
1.	Agriculture	R	0.4	0.6	–0.2	–.04	0.9	1.2
		ST	5.9	6.2	2.6	3.0	9.3	8.1
		CBM	2.2	2.8	0.9	1.2	0.9	1.0
2.	Non-Agriculture	R	3.0	2.8	2.5	2.5	2.2	2.3
		ST	4.4	4.3	2.9	3.0	3.4	3.2
		CBM	3.7	3.7	1.9	1.8	1.2	1.2
	i. All Manufacturing	R	1.5	0.6	1.1	1.1	0.6	0.6
		ST	3.5	2.8	2.0	1.8	2.3	1.7
		CBM	2.2	2.1	0.9	1.1	–0.2	0.1
	ii. Construction	R	6.2	6.2	5.1	4.9	5.8	5.7
		ST	8.8	8.7	8.6	8.9	9.6	9.5
		CBM	9.4	9.6	6.0	6.0	4.8	4.8
	iii. All Services[1]	R	3.6	3.4	3.3	3.2	3.3	3.0
		ST	4.6	4.5	3.2	3.1	3.8	3.6
		CBM	4.0	3.8	2.0	1.6	1.7	1.4

Source : Same as Table 4.1

Notes : 1. All Services include Trade and Commerce, Transport and Communication and Other Services.

2. Spatial categories have been defined using the continuous method.
R - rural; ST - small towns; CBM - cities, big and medium towns; P - Persons; M - Males

From Table 4.6 it may be noted that population, both in the rural and urban areas, has grown most rapidly in the northern region which continues to have a higher birth rate compared to Travancore-Cochin, despite considerable narrowing of the gap since integration.[23] The employment growth rate however, has fallen short of the growth in the labour force in the northern region especially in rural areas. The labour absorptive capacity of agriculture appears to be low in all regions; in the central region growth in agricultural employment in rural areas was negative. In small towns in all the regions, agricultural growth was high on account of the rapid growth in allied agricultural activities (primarily livestock and horticultural production)noted earlier. Growth of employment in non-household manufacturing in rural areas has been most rapid in north Kerala followed by the central region. While it was lower than employment growth rate of all non-

[23]For instance in 1966 rural birth rate in Kerala was 42 per thosand population compared to 33 per thosand in Travancore-Cochin. By 1991 the rates were about 22 for Malabar and 15 for Travancore-Cochin.

Table 4.7: Distribution of Employment by Select Industry Groups: Region-wise 1971 and 1991

Industry group		Region								
		North			Central			South		
		1971	1991	Change %	1971	1991	Change%	1971	1991	Change%
1. Agriculture	R	66.2	54.2	–18.1	54.9	41.8	–23.9	61.3	55.3	–9.8
	ST	30.6	37.0	20.9	33.9	32.5	4.1	31.2	57.8	85.3
	CBM	24.4	19.5	–20.1	9.9	8.4	–15.2	20.5	19.5	–4.9
2. Non–Agriculture	R	33.8	45.8	35.5	45.1	58.2	29.0	38.7	44.7	15.5
	ST	69.3	63.0	–9.1	66.1	67.5	2.1	68.8	42.2	38.7
	CBM	75.6	80.2	6.1	90.1	91.6	1.7	79.5	80.5	1.2
i. All Manufacturing	R	11.5	11.6	0.9	18.1	17.9	–.01	15.7	13.3	–15.3
	ST	21.2	16.3	–23.1	19.3	16.4	–15.0	23.7	11.6	–51.1
	CBM	23.8	18.9	–20.6	24.2	20.8	–14.0	20.4	15.4	–24.5
ii Construction	R	1.4	3.5	150	2.6	5.4	7.6	1.3	3.0	131
	ST	1.9	4.0	110	2.0	6.1	205	1.5	2.9	93.3
	CBM	1.8	5.6	211	3.4	7.6	123	2.4	4.9	104
ii. All Services	R	20.3	25.9	27.5	23.7	34.0	43.4	21.3	27.8	30.5
	ST	45.5	41.4	–19.0	43.9	44.5	1.4	43.1	27.4	–36.4
	CBM	49.7	55.3	11.3	62.0	63.1	1.7	56.6	50.0	6.0

Source: Same as Table 4.1

Notes : 1. R - rural; ST - small towns; CBM - cities/big/medium towns

agricultural activities, the latter was also higher for the north resulting in higher rates of rural diversification in that region followed by the central region. The south has witnessed the slowest growth in manufacturing employment. As a consequence of these differential rates of growth there has been a change in the employment pattern across the regions.

Focussing on broad industry groups we find that the share of rural non-agricultural employment has increased in all the regions; the largest increase is in the north (Table 4.7). There is no doubt that the service sector contributed to the major share of the increase, which was particularly high in the central region. The percentage increase in manufacturing was small but positive only in the north. It is interesting to note that there was a substantial decline in the share of manufacturing employment in the large urban settlements that is, CBM, in the three regions. However, the absolute numbers declined only in the south. Has there been a narrowing of the gap in the distribution of employment between agricultural and non-agricultural activities in north and central-south Kerala? We use the Chi-square Statistic to measure this for rural areas (Table 4.8)

Table 4.8: Distance between Distribution of Workforce across Industry Groups Measured by the Chi-square Statistic

Industry groups	Chi-Square statistic					
	1971			1991		
	N-C	S-C	N-S	N-C	S-C	N-S
1. Disaggregated Industry Groups	8.10	2.68	2.79	8.42	9.26	3.29
2. Broad Agriculture-Nonagriculture groups	5.07	1.60	1.07	6.53	7.95	0.07

Source : Derived from data source given in Table 4.1

Notes : N-C North-Central Kerala; S-C South-Central Kerala; N-S North-South Kerala.

We examine the distance in terms of the nine-fold industry groups first and find that the distance was high between the north and central regions in 1971 but was much less between north and south as also south and central Kerala. However, by 1991 while there was hardly any increase in the gap between occupational structures between north and central Kerala, both north and central regions moved further away from the south; the distance between the south and central regions has risen very sharply. With a broader agriculture-non-agriculture industry grouping – the south-central gap has increased sharply in this case too. However, the north-south gap has declined and the north-central distance has increased marginally. This suggests that the large scale diversification of rural areas in the north and central regions resulting in the emergence of a number of new towns has widened the gap between these two regions and the south; however the distance between the north and central regions did not register a decline as expected. Perhaps the higher non-agricultural base in the central region and further diversification since 1971 resulting in a negative growth in the agricultural work force has moved it further away from the north.

4.5 The Process of Rural Diversification: Some Linkages Explored

4.5.1 Data Base

In this section we attempt to understand the process of structural transformation of the rural work force at the village level in terms of certain linkages discussed earlier. Village level data pertaining to the rural settlements that have become urban are examined. There were about 128 villages which became urban between 1971 and 1991. These constituted about 12 percent of the total rural population in 1971 and over one third of the urban population in 1991. Hence their contribution to the process of urbanisation was substantial.

The major source of socio-economic information at the village level in India is the District Census Handbook, covering all the districts of a state, brought out after each decennial Census, though with considerable delay. It gives a directory of the towns and villages in each district and information on characteristics relating to the pattern of employment, agricultural production base and some aspects of infrastructure (Vaidyanathan 1996). These data provide certain initial conditions existing in each village in 1971, like the extent of area cultivated, the proportion of irrigated area, cultivated area per agricultural worker, incidence of agricultural labour, distance from the nearest town and literacy levels.[25] We attempt to capture the relative significance of these socio-economic characteristics, some of which can be used as proxies for the presence of certain linkages, in the growth of rural non-agricultural employment. However, in the absence of similar data on these characteristics for 1991, we were unable to capture the extent to which changes in initial conditions impact on the process of economic transformation. This is a serious limitation, since the mid-seventies mark a turning point in Kerala's path of development with large-scale migration of (primarily) male work-seekers from rural and urban areas, to oil-rich countries in West Asia. The consequent inflow of remittances by workers in the Gulf has had a deep impact on the economy of Kerala, particularly in respect of a rapid growth of consumer demand for goods and services and investment demand reflected primarily in a building "boom" (Eapen 1994). This would have been a major exogenous factor inducing the diversification of the rural economy since the late seventies. Since inflow of remittances is external to the rural economy and migration would have been

[25]Some village level data on schools, post office and communication-road and rail, are available from the same source. All the villages under study possess these facilities which did not show much variation among the villages.

facilitated in rural areas close to large urban towns, it would strengthen the impact of "urban" linkages. Data on migration at the village level are not available; neither was it very significant in 1971.

Ours is a cross section analysis, attempting to relate the proportion of male non-agricultural employment in 1971 (or the proportion of manufacturing employment in particular)[26] to the above stated characteristics across the villages. (In this section most of the worker related characteristics are in terms of male workers). The basic thrust of our argument has been to highlight the significance of a relatively endogenous process of rural diversification in general and rural manufacturing in particular in which linkages play a critical role. As discussed in Chapter 2, agriculture induced linkages constitute an important component of rural linkages. However, growth in non-agricultural employment is not merely an adjunct of agricultural growth; other non-agricultural sectors contribute to its growth. It was also argued that external or urban linkages appeared to play a more important role in generating rural non-agricultural employment. Moreover, as a critique of the linkage approach it was pointed out that an excess labour situation also induces a diversification of the work force. Given these various paths through which a structural transformation of the rural work force occurs, we examine the nature of the socio-economic data given for each village in an attempt to understand their contribution to the different paths. (Since we are examining the data in 1971 during which these settlements were rural, we refer to them as villages though in the earlier sections these were being referred to as new towns).

4.5.2 *Approximating Agriculture-induced Linkages from the available Socio-Economic Data*

Given the nature of data available which precludes the estimates of agricultural output and incomes at the village level, we use the percent of cultivated area (CA%), ratio of cultivated land per male agricultural worker (CA/MAW) and the extent of land irrigated (IR/CA) as agricultural growth induced production and consumption linkages which generate non-farm activity. It would be difficult to estimate production linkages from secondary data unless we have rural input-output tables quantifying the backward and forward production linkages of small-scale enterprises with agriculture. However, consumption linkages are approximated to a limited extent since villages

[26] An examination of the data revealed that the proportion of male work force in manufacturing moves in tandem with the proportion of male non-agricultural employment but its rate of change is lower. The rank correlation coefficient between the two in 1971 was 0.46 while the linear correlation coefficient was 0.47.

which combine a high proportion of cultivated area, high cultivated area per agricultural worker and a high incidence of irrigation would generate relatively higher rural incomes. The latter imply a high consumer demand for goods and services and the rural income multiplier would be large depending on the consumption behaviour of the agriculturists. Production linkages would depend on the nature of farming practices in use and the prevailing agrarian structure. The use of chemical fertilizers and other inputs as also heavy labour-saving machinery results in poor local multiplier effects. However, a high incidence of irrigation, including the use of pumps, new variety of seeds, mechanical threshers, and repair services generate greater local linkages. Hence the higher are rural incomes and the more egalitarian is the landholding structure, the greater is the local multiplier effect since smaller farmers tend to demand relatively labour intensive goods such as non-foodgrain agricultural commodities and simple manufactured consumer goods which could be produced locally. Kerala's land reforms as argued earlier have resulted in a dramatic reduction in landlessness and abolition of tenancy broadening the land ownership base. The incidence of commercial cropping too, rubber, coconut, pepper among others, is high on small landholdings resulting in a much wider spread of benefits from increases in prices or productivity of such crops. This should result in a broad based rural demand. However, a severe limitation of this analysis is the implicit assumption that agricultural incomes dominate the rural economy and linkages flow only from agriculture, while we have emphasised the need to explore the linkages with other sectors of the rural economy, particularly the service sector. It appears to be difficult to overcome this data constraint.

Worker participation rates (WPR) or level of employment should also have a positive impact on rural incomes. However, this may not necessarily be so given the "residual sector" role played by agriculture in most large agrarian developing economies. An increase in the proportion of economically active population in agriculture may not always reflect a response to rise in agricultural production but could be due to a sluggish growth in employment opportunities in other sectors. Hence worker participation rates tend to be negatively correlated with the extent of non-agricultural employment (Eapen 1994). Furthermore, higher levels of employment may be the consequence of low wages forcing more family members to join the labour force, a distress factor (Bar-el 1984). The role played by this characteristic in buttressing rural incomes is uncertain because of its ambiguity.

There is of course a linkage too in terms of availability of local capital from higher agricultural incomes since a potential exists for increased savings by the cultivating classes. The questions is: To what extent does agricultural surplus finance non-agricultural activities, in particular rural small-scale manufacturing? While this question cannot be answered from the secondary data we will attempt to provide answers to it in the chapter based on the field survey.

4.5.3 Distress Induced Diversification

Rural non-agricultural employment could be a reflection of the sluggish growth in agricultural employment pushing work seekers into certain types of low productivity, non-agricultural work. While we have used the ratio of cultivated area per agricultural worker (CA/MAW) as one of the indicators of rural prosperity, a rapidly declining land-man ratio would indicate a push factor out of agriculture as less land is available per person for cultivation. A high proportion of male agricultural labourers to male agricultural work force (MAL/MAW) suggesting a relative surplus labour situation in agriculture, would also compel labourers to seek work outside agriculture. MAL/MAW also measures the extent of inequality among agricultural classes (Vaidyanathan 1996).

4.5.4 Urban Linakges

The distance from towns is a measure of the intensity of urban linkages (URB). "Urban" is defined in terms of the distance from the nearest town which could be a city, big, medium or small town. The closer it is, in kilometres, the higher the chance of the village economy responding to impulses generated from the urban centres and sooner or later being absorbed into the urban agglomeration. Demand for unskilled and semi-skilled rural labour in nearby urban centres to which the workers commute, is one way in which the urban linkage promotes the growth of non-agricultural employment for rural residents. Another way is through the rural areas catering to the demand for non-agricultural goods and services emanating from nearby urban areas, generally in the nature of sub-contracting work for urban units. The latter may take advantage of lower rural wages and/or land prices. For instance with land prices generally rising much faster in urban locations, land available in rural hinterland is very often purchased by urban settlers for commercial or domestic purposes. This results in the decline of land based activities in the hinterland. Moreover, the more educated rural persons would seek work in the nearby urban area. Nearness to a town also indicates a relatively better availability of certain infrastructural services such as electricity, water, roads, post and telecommunication, schools and hospitals as a spill over of being near the town. This too would have a positive impact on the generation of non-agricultural activities in rural areas. We would expect urban linkages to be relatively higher than rural linkages, that is, agricultural linkages in this analysis, for villages that are extensions to UAS.

4.5.5 *Literacy – Accumulation of Human Capital*

Village level data on literacy are also given for males (MLIT) and females (FLIT). The spread of literacy raises the quality of labour helping rural labour to upgrade and diversify their skills. It also helps work-seekers to move out of traditional occupations (Jayaraj 1996). Rising levels of literacy thus raise the supply of labour for non-agricultural work, since literate and educated workers do not want to work in agriculture or low productivity traditional occupations. Some have argued that growth of education results in the generation of surplus labour because of the desire of educated people to seek non-agricultural work (Jayaraj 1996). Besides the labour supply side stimulus, high literacy levels have an impact on the demand side too, since the potential for setting up modern non-agricultural enterprises is higher among the educated entrepreneurs. This is even more true of the technically educated persons. In a state like Kerala where literacy is widespread, this characteristic may not show much variation between villages except for the educated[27] and above. The question is to what extent does this fund of human capital in a literate state help in the process of rural diversification and (an issue to be discussed in our chapter on the field survey) how does it affect earnings?

The above is a very broad attempt at deriving some of the possible determinants of rural non-agricultural employment from the available data on socio-economic characteristics of villages, some of which may be in the nature of linkages. A distinction is also made between "agricultural" and "urban" linkages. We attempt first to assess the extent to which variations in non-agricultural employment across villages could be explained in terms of these determinants. Subsequently to explore the differences in the nature of linkages that may have facilitated occupational diversification we examine the village data classified by extensions and independent/isolated towns.

4.5.6 *The Correlation Matrix*

Table 4.9 presents a matrix on inter-correlations among the proportion of male non-agricultural workers and the various possible determinants discussed above.

From the first column of the inter-correlations, it can be seen that the proximity to urban centres (URB) has the highest correlation with the proportion of male non-agricultural workers (–0.41), followed by the literacy variables (MLIT and FLIT) and the extent of irrigation (IR/CA). It is also to be

[27]The "educated" are defined as those with matriculation, that is 10 years of schooling.

Table 4.9: Inter-correlation matrix of Proportion of Male Non-agricultural Workers and its Determinants

	mnaw/mw	wpr	mal/maw	ir/ca	Log (IR/CA)	ca/maw	ca/mal	ca%	milt	flit	urb
mnaw/mw	1.0000										
wpr	–0.1591	1.0000									
mal/maw	0.0100	–0.0930	1.0000								
ir/ca	0.1204	–0.0669	0.1354	1.00000							
Log (IR/Ca)	0.2284 *	–0.2053	0.2713 *	1.8334 *	1.0000						
ca/maw	0.1327	–0.0202	–0.2290 *	–0.0665	–0.4777 *	0.9904 *					
ca/mal	0.0908	0.0152	–0.2290 *	–0.0665	–0.4777 *	0.9904 *	1.0000				
ca%	0.1218	–0.2294 *	0.0074	0.0991	–0.2791 *	0.1488	1.0000	1.0000			
mlit	0.3041 *	–0.1069	0.0018	0.0102	0.1126	–0.0169	0.0790	0.1182			
flit	0.2842 *	–0.2048 *	–0.1337	0.1203	0.2717 *	–0.0863	–0.0386	0.1790 *	0.8311 *	1.0000	
urb	–0.4073 *	0.4209 *	–0.1826	–0.4771 *	0.0607	0.8858	–0.0959	–0.1626	–0.1794 *	–0.3421 *	1.0000

Note: *denotes statistical significance at 5% level. As the relationship between MNAW/MW and IR/CA seemed non-linear, we had considered log transformation of IR/CA for examining the correlation co-efficients.

Legend:
- MNA/MW – male non-agricultural workers as proportion of male workers.
- WPR – worker participation rate
- MAL/MW – male agricultural labourer/male agricultural workers
- IR/CA – irrigated area as percent of cultivated area
- CA/MAW – cultivated area/male agricultural worker
- CA/MAL – cultivated area/male agricultural labourer
- CA% – percent of area cultivated
- MLIT – male literacy in percent
- Flit – female literacy in percent
- urb – proximity to urban centre

noted that most of the determinant variables are correlated with the proximity of urban centre (URB).[28]

Proximity to urban centres (URB) appears to be most important when we look at all the villages together. One of the reasons why many of the determinants are not found to be correlated like URB with the proportion of male non-agricultural workers (MNAW/MW) is precisely the point we were making earlier viz. linkages that promote occupational diversification vary across villages. Villages which are far from the urban centres may have different determinants than those which are close to the urban centres. This fact may not be evident when we look at correlation co-efficients taking all villages together.

4.5.7 Village Data Classified by Independent and Extension Villages

In order to pursue this point, we examined the village data classified by independent/isolated and extended villages. The latter being a part of the urban agglomeration would be much closer to a town and responsive to demands for workers in urban areas who could commute to work. On the other hand, the independent villages being more distant, we would expect the extent of agriculture and related activities to be higher.

The distance from the nearest urban centre varies within a narrow range in the case of the extended villages, between 1 and 22 kilometers with an inter-quartile range of 3 kms only. But it varies widely in the case of isolated villages, between 1 and 72 kilometers with an inter-quartile range of 10 kms. The isolated villages as a category, therefore, do not necessarily represent villages without the impact of the urban centers. For this reason, we further classified the isolated villages into two groups-those near urban centers and those far off-on the basis of the median distance of 14 kms.

In the next step, we identified the villages with relatively high level of occupational diversity in all the three categories viz. isolated villages nearer to and further away from the urban centres, and the extended villages. On the basis of the means and medians of the percent of male non-agricultural workers to total male workers, we have taken 75 percent as the cut off point for this purpose. It is

[28]Since we are examining the complete list of villages in Kerala which became urban over the period of 1971–91, statistical test for the correlation co-efficients is not strictly valid. We have nevertheless indicated (by *) the coefficients which were found to be statistically significant at 5% level, if one were to consider these villages to constitute a random sample from a hypothetical population with relevant characteristics similar to that of Kerala.

Table 4.10: Number of Villages Classified by the Proximity to Urban Centres and Percentage of Male Non-agricultural Workers to Total Male Workers

Percentage of Male Non-agricultural Workers	Extended Villages	Isolated Villages with distance From the nearest urban center	
		<=14 Kms	>14 Kms
(MNAW/MW)			
Less than or equal to 75%	33	18	19
Greater than 75%	32	15	7
Mean (MNAW/MW)	71.60	69.31	62.81
Median (MNAW/MW)	73.95	72.87	65.33

Note: MNAW/MW – male non-agricultural workers/male workers

also the cut off point in respect of the occupational criterion for being designated as urban (see footnote 16). The relevant figures are presented in Table 4.10.

Our examination of linkages is based on a comparison of the averages of the various indicators between the less and more (below and above 75 percent) diversified villages across the three categories defined above. In particular, we compare between isolated villages far off from the urban centre and the extended villages in respect of the indicators. The relevant figures are presented in Table 4.11.

The average extent of irrigated area (IR/CA) is very similar between highly diversified and less diversified villages in the case of extended villages (31.4 percent and 30.3 percent). However, the difference is considerable in the case of far off isolated villages (46.6 percent and 13.8 percent). Same patterns are observable in the cases of cultivated area per male agricultural worker (CA/MAW) and percent of cultivated area (CA%).[29] In other words, higher agriculture linked indicators are associated with the highly diversified isolated villages and not so with the extended villages. On the other hand, literacy levels do not appear to be associated with diversification in the case of far off isolated villages. Male agricultural labour to male agricultural workers, an indicator of excess labour pushing persons out of agriculture into any available activity, does not appear to be different between the highly diversified and not so highly diversified far off villages. This implies that other positive indicators of diversification seem to be playing a more important role.

The above analysis reveals that both "agricultural" and "urban" linkages play an important role in promoting rural economic diversification depending on the location of the village. A serious

[29] As stated earlier, we are analysing the complete list of villages. However, we checked with Oneway Analysis of Variance and the tests were significant in the case of IR/CA and CA/MAW at 5% level.

Table 4.11: Average of the Linkage Indicators by Categories of Villages

Indicators	MNAW/MW	Extended Villages	Isolated villages with distance from the nearest urban centre	
			< = 14 Kms	> 14 Kms
WPR	<=75%	42.86	43.36	45.19
	>75%	42.62	42.65	43.33
MAL/MAW	<=75%	0.57	0.58	0.48
	>75%	0.47	0.48	0.48
IR/CA	<=75%	31.45	16.53	13.79
	>75%	30.34	22.08	46.55
CA/MAW	<=75%	0.86	0.99	0.91
	>75%	1.45	1.30	6.73
CA%	<=75%	73.68	78.52	64.59
	>75%	77.19	77.26	87.38
MLIT	<=75%	68.66	70.55	68.59
	>75%	71.72	73.23	70.40
FLIT	<=75%	56.66	57.55	52.03
	>75%	61.73	61.85	53.29

Legend: MNAW/MW – male non-agricultural workers/male workers
MAL/MAW – male non-agricultural labours/male agricultural worker
IR/CA – irrigated area as per cent of cultivated area
CA/MAW – cultivated area/male agricultural worker
CA% – percent of area cultivated
MLIT – male literacy (in percent)
FLIT – female literacy (in percent)

limitation of the data is that only agriculture-based linkages could be discussed leaving out other rural linkages. We have emphasised later that the service sector in rural areas can exert a powerful influence on the establishment of small-scale manufacturing enterprises. However, that rural linkages can generate a high level of rural non-agricultural activity appears to be supported by the evidence. It also links up with the question of the extent of "local" linkages: villages more distant from urban centres would tend to display relatively higher local production and consumption linkages since the impulses are rurally generated. This is supported by our field survey for two differently located areas, one in which the average distance of the panchayats from a nearby town is almost half that of the other. The study of Tambunan (1994) also suggests a similar relationship between distance from a town and market orientation of output and raw materials of small producers. However, it is stronger in terms of raw material supplies than the demand for their products.

We now examine the size structure of manufacturing activity in the state focussing on the small-scale sector in the following chapter.

5

Size Structure of Manufacturing Industry in Kerala:Growth of the Small Scale Sector

5.1 Introduction

An earlier study on the Indian industrialisation process from a regional perspective highlighted the emergence of two broad patterns in the period 1961–71: one in which growth is agglomerated, based largely on capital intensive, large-scale manufacturing units located in big cities, and the other in which the pattern is more dispersed in rural settlements and small towns (Kundu and Raza 1982). Kerala (and a few other states)[1], was identified as a region in which industrial growth was more dispersed based on the small sector. The state's mixed rural-urban settlement pattern and mix of agricultural – non-agricultural activities is regarded as a critical factor underlying the dispersed pattern of industrial growth (Bharadwaj 1982). However, we have argued in Section 3 of Chapter 3 that the dispersed nature of surplus generation, given the broad-based growth of the economy, would have also contributed to the observed pattern.

While the dispersed pattern of growth of manufacturing continued in Kerala during the period since then, that is 1971–91, as revealed by the evidence presented in the preceding chapter, there has also emerged a tendency towards agglomeration. However, the latter appears to be mostly in the nature of a concentration of tertiary sector activities, the share of which has grown in the urban agglomerations (UAs) while manufacturing is growing faster in the extensions of the core cities/big/medium towns of UAs and other rural areas. There is a tendency therefore, for manufacturing activity to continue to be dispersed.

In this chapter we examine the size structure of manufacturing industry in Kerala focussing on the growth of small scale enterprises (SSEs). It is organised in 4 sections. In Section 5.2 we briefly discuss the data base and its inadequacies particularly in respect of the small sector, which have been discussed at length elsewhere (Nagaraj 1985; Suri (ed.) 1988; Kashyap 1988).

[1]Certain parts of Andhra Pradesh, Karnataka, Haryana, Gujarat and parts of Maharashtra were the other regions identified as having experienced a dispersed pattern of industrial growth (Kundu and Raza 1982).

Earlier attempts to build a size structure of manufacturing industry in Kerala are examined in Section 5.3 and updated for the eighties. In Section 5.4 we focus on the small-scale sector examining its growth and hetrogeneity in various ways, given the diverse sources of information available which are not always compatible. Our emphasis is on its product structure which continues to be dominated by agro and natural resource based industries.

5.2 Data Base and its Limitations

The problem of estimating the size structure of the manufacturing sector lies in the fact that there is no single source of data (or complementary sources) which adequately covers, in a non-overlapping sense,[2] its different segments (Sundaram and Tendulkar 1988). While in terms of employment the problem is less acute, in respect of value added and other economic characteristics, the inadequacy and non-compatibilty of data for the different segments is more severe. Basically we would like to distinguish between the large and medium scale undertakings on the one hand and the small-scale units on the other, by a rural urban break up. In the Indian context while the former, that is, units employing 50 and more workers with power or 100 and more wokers without power,[3] lie entirely within the factory sector (that is registered under the Factories Act 1948) and are covered by the Census sector of the Annual Survey of Industries (ASI), the small sector has a factory and non-factory component. Small-scale factories, that is units employing 10 to 49 persons with power and 20 to 99 persons without power are enumerated by the Sample sector of the ASI.[4] The ASI is very comprehensive in its coverage giving information on major economic characteristics of large and small factories, state wise and industry wise at a three-digit level of disaggregation; however, it does not give a rural-urban break up.

Although a lower size limit is not imposed on a factory, generally those units with less than 10 workers with power and less than 20 workers without power need not register as factories.

[2]For instance the decennial population Census, classifies manufacturing into household and non-household manufacturing. The latter includes the factory and non-factory sectors. To separate the non-factory sector, data collected by the Small Industries Development Organisation (SIDO) on unregistered units could be used. However, these data are found to include a number of small-scale fatories too, which implies an overlapping of factory and non-factory sectors.

[3]The Indian definition of large and small in terms of employment is rather unique, combining as it does two generally used definitions of small (upto 50 workers or upto 100 workers) by specifying use of power: those units employing 10–49 workers and using power or employing 20 to 99 workers without power are defined as small.

[4]While the large and medium scale factories are covered on a census basis, the smaller factories, that is factories employing 10–49 workers with power and 20–99 workers without power, are covered on a 50 percent sample basis. The scope of the Annual Survey of Industries in respect of the small factories is fairly complete except for variation in coverage from year to year due to non-response. This implies that even if the data relating to an industry covers the same number of units in two years there is no guarantee the data would refer to the same set of units in the two years (Saluja 1988).

This non-factory component of the small scale sector, also referred to as the unorganised manufacturing sector, is made up of the following segments:

- unregistered enterprises organised mainly as single proprietorships or at times partnerships, where productive activity is carried on by the proprietor or partner(s) with the help of hired labour; and
- the household sector (which we have categorised as family enterprises)[5] based almost entirely on family labour.

Information on the household component is directly available from the decennial population Census. However, the non-factory segment is derived as a residual (after subtracting employment in large, medium and small-scale factories given in the ASI from employment in non-household manufacturing as given in the Census) or more directly from relatively recent (that is since the late seventies) surveys of the NSSO.

While the larger proportion of small units are "micro" or "tiny" in nature,[6] there is also a bunching of units at the cut-off point for a factory, with a number of factory size units not registering as factories. Since the Factory Act registration imposes certain regulations on units[7] there is a tendency to evade it. A further complication in delineating the different segments of the manufacturing sector in the Indian context is the use of a dual scalar definition: while most information on size structure comes from sources which define it in terms of employment, for official purposes, especially for Governmental assistance schemes, the small units are defined in terms of original value of investment in plant and machinery (Kashyap 1988).[8] Again, with the investment limit being frequently revised upwards[9] it is very likely that small units so defined

[5]Since the household sector is viewed as being virtually synonymous with traditional industries, it underplays the tenacity of this sector which is found even within the modern small-scale enterprises (as our own findings reveal). We prefer to categorise it as family enterprises (see Lipton 1990). Moreover, the Census defines it in terms of location, that is, within the village in rural areas but in the premises of the producer in urban areas. The latter appears to be an unnecessary condition.

[6]A micro enterprise is normally defined as one with 0–4 workers (UNDP *et al* 1988); sometimes the cut off limit is stated as 0–10 workers (Boomgard *et al* 1992). In India the concept of "tiny" was introduced in 1977 being defined as a unit with investment in plant and machinery of Rs. 200,000 which was raised to Rs. 500,000 in the New Industrial Policy of 1991.

[7]This is particularly so in respect of protective legislation regarding employment of labour.

[8]However since some sources do cross classify units by employment and investment in plant and machinery, a broad correspondence can be derived although the nature of information given in this manner may be limited.

[9]The investment limit in the 50s was Rs. 500,000 in plant and machinery at purchase price and Rs. 750,000 for ancillary units (that is those supplying one-half or more of their total output to one or more parent units). By mid-sixties the limit had been raised to Rs. 750,000 and Rs. 1 million respectively. Since the mid-seventies there was another hike to Rs. 1 million and Rs. 1.5 million respectively, in the early eighties to Rs. 2 million and Rs. 2.5 million and by late eighties the limits stood at Rs. 6 million and Rs. 7.5 million respectively. (Another category with higher limits was of the exporting units). In 1997 there was a policy initiative to raise the limit very sharply to Rs. 30 million.

would qualify as small-scale factories or medium size units in terms of employment[10]

The inadequacies of data for a detailed analysis of the non-factory sector are severe. These are discussed at greater length in the section focussing on the small-scale sector. Despite these limitations, the structure of manufacturing by scale of activity, and the relative importance of each in total manufacturing employment, can be approximated with the use of the decennial Censuses and ASI factory data. However the Census does not give any information on value added. We examine first some early attempts at building up the size structure of manufacturing activity in Kerala.

5.3 Earlier Attempts at Building up the Size Structure of Manufacturing Industry in Kerala

Some attempts have been made to approximate the size structure of manufacturing industry in Kerala, which we discuss below. These deal with the sixties and seventies. Our effort would be to collate the data for the eighties. The simplest method, defining size in terms of employment, by which we can derive a broad picture of the size structure of manufacturing industry, is based on juxtaposing the decennial Census estimates of total workers in manufacturing, classified into household and non-household manufacturing, with the ASI data on factories. In line with much of the literature on structure of manufacturing by scale of activity, the various segments which can be approximated are:

- large and medium-scale factories;
- small-scale factories;
- non-household, non-factory units or the unregistered sector; and
- household sector.

While (a) and (b) are taken from the ASI, (c) is derived by deducting (a) and (b) from non-household manufacturing given in the Census as noted earlier, and (d) is available from the Census. This exercise has been done for the period 1961–81 from which we draw the evidence (Vaidyanathan and Eapen 1984; Albin 1988).

[10]For instance the 1987–8 Census of Small-scale Industrial Units revealed that about 16 percent of the SIDO units were registered factories. A small proportion (less than 1 percent) would also qualify as medium size units employing 50–100 workers (DCSSI 1992).

The data given in Table 5.1 relate to total work force since ASI estimates are not available for rural and urban areas separately. It highlights the tremendous growth of employment in the non-factory, non-household small sector, the share of which rose dramatically from about 35 percent of the manufacturing work force in 1961 to considerably more than half by 1981. The relative and absolute shares of the household sector in employment have shrunk considerably while there was a marginal decline in the share of the small-scale factory sector. On the other hand the share of the large factories increased from about 12 percent to 16 percent of the work force. However, growth of the total work force was higher resulting in an overall decline in the relative share of manufacturing in total work force, from 18 percent to 16.6 percent.

What does the picture look like during the eighties when we juxtapose the 1991 census estimates of manufacturing[11] with the ASI data on registered factories? The growth in the unregistered sector continued, though at a much slower pace and its share increased to 60 percent of total employment in manufacturing. While the share of household industry declined further to about one fifth of the manufacturing work force, its rate of decline slowed down considerably. Factory employment, for which the break-up between large and small factories was not available, registered a very small increase. While total employment grew at 1.6 percent per annum between 1981–91 (data not shown here), almost the same rate as in the earlier period, the rate of growth of manufacturing employment was much less, resulting in a further decline in the relative share of manufacturing in total workforce to about 15 percent.

The above data reveal a significant growth in the small unregistered sector in the sixties and seventies in Kerala, which was true for most states in India, as also in the eighties. It supported the growing evidence of the emergence of a "modern"[12] small-scale industrial sector in Indian manufacturing (Nagaraj 1985b). Kerala ranked first among all the major states in terms of the relative importance of the non-household, small-scale sector in 1961 and 1981 and was among the last in terms of large factory employment (Vaidyanathan and Eapen 1984). The small sector in Kerala, including also the household sector, accounted for a little over 80 percent of the manufacturing employment in 1991.

5.3.1 Comparing Scalar Changes in Manufacturing Employment in Kerala with Anderson's Phases

This changing composition of the manufacturing sector in Kerala, when classified according to scale, reveals that the state has passed out of the first phase as discussed by Anderson (1982), in

[11]Main and marginal workers for 1991 were taken to make the figures comparable with 1961. However, since the esindustrial distribution of marginal workers was not available for 1991 it was estimated for manufacturing by assuming that the proportion of marginal workers in 1981 remained the same in 1991.

[12]Modern is defined in terms of being non-traditional.

Table 5.1: Size Structure of Manufacturing Industry in Kerala: 1961, 1981 and 1991

		Actual Employment			As % Total Manufacturing			As % Total Workers		
		1961	1981	1991	1961	1981	1991	1961	1981	1991
1.	Total manufacturing (a+b)	1,018,034	1,285,775	1,359,364	100	100	100	18.1	16.6	14.9
a.	Non-household sector	529,472	971,700	1,088,846	52.0	75.6	80.1	9.4	12.5	11.9
a.1	Large/Medium factories	120,581	212,046	271,961*	11.8	16.5	20.0*	2.1	2.7	2.9*
a.2	Small factories	44,477	52,954		4.4	4.1		0.8	0.7	
a.3	Non-household non-factory sector	364,144	706,700	816,885	35.8	55.0	60.1	6.5	9.1	8.9
b.	Household sector	488,562	314,075	270,518	48.0	24.4	19.99	8.7	40	3.0

Source: Eapen (1986); Albin (1988)

Notes: 1. Data in the 2 cited papers has been updated for 1991, using Census of India, Series 12, Kerala, Economic Tables

* Data relating to large, medium and small factories are given together

which household manufacturing is predominant, accounting for almost one half or three quarters of total manufacturing employment. The table shows that in 1961 household manufacturing accounted for about 48 percent of employment in manufacturing and its share declined sharply between 1961–81. Manufacturing activity in the state appears to be in the second phase in which small workshops and factories emerge at a comparatively rapid rate. Kerala has a higher than all-India average share of such undertakings (Albin 1988). However, a few differences from the Anderson scenario need to be noted:

- most of the growth is in the unregistered small sector. The factory sector both small and large is more or less stagnant in terms of employment between 1981–91;
- there does not seem to be any emerging tendency towards a growing relative importance of large-scale production, which would displace a large share of the workshop and small factory production by the end of the second phase;
- the household sector shows a certain persistence and its rapid decline appears to be arrested in the eighties. The latter possibility is conceded by Anderson in the light of studies which draw attention to its role in providing earning opportunities to a section of the population over a long period of the development process; and
- the higher (than all-India) share of the non-household sector in Kerala is not positively associated, as expected (cf. Anderson 1982), with a high level of per capita income or per capita manufacturing value added. However, it is positively related with the percentage of state domestic product (SDP) originating outside agriculture (Albin 1988). While the above anomaly is to some extent related with estimation problems of SDP in Kerala, discussed earlier in the context of large accruals of remittance incomes, it is evident that the nature of the small or unregistered sector has to be probed deeper.

The above appears to support our earlier argument that the pattern of industrial growth in Kerala would tend to be more dispersed and small-scale in nature reflecting the relatively small size of capital in the region. This also answers to some extent a question raised earlier: Does it necessarily progress to large-scale production? From the data on size structure of manufacturing activity, there does not appear to be any tendency towards a growing share of large-scale manufacturing industry in the state. The share of the factory sector, large, medium and small, continues to account for about one-fifth of the manufacturing work force in 1981 and 1991. Is it possible that the nature of small-scale production emerging in the state is compatible with sustainable industrial growth? Or will the small units stagnate and eventually die out? While it may not be possible to arrive at very definite answers to such questions, a more detailed examination of the small-scale sector, especially its product structure and value added, is warranted.

5.4 The Small-Scale Sector

The difficulty in obtaining a complete picture of the totality of the small sector lies in the "simultaneous presence of various historical stages" (Aubrey 1951; Staley and Morse 1965) from the artisan to the factory, in the process of industrialisation. Historically, since the lower forms of production, particularly in rural areas, were expected to disappear or stagnate with the advent of capitalism, which view has now been challenged as noted earlier, they were not considered significant enough to warrant any serious enumeration (Mendels 1972). However their persistence as also relevance for the large work force they supported, the emergence of modern small-scale enterprises, and the changing nature of technology favouring small size (Piore and Sabel 1984) created an urgent need to understand the nature of the small-scale sector in developing and developed economies (Chuta and Liedholm 1985; Acs et al 1996).

What would be very useful for assessing the nature and growth of the small-scale sector and its constituents are comparable estimates of the number of units, their spatial and industry-wise distribution in terms of employment and value added, at least for a few points of time. Very often one has to suffice with growth in numbers of such units, with virtually no information on employment and value added. While for the small-scale factory sector, the ASI is the main source of information, as observed earlier, with respect to the unregistered small sector there are two major sources of data which provide some details:

- the Economic Census and the NSSO follow up sample surveys;and
- the Census undertaken with no fixed periodicity, by the Development Commissioner of Small-scale Industries on small "registered" units better known as the Small Industries Development Organisation (SIDO) units.

However, a longitudinal analysis is constrained by availability of very few comparable time points as also an overlap of different segments of the small sector. The two sources themselves are not very comparable, the former defining "small" in terms of employment and value of output, the latter in terms of investment in plant and machinery. Both sources have been used in earlier studies on the nature and growth of the unregistered small-scale sector in Kerala, which also focus on the inadequacies of these data.

5.4.1 Growth and Structure of the Small-Scale Sector as derived from the NSSO/CSO *Surveys*

The NSSO is the main agency for the collection of data on unregistered manufacturing enterprises. However the earlier Rounds covering the periods 1958–59 (14th Round), 1968–69 (23rd Round) and 1974–75 (29th Round) related essentially to household units. While information was collected on employment, capital, value of output and value added, the inadequate coverage of unregistered, non-household enterprises, the fastest growing segment in the manufacturing sector, left the picture rather incomplete. In order to fill this gap, a massive programme for conducting periodic Economic Censuses by the Central Statistical Organisation (CSO) was undertaken since the late seventies, which adopted the "site" approach for preparing a frame of manufacturing enterprises by a house to house visit. This frame was used for follow up surveys on the unorganised sector, covering both household and non-household unregistered units and giving more detailed economic information.

The first Economic Census was conducted in 1977 on the basis of a complete house listing approach in both rural and urban areas. It defined an "establishment" as a unit or a household which undertakes non-agricultural activities and employs at least one hired worker on a fairly regular basis. The establishments covered by the census were classified into two categories:

(a) directory manufacturing establishments (DME), having six or more workers and/or an annual output of Rs. 100,000 or more; and

(b) non-directory manufacturing establishments (NDME) with less than six workers and the annual output less than Rs. 100,000[13].

While it covered the non-factory units in all sectors of the unorganised economy, viz. manufacturing, trade, transport and services, such a definition left out own account enterprises using family labour, seasonal enterprises as also agricultural (other than crop production and plantation) enterprises. To that extent the 1977 Census had a relatively restricted coverage compared to subsequent Censuses of 1980 and 1990 which were undertaken along with the houselisting operations of the decennial population Censuses of 1981 and 1991. The scope of the latter was broader, including all enterprises, engaged in agricultural[14] and non-agricultural activities, whether employing hired labour or not. However, it may be noted that despite the restrictive coverage of the 1977 Census, the follow up survey on the unregistered manufacturing sector, viz. NSSO 33rd Round for the year 1978–9, broadened its coverage to include enterprises using primarily family labour, that is, own account enterprises (OAE). It used the 1971 population

[13]These arbitrary cut-off points such as 6 workers and Rs. 100,000 as value of output, not used by other sources, creates a problem of comparability.

[14]Agricultural enterprises include livestock production, hunting, forestry and fishing, but exclude those engaged in crop production and plantation activity.

census household enterprise definition. Hence it was fairly comparable with the two later follow up surveys of the 1980 and 1990 Economic Censuses on the unorganised manufacturing sector with slight changes in the concepts used.[15] The non-directory manufacturing establishments (NDME) and own account enterprises (OAE) of the manufacturing sector were surveyed by the NSSO as part of their normal Rounds, 33rd Round for the year 1978–9, 40th Round for the year 1984–5 and the 50th Round for 1989–90. However, the larger establishments, the directory manufacturing establishments (DME) were surveyed separately under the supervision of the Central Statistical Organisation (CSO).[16]

While it may be tempting to conclude that the NDME+OAE+DME constitute the unregistered manufacturing sector (that is non-factory and household segments), there are two serious limitations which inhibit us from using these data for assessing the total size of the unregistered sector as also its relative significance vis-a-vis the large and medium-scale manufacturing sector:

- The report on the DME units for 1978–9 revealed that almost 8 percent of the units at the all-India level were registered factories and another 31 percent employing 10–19 workers with power should have been registered as factories (Saluja 1988). There is an overlap with factories and hence the data do not pertain only to the unregistered sector;
- employment in the unregistered sector as estimated by these sample surveys appears to be overstated vis-a-vis the population Census estimates. On the other hand, value added is considerably understated compared to estimates of unregistered manufacturing compiled at the national and state levels. The limitations become clearer as we examine these data.

5.4.2 *A Comparison of the 33rd Round of* NSSO *(1978–9) on Unregistered Manufacturing with the 45th Round (1989–90)*

An attempt was made in Albin's study, mentioned earlier, to build a picture of the small unregistered sector and its relative significance, both in terms of employment and value added, using the NSSO 33rd Round data on own account enterprises (OAE) and non-directory manufacturing establishments (NDME) and the data on directory manufacturing enterprises (DME) collected separately for the year 1978–9. We have included the latest year for which similar data are available, 1989–90[17]. Taking employment first (see Table 5.2), we find that within the

[15]The directory establishments since the 1980 Census are defined only in terms of workers irrespective of the value of output.

[16]These establishments were surveyed by the special staff appointed by both the Central and State governments under the supervision of the CSO.

[17]Data are also available for 1984–5 (NSSO 40th Round), the second follow-up survey on unregistered manufacturing which we have not presented here.

non-factory sector in Kerala, OAEs contributed the largest share in terms of employment (about 54 percent) which however, was lower than at the all-India level, viz. 64 percent in 1978–9. The share of NDMEs which accounted for almost a quarter of the employment was higher in Kerala. As far as the larger (DME) units were concerned their shares in employment and number were almost the same as that for all-India. It may be noted that while these units accounted for less than 5 percent of the total number of units both in Kerala and all-India, they contributed almost a fifth of total employment in the small sector. The total unregistered sector in Kerala as defined by OAE+NDME+DME, accounted for almost 90 percent of total employment in the manufacturing sector in 1978–9. This is much higher than its share as thrown up by the earlier estimate given in Table 5.1 for 1981, about 79 percent.

What is noteworthy is the much smaller difference between rural and total figures in the case of Kerala; the structure of the unregistered sector in terms of employment shares is not very different in rural areas. Even the proportion of employment contributed by the larger of the small units, viz. DME units, is about the same in rural locations. This is unlike for all-India where the share of OAEs is much higher in rural areas and of DME units much lower.

By 1989–90 some interesting changes occur. There is an increase in the proportion of the smallest (OAEs) and (marginally), the large (DME) units in Kerala. However, there is a decline in the share of the former in employment while that of the latter registered a sharp increase. The pattern though similar in rural areas is less sharp. On the whole the larger of the small units are gaining in relative importance in terms of employment in Kerala but the shift is more gradual in rural areas. However, given the increase in the proportion of OAEs in the small-scale sector, the average size of a unit has not increased. The total non-factory sector employment in 1989–90 obtained by adding OAE+NDME+DME units accounted for almost 98 percent of total manufacturing employment in Kerala, and is once again much higher than the estimate derived from Table 5.1 for 1991 (about 80 percent). In the rural areas, it is higher than total employment in manufacturing. At the all-India level, the larger sector has registered a decline in its share of employment over the period.

Table 5.2: Structure and Growth of the Unregistered Manufacturing Sector in Kerala and India Derived from the NSSO/CSO Surveys: 1978–9 to 1989–90

	Total						Rural					
	Kerala		%	All-India		%	Kerala		%	All-India		%
	1978–9	1989–90	change	1978–9	1989–90	change	1978–9	1989–90	change	1978–9	1989–90	change
I OAE												
1 Number (000)	411	494	20.2	7178	15731	193.5@	346	422	22.0	5725	12019	193.1@
	(79)	(81)		(85)	(96)		(80)	(84)		(90)	(98)	
2 Employ-	619	689	11.3	11614	29629	205.8	520	594	14.2	9217	21706	104.4
ment (000)	(54)	(52)		(64)	(84)		(56)	(57)		(74)	(81)	
3 Value added	718	1090	51.8	18161	77470	180.8	593	871	60.4	11927	40731	162.2
(Rs. million)	(32)	(30)		(40)	(69)		(38)	(40)		(58)	(81)	
4 VA/employee (Rs.)	1158	1582		1563	2614		1140	1466		1294		
II NDME												
1 Number (000)	92	87	-5.4	957	@		71	61	-12.8	503	@	
	(18)	(14)		(11)			(16)	(12)		(8)		
2 Employ-	268	264	-1.5	2785	@		204	179	-12.3	1403	@	
ment (000)	(24)	(20)		(15)			(22)	(17)		(11)		
3 Value added	616	1236	100.6	9424			399	816	104.5	3607		
(Rs. million)	(28)	(34)		(21)			(26)	(37)		(18)		
4 VA/employee (Rs.)	2296	4682		3383	@		1956	4556		2571	@	
III DME												
1 Number (000)	20	30	50.0	335	567	69.2	15	18	20.0	140	224	60.0
	(4)	(5)		(4)	(4)		(3)	(3)		(2)	(2)	
2 Employ-	249	376	51.0	3813	5846	53.3	200	265	32.5	188	275	46.3
ment (000)	(22)	(28)		(21)	(17)		(22)	(26)		(15)	(11)	
3 Value added	877	1344	53.2	18403	34583	87.9	554	506	-7.0	5021	9411	87.4
(Rs. million)	(40)	(36)		(40)	(31)		(36)	(23)		(25)	(19)	
4 VA/employee (Rs.)	3526	3548		4826	5916		2770	1909		2668	3420	

Table Contd ...

		Total						Rural					
		Kerala		%	All-India		%	Kerala		%	All-India		%
		1978–9	1989–90	change	1978–9	1989–90	change	1978–9	1989–90	change	1978–9	1989–90	change
	All Enterprises												
1	Number (000)	522	611	17.0	8469	16298	92.4	432	500	15.7	6368	12243	92.2
		(100)	(100)		(100)	(100)		(100)	(100)		(100)	(100)	
2	Employ-	1135	1329	17.0	18213	35475	94.8	923	1037	12.4	12502	24458	95.6
	ment (000)	(100)	(100)		(100)	(100)		(100)	(100)		(100)	(100)	
3	Value added	2212	3660	65.4	45987	112054	143.7	1546	2193	41.8	20555	50142	143.9
		(100)	(100)		(100)	(100)		(100)	(100)		(100)	(100)	
4	VA/employee (Rs.)	1947	2754		2525	3159		1674	2114		1644	2050	
	Ratio of Total/Rural VA/employee	1.16	1.30		1.54	1.54							

Source: 1.i For OAE and NDME, 1978–79, NSSO 33rd Round (July 1978–June 1979) Tables with Notes on Survey of Unorganised Manufacturing, 1987, Department of Statistics, New Delhi

ii For DME, Directory Manufacturing Establishment Survey, 1978–79, Summary Results for Central Sample, CSO, 1983.

2.i For OAE and NDME, 1989–90, NSSO, 45th Round (July 1989–June 1990) Tables with Notes on Survey of Unorganised Manufacturing, 1997, Department of Statistics, New Delhi.

ii For DME, Directory Manufacturing Establishment Survey, 1989–90, CSO, 1995

Notes: 1. Figures in brackets indicate percentage of All Enterprises

@ OAE and NDME estimates are given together for 1989–90 at the all-India level

OAE - own account enterprises; NDME - non-directory manufacturing establishment; DME - directory manufacturing establishment

Looking at the corresponding data on value added we find that OAEs in Kerala contributed only about one third of value added in 1978–9; almost 40 percent was generated in the DMEs. While the situation was no different for India, value added per employee (derived by juxtaposing the two sets of data) was higher in respect of each category compared to Kerala (though not for DMEs in rural areas). Over the period 1978–9 to 1989–90 the increase in value added (deflated by the index of wholesale prices for manufactured products with base 1981–2=100)[18] per employee for the small sector as a whole was higher in Kerala. However, growth in productivity in the larger units (DMEs) was much lower. These were the units in which the share of employment had increased considerably in 1989–90.

From the above analysis of recent tendencies within the small sector we find that some disparities have appeared between the rural and all-Kerala picture: there was a decline in value added per worker in DMEs in rural areas between 1978–9 and 1989–90, while the share of the smallest units, OAEs has increased. The ratio of total/rural average productivity which was 1.16 in 1978–9 increased to 1.30 in 1989–90 while at the all-India level the gap was higher(1.54) and has remained the same.

Value added by the unregistered manufacturing sector estimated in this manner, that is OAE+NDME+DME, constituted about 35 percent of total manufacturing value added in 1978–9 while value added by unregistered manufacturing as available from the estimates of State Domestic Product (SDP) was almost 47 percent. Similarly in 1989–90, value added by the OAE+NDME+DME declined as a proportion of manufacturing SDP to about 32 percent while the share of unregistered manufacturing in SDP reveals an almost constant share at 46.7 percent. This is surprising given the afore-mentioned possibility of small factories and what should have been registered as factories being included in these data. These data do not permit us to draw a very precise picture of the relative importance of the small unregistered sector other than providing us with a broad idea, in a comparative perspective with India, of its composition. The lower level of productivity in the DMEs which account for over a quarter of the employment in Kerala, is disturbing.

5.4.3 *Small-Scale Units Registered with the Small Industries Development Organisation (SIDO)*

Even before the initiative taken by governmental agencies in the seventies to generate comprehensive data on the unregistered sector through periodic censuses and sample surveys, a scheme

[18]All value figures in 1978–9 and 1989–90 have been deflated using the all-India index of wholesale prices (base 1981–2=100)of manufactured products. This procedure has certain limitations:(a)the index is the all-India index since there is no state level index of wholesale prices, as yet available; and (b) it relates primarily to prices of manufactured goods in the organised sector which may have risen faster than in the unregistered manufacturing sector

did exist to build up a frame for the non-factory enterprises. Since 1960, small scale units were obliged to register voluntarily with the Directorate of Industries in each state and the Small Industries Development Organisation (SIDO) under the Central Ministry of Industry acted as the nodal agency for their promotion and development. The SIDO dealt mainly with the "modern" units as distinct from the "traditional" industries. The latter came under the purview of different specialised Boards or agencies.[19] However, modern units could be organised as household units, as also proprietorships, (sometimes) partnerships and a few as private limited companies. It was noted (Saluja 1988), that a number of small registered factories were also covered by the SIDO.

Some preliminary information on employment, capital invested and installed capacity also had to be provided by the units at the time of registration. Subsequently the units were expected to submit quarterly production returns, to enable an assessment of their progress which was rarely done. The data generated could hardly be used. With the launching of the District Industries Centre programme in the states in 1978[20] enabling a certain decentralisation of the registration procedures, the coverage improved to some extent. However, its definition of "small" in terms of the investment limit which underwent revision a number of times, was problematic (as noted earlier). Nonetheless, the SIDO units constitute a very significant segment of the small-scale sector whether registered as a factory or not.[21]

5.4.3.1 Growth in Number of SIDO *Units*

Data on the number of units registered each year since the early seventies and the cumulative totals, are put out by the District Industries Centre (DIC), State Directorate of Industries. However, a break up of the units by rural-urban location is not published by the DIC. The use of these data is limited for the following reasons:

- the figures do not take into account mortality of small-scale units, information on which is not available for each year. In 1972–3 the year for which the first all-India Census of registered units was undertaken, almost 40 percent of the units in Kerala were found to

[19]For instance there is an All-India Handloom Board, All-India Handicrafts Board, Central Silk Board, Coir Board and the Khadi and Village Industries Commission, for the different traditional industries.

[20]The District Industries Centre (DIC) programme was launched by the Government of India in 1978 and was deemed to have come into existence in all districts of Kerala in that year. It was to provide a focal point at the district level for the promotion of small-scale units providing essential services and support under one roof (Government of Kerala 1989).

[21]The results of the first all-India Census of these units relating to the year 1972–3 were widely used for estimating value added per person in the non-household segment of unregistered manufacturing in the National Accounts Statistics (Saluja 1988).

be closed (DCSSI 1987–8). A survey conducted by the Directorate of Industries (DI) and Commerce, Government of Kerala on the registered small-scale industrial undertakings as on March 31, 1985 showed that almost 20 percent of the units were closed or sick (GOK 1988). The second all-India Census for 1987–8 revealed that 31 percent of the units were closed. Another estimate for 1993–4 puts the proportion of sick and closed units at only 4 percent (GOK 1995).[22]

- There is a possibility of double counting since a unit may be registered more than once depending on the number of products it proposes to manufacture.[23]

- While it is stated that since 1976 additions to the stock of existing units include only those with permanent registration[24] it is very likely that units with provisional registration which may or may not be finally set up, continue to be included.

- There is still a proportion of the non-factory units that do not register with the DIC, the extent of which is not known.[25] At the same time a number of factory units are covered by these data as noted earlier. It is difficult to use this information in a non-overlapping manner with other data sources.

Thus while we give the year wise data on the growth in number of registered units in the state in Diagram 5.1 and its three regions in Diagram 5.2, we focus on data for the two years, 1972–3 and 1987–8 in which a Census of such units was undertaken, which appear to be relatively more reliable. A third year, 1993–4 is also included since it is a recent year for which certain other characteristics of small-scale units have been compiled besides the number of units.

Diagram 5.1 shows that the annual registrations of small-scale units show a sharp increase in the second half of the eighties. Interestingly the number of units registered each year appears to have grown more rapidly in the southern region (Diagram 5.2) where absolute numbers in manufacturing had declined between 1971–91 as we saw in the preceding chapter. The decline in employment in household manufacturing constituting primarily the two major traditional industries, coir and cashew, located in the south appears to have been overwhelming.

[22]A comprehensive programme for revival of closed and/or sick units is in existence since the late seventies. However its record of achievement is very low; less than 100 units were assisted by the DIC upto the end of 1984–5 and the number increased to about 150 by 1987–8 which constitute 1-2 percent of the total number of closed units.

[23]We were told by officials at the Directorate of Industries that the possibilty of double counting exists but its extent was not known.

[24]Registration with the DIC is a two-stage process. Provisional registration is granted to enable an entrepreneur to set up his/her unit. It entitles a unit to approach different agencies for inputs at pre-production stage. Permanent registration is granted to the functioning units or those which are ready to start production. All those who take provisional registration need not necessarily set up the unit.

[25]In 1977–8 a guessestimate for the country put it almost on par with the registered units, 296,00,000 units against 374,00,000 registered units (Sandesara 1988). However, the situation has improved since then and in Kerala, we were informed by a number of officials in the Industries Department, that the number of unregistered units is very small especially in manufacturing industry.

Diagram 5.1. Registered SSEs

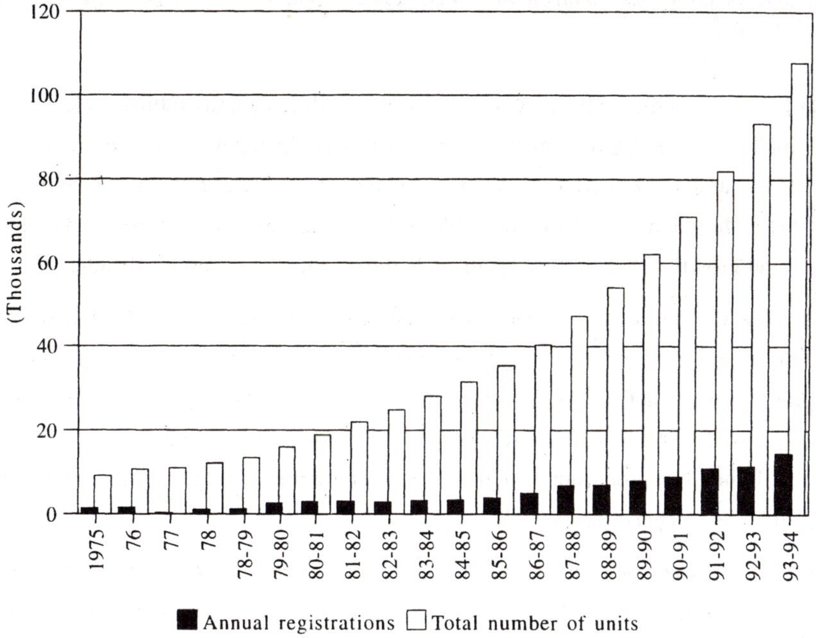

Diagram 5.2. Annual registration of SSEs – Region wise

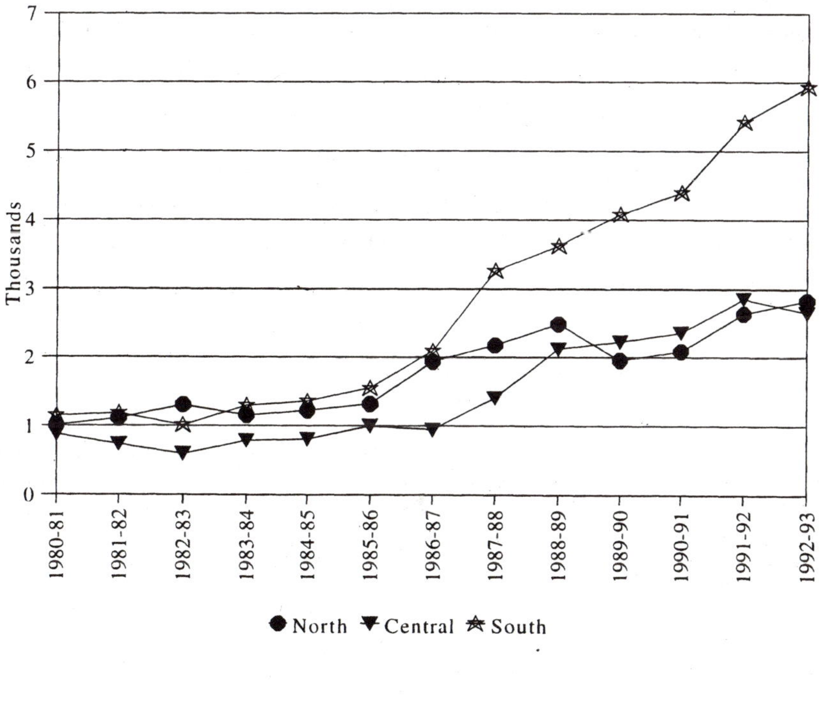

5.4.3.2 Overview of the Small-Scale Units: 1972–3 and 1987–8 as Derived from the SIDO *Data*

Two fairly comprehensive all-India surveys of the small-scale units falling under the purview of the Small Industries Development Organisation, were undertaken on a census basis for the years 1972–3 and 1987–8 which have been examined in an earlier study (Subramanian and Pillai 1994). Though not strictly comparable[26], these data were used to throw some light on the structure and growth of the modern small-scale units in Kerala vis-a-vis all-India.

In 1987–8, the state contributed less than 5 percent to the total number of small-scale units in the country as also of employment and even less in terms of value added or total production. A larger proportion of small units in Kerala are manufacturing units (60 percent, against 50 percent for all-India) and 70 percent are located in rural areas compared to a much lower proportion, 42 percent, in India. The proportion of female-headed enterprises (14 percent) is higher in Kerala than all-India (8 percent) (DCSSI 1992).

Table 5.3 gives a broad comparative picture of growth between 1972–3 and 1987–8 in Kerala and all-India. While growth in the number of small-scale units has not been very different between Kerala and all-India, the rate of growth of employment was much higher for all-India (5 percent compared to 2 percent for Kerala). Average size of a unit in terms of workers declined for both Kerala and India, but was sharper for the state.[27] In terms of workers, size of unit was slightly larger in Kerala which is also borne out by the NSSO data.[28] On the other hand size of a unit in terms of investment in plant and machinery is smaller in Kerala. This implies that units are relatively more labour intensive in Kerala. Indicators such as value added and production grew at a much higher rate at the all-India level.

The study by Subramanian and Pillai (1994) revealed that structural ratios like investment in plant and machinery per unit (at 1972–3 prices)[29] and net value added per unit (at 1972–3 prices) had declined more sharply in Kerala than at the all-India level. While labour productivity registered an increase over the period in the case of both, it was higher for the country as a whole; in terms of production or output (at 1972–3 prices) the per unit value declined in Kerala

[26]The upper investment limit for small units was prescribed as Rs. 0.75 million in 1972–3; by 1987–8 it had been raised to Rs. 3.5million and to 6.0 million in 1991. Although comparable (to 1972–3) data are not given in the 1987–8 census Report, it has been generated in the study by Subramanian and Pillai (1994).

[27]The average size of a unit had declined in Kerala from 20 to 7 persons (for India it was from 10 to 6 persons).

[28]The share of the smaller units viz. own account enterprises (OAE) and non-directory manufacturing establishments (NDME) in employment was about 72 percent in Kerala while for all-India it was over 80 percent in 1989–90.

[29]This study used the all-India index of wholesale prices keeping the first Census year 1972–3 as the base=100 to deflate the 1987–8 value figures.

Table 5.3: Growth of the Small-Scale Sector (SIDO units) in Kerala and All India - A Comparative Perspective: 1972–3 to 1987–8

	Indicators	Kerala			All-India			Annual compound growth rate (1972–87)	
		1972–3	1987–8	% change 72–87	1972–3	1987–8	% change 72–87	Kerala	India
1	No. of units in census frame ('000)	11	38	245	258	987	282	8.62	9.36
2	No. of working units ('000)	7	25	257	159	594	273	8.86	9.18
3	Employment ('000)	126	169	34	1650	3666	122	1.98	5.45
4	Investment in plant & machinery (Rs. million)	220	660*	200	5370	17450*	224	7.60	8.15
5	Production (Rs. million at 72–73 prices)	1160	3580*	209	26030	135280*	420	7.80	11.61
6	Value added (Rs. million at 72–73 prices)	360	710*	97	8410	32300*	284	4.63	9.39

Source: Compiled from Subramanian & Pillai (1994)

Notes: *All financial values in 1987–88 have been taken at 1972–73 prices using the all-India index of wholesale prices for manufactured products.

but increased for the country. It is interesting to observe that capital productivity or the output-capital ratio (defined as value of production divided by investment in plant and machinery)[30] was higher in Kerala in the initial year compared to all-India. However, it increased much faster for the latter (at 72-73 prices) while the figure was almost stagnant for Kerala. Another striking difference between the state and the country in respect of the small-scale sector is to be noted. While the share of the smallest units (that is upto an investment of Rs. 300,000 in plant and machinery)[31] declined in terms of numerical strength with the larger units (Rs. 300,000 and above) gaining in relative importance in the state and the country, in respect of production, the contribution of the larger units increased to over half the output by 1987–8 at the all-India level while the smaller units still accounted for over 60 percent of the output in Kerala. To some extent this tendency appears to contradict our findings from the NSSO data which defines size in terms of workers. According to the latter, the share of the smallest units, viz.OAEs and NDMEs in total number of units has remained almost the same at 95-96 percent between 1978–9 and 1989–90, in respect of both Kerala and all-India while their share in value added has increased. The relative contribution of the larger (DME) units to value added has declined; however, value added per DME unit was higher at both time points for all-India. That the smaller (capital) size

[30]Fixed capital is taken as investment in plant and machinery (at original cost) excluding land and buildings due to a tendency to over-value the latter in smaller units (Ishikawa 1962).

[31]It must be remembered that "small" is defined in terms of investment in plant and machinery at original cost.

of the units in Kerala could be related to the product structure of the small sector is discussed below.

However, before we examine the product structure we up-date some of the information on the SIDO units in Kerala beyond 1987–8, with more recent data for the year 1993–4 (Table 5.4). It may be noted that in this table the figures for total investment and value of production for 1972–3 and 1987–8 are different than in the earlier table since we have deflated the values with the wholesale price index of manufactured products (base 1981–2=100). The data appear to support the earlier finding that there was a sharp increase in the rate of growth of small-scale units in Kerala and employment generated since the latter half of the eighties. The decline in the average size of a unit in terms of workers is continuing. While growth in total investment[32] at constant prices recorded a substantial increase since the late eighties (11 per cent per annum), per unit investment tended to decline rather sharply. However, production of goods and services or total output, increased at a slightly higher rate (than total investment) and hence there was a mild increase in the output-capital ratio from 2.6 to 3.1. Looking at the output - labour ratio we find that in the first period it increased sharply. However there was a decline in the later period when employment grew much faster than the rate of growth of output. This suggests that the increase in output in the early ninities was due largely to an increase in capital productivity, a positive finding in a situation when per unit investment in plant & machinery has declined. The proportion of female-headed units has more than doubled.

5.4.4 *Product Structure of the* SIDO *Units*

The product structure was examined by Subramanian and Pillai (1994) for the two time points at a two-digit level of disaggregation in terms of value of output. Similar data were not available in terms of value added or employment for 1972–3. Growth between 1972–3 and 1987–8 was estimated by working out the latter figures at 1972–3 prices. While the output of different industry groups grew at varying rates and some industries such as food, wood, rubber and plastic products recorded higher than the all-industry average growth rate, more than three-fourths of the total output in 1987–8 in Kerala was accounted for by 5 two-digit groups, viz. (1) food products (2) wood products (3) rubber and plastics (4) chemicals and (5) metal products. These same 5 industry groups had also shared more than 75 percent of the total output in 1972–3 although the inter se shares were slightly different. A comparison with the all-India product structure brings out interesting differences.

The all-India pattern was much less concentrated in 1972–73: More than 75 percent of the output was shared by 9 industry groups the top three being metal products, chemicals and basic

[32]We were not able to procure figures on investment in plant and machinery for 1993–4.

Table 5.4: Some Recent Indicators of Growth of SIDO units - 1972–3 to 1993–4

Year	Units in census frame	Units working	Employment (number)	Employment per unit @	Total investment (Rs. million)	Investment per unit (Rs.'000) Rs.	Total production (Rs. million)	Production per unit of investment	Production per employee (Rs.'000)	Women's units (%)
1972–3	11,427	6903	126,415	20@	980	158@	2569	2.60	20	
1987–8	38,030	25717	169,309	7	2566	100	7529	2.90	44	6*
1993–4	110,384	105780	602,987	6	4836	46	14847	3.10	25	13.4*
Annual compound growth rates										
72–87		9.2	2.0		6.6		7.4			
87–93		26.6	23.6		11.1		12.0			
72–93		13.9	7.7		7.9		8.7			

Source: 1. For 1972–3 and 1987–8, Subramanian & Pillai (1994). However all values are deflated by Index of wholesale prices for manufactured products with base 1981–82 =100.

2. For 1993-4, Economic Review, 1994, State Planning Board, Government of Kerala, Thiruvananthapuram.

Notes: @ Estimated for units for which data were tabulated, viz 6205 units.

* As percent of total units.

metals. While for India too, the pattern did not alter much by 1987–8, it was already more diversified. It is interesting to note that the share of food products is much lower for all-India, 22 percent in 1987–8 (though it registered an increase since 1972–3), compared to about 40 percent in Kerala (where in fact it declined from about 42 percent). It may be noted that with the entry of food processing as a major activity since the eighties (Singh 1992) the food group has become a fairly dynamic sector; however in Kerala coconut oil accounts for the largest share in total production with cashew being the fourth most important.

A further attempt in the study cited above, to look at diversification of the industrial structure in terms of regional base study concepts like location quotient[33] and specialisation quotient[34] confirms the above finding: the industrial base in Kerala is narrow and marked by the low share of enginnering industries even in the late eighties. Although there was some diversification (as shown by the specialisation quotient), its extent was far lower than at the all-India level (Subramanian and Pillai 1994).

5.4.4.1 Product Structure in Terms of Employment: 1987–8

The product structure of the small-scale sector in terms of employment (1987–8) is almost as concentrated in Kerala as in India (Table 5.5). About 70 percent of the employment is shared by 5 industry groups in Kerala (food products, wood products, non-metallic mineral products, metals and products and rubber/plastic products) and 6 at the all-India level (metals and products, food products, machinery and parts, non-metallic mineral products, chemicals and products and wood products). However, what distinguishes the Kerala structure is the heavy concentration within these groups of agro and natural resource based industries. About 60 percent of employment was accounted for by the latter while the proportion was about one-third for all-India. The latter, as can be seen from the table, tend to use much less fixed capital (plant and machinery) per unit on average.

5.4.5 Growth of Value Added in Unregistered Manufacturing

Another way of looking at growth in the small-scale sector is in terms of its contribution to value added in manufacturing. The estimates for two time points on value added presented earlier indicated a relative under estimation of its share. We therefore examine the State Domestic Product figures which give estimates of income originating by industry group (Table 5.6). The

[33]It can be used as a meaure of relative regional concentration of a given industry compared to total national magnitude.

[34]It measures the extent to which a region showed a diversified pattern as compared to all-India.

Table 5.5: Structure of the Small-Scale Sector: Product Group Wise by Percentage Share in Total Employment: SIDO units: 1987–8

	Product group	SIDO units (Percentage share in total employment) 1987–8			
		Total		Rural	
		Kerala	India	Kerala	India
1	Food and beverages	27 (51)	15 (80)	31	22
2	Garments, hosiery	4 (16)	6 (40)	4	5
3	Wood products	14 (41)	6 (33)	16	9
4	Leather products	*	2 (28)	*	2
5	Non-metallic mineral products	13 (55)	12 (120)	16	23
6	Rubber and plastic products	8 (88)	5 (198)	7	4
7	Printing	7 (67)	5 (136)	5	3
8	Chemicals & products	6 (63)	9 (199)	5	9
9	Metals and products	9 (56)	16 (119)	8	11
10	Machinery and parts	5 (69)	12 (154)	3	4
11	Transport equipment	1 (85)	3 (164)	1	1
12	Repair	5 (32)	5 (20)	3	5
13	Miscellaneous industries	1 (40)	2 (101)	1	1
14	Total	100 (54)	100 (95)	100	100

Source: Same as Table 5.3

Notes: 1. Figures in brackets indicase investment in plant and machinery per unit (in Rs.'000) which has been given for Total units

focus is on the eighties and early nineties, the period of relatively higher growth of this sector. The estimates are at constant 1980–1 prices. Manufacturing income is classified under registered and unregistered manufacturing. The former relates to the total factory sector, that is enterprises employing 10 or more workers with power and 20 or more workers without power. Unregistered manufacturing covers the non-factory, non-household and household sectors constituting the bulk of the small sector. However, while the small-scale factories are to be included under registered manufacturing, we noted earlier that the (SIDO) data covered a substantial pro-

Table 5.6: Net State Domestic Product at Factor Cost in Unregistered Manufacturing, Manufacturing and all Industry group

Year (1)	Unregistered manufacturing (2)	Manufacturing (3)	SDP (4)	Percentage of 2 to (3)	Percentage of 3 to (4)
1970–1	2032	3788	30523	53.6	12.4
1975–6	2403	4448	34624	54.0	12.8
1980–1	2412	5315	38227	45.4	13.9
1985–6	2737	5846	39692	46.8	14.7
1986–7	2690	5402	38991	49.8	13.8
1987–8	2522	5396	40470	46.7	13.3
1988–9	2014	5978	44443	33.6	13.4
1989–90	1899	6379	47054	29.8	13.6
1990–1	3916	7987	52623	49.0	15.2
1991–2	3810	8244	53647	46.2	15.4
1992–3	4292	8938	57516	48.0	15.5
1993–4	4370	9262	63805	47.2	14.5
1994–5	4739	10045	68688	47.2	14.6

Source: Economic Review, Kerala, various issues, State Planning Board, Government of Kerala, Thiruvananathapuram.

portion of small-scale factories.

From the table we find that in the 70's when the share of manufacturing was relatively lower in SDP, unregistered manufacturing contributed more than half of total value added in manufacturing. However, in the 80's, manufacturing registered a small increase, but the share of unregistered manufacturing declined to 45–50 percent, very sharply in the late 80's, which marked a sharp growth in its numbers. Since then the share of manufacturing has remained sluggish at around 15 percent of the SDP. Unregistered manufacturing as a proportion of total manufacturing increased to its early 80's level. It has very often been stated that the contribution of the unregistered sector of manufacturing to output and value added tends to be underestimated given its hetrogenous nature. However, what is puzzling is that even indepth surveys of different segments of this sector throw up a poor aggregate performance of this sector. This of course does not deny the fact that the sector also contains dynamic segments.

5.4.6 *Summing-up*

In the foregoing analysis we have looked at the growth and diversity of the small-scale sector in different ways given the different data sources. In terms of numbers, while the rate of growth in registered SIDO units was not very different in Kerala from all-India, in respect of own account enterprises (OAEs) and non-directory manufacturing establishments (NDMEs) the change was much smaller in the state. Smaller units, in terms of workers, are on average larger in Kerala than their counterparts at the all-India level. However, the units use much less of capital equipment resulting in a larger share of "tiny"[35] units in Kerala. In terms of employment the share of the larger units has increased in Kerala; however, in terms of value added it has declined. Size in terms of both workers and fixed capital investment appears to be declining. While the structure of the small sector in rural Kerala did not show any sharp differences with the all-state picture in the late seventies, some disparities did appear by the early nineties. The proportion of OAEs has increaed relatively more in rural areas and there was a negative growth in value added per unit in the larger units. In terms of employment the share of the small sector appears to have increased marginally to 80 percent in Kerala. However, its share in value added in manufacturing shows a declining tendency according to the different sources, varying between one-third to a little less than half. The larger proportion of employment is accounted for by agro-based industries which are relatively small in terms of investment in plant and machinery. In terms of the value of output, the structure of the small-scale sector is very concentrated relative to the all-India picture; the extent of diversification is much lower.

Overall it appears that the growth in the large-scale manufacturing sector in Kerala has been very sluggish in the eighties and its structure was characterised by a concentration of agro-based processing industries as we observed in Chapter 3. The small-scale sector grew relatively fast since the latter half of the eighties; however its structure too is centred on agro-natural resource based product groups. While its growth performance in the aggregate has been relatively poor, however, the increasing tendency in the output-capital ratio in the recent period is an encouraging trend.

We now present the data from our field survey of a sample of recently set up rural small-scale enterprises in a district of north Kerala. Our attempt is to probe further into the nature and type of such enterprises focussing in particular on their linkages with the rural sector and growth potential.

[35]"Tiny" was defined as units with an investment in plant and machinery of Rs. 200,000 which was raised to Rs. 500,000 in 1991.

6

Rural Industry and its Linkages: Evidence from Secondary and Primary Sources of Information

6.1 Introduction

In this chapter we attempt to analyse the linkages of rural small-scale enterprises (RSSEs) with the agricultural-rural sector[1] which correspond to the types discussed earlier:

- geographical and sectoral origin of the entrepreneur[2] and mobilisation of initial capital;
- geographical origins of labour employed;
- production linkages both backward (in terms primarily of raw materials, industrial intermediates and capital equipment used by these units) and forward (in terms of use of their products by other sectors of the rural economy);
- consumption linkages or the source of demand for the final goods produced by these units.

An input-output table at the regional level would be very useful in understanding linkages. However, relatively few input-output studies incorporate the small-scale enterprises, especially those in rural areas and thus tend to underestimate linkages. For Kerala, besides a very early attempt at constructing an input-output table for the state no similar exercise was done at an aggregate or disaggregate level for a recent year. In the absence of such information, we derive an approximate picture of agriculture-small-scale industry linkages based on the available secondary data on small-scale units for the district under study. These data, taken from the registers of the District Industries Centre (DIC), (which come under the nodal agency SIDO give basic information on location of small-scale enterprises and product group. Culling out the rural based units and classifying them by product group we can roughly discern the nature of

[1] It may be noted again that we have defined linkages in terms of the RSSEs being the sector of origin.

[2] The terms owner-producer, producer, entrepreneur, operator and proprietor have been used interchangeably.

their linkages with agriculture according to whether it is backward or forward production or consumption linkages. However to what extent the linkages of, as also the resource flows into, small-scale units are local rural (or lie outside the rural economy), can be assessed only by a field survey which is the second exercise we undertake to understand the nature of linkages.

This chapter is organised in five sections. We start in Section 6.2 with some basic socio-economic information on the district of Palakkad and its two blocks[3] selected for the field survey on SSEs in Section 6.3 the information on small-scale enterprises registered with the DIC, Palakkad in the two blocks, in terms of product group was used to broadly approximate the nature of linkages with agriculture based on secondary information. It also discusses the design of the sample survey in these two blocks. Section 6.4 gives the pattern of linkages based on secondary (DIC) data a descriptive profile of the sample units, classifying them by major type, size, product group and location and in Section 6.5 we examine the linkages in terms of the socio-economic origins of the sample producers and sources of initial capital and labour supply. This has important implications for the development of rural linkages. Information on the type of household (in terms of father's occupation) the entrepreneur comes from also enables us to observe the patterns of diversification as between the different types of rural households. The production and consumption linkages of the sample units are discussed in the following chapter.

6.2 The Study Area: Socio-economic Profile of Palakkad (erstwhile Palaghat) District and Selected Blocks

Palakkad lies in the north-east of Kerala, at the foothills of the Western Ghats with the state of Tamil Nadu bordering it on the east, the district of Trichur in the west and south and the district of Malappuram in the north (see Map 2). The most striking feature in its configuration is the extensive gap historically known as the "Palghat gap" in the otherwise unbroken great range of the Western Ghats which opens to the Coimbatore district in Tamil Nadu. The largest town in the district bears the same name, Palakkad and given its geographical proximity to Coimbatore, the second largest city of Tamil Nadu to which it is connected by the Palakkad-Coimbatore road (a distance of only 48 kms.), the latter has had considerable impact on its

[3]As noted earlier a block is the second tier of local development administration with the village panchayat below it and the district panchayat above it. A panchayat is a group of revenue villages (or census villages) constituted to form a viable unit of development. However, in Kerala given the large average size of a village, most panchayats are single village panchayats or may include another village or a portion of a village. In North Kerala, panchayats may sometimes include two or three villages. At present there are 990 panchayats and 1384 revenue villages in Kerala; 156 villages, 90 panchayats and 13 blocks in Palakkad. Since there would be very few newly registered units in a panchayat, we selected a block as the unit of analysis. The average size of a village panchayat for the state is 25,000 persons and of a block is 170,000 persons (GOK 1998).

Map 2: Palakkad District and the Two Blocks, Kollengode and Malampuzha

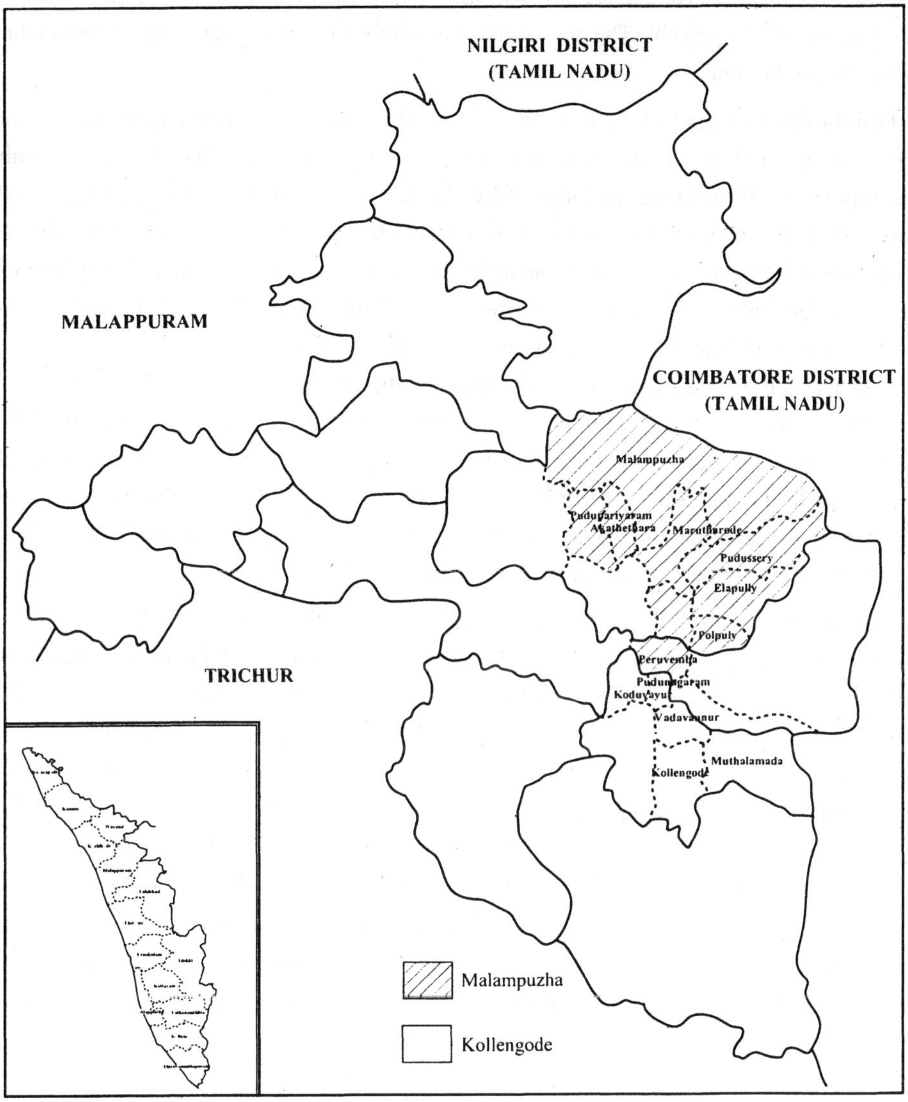

industrial growth. Table B.1 in Appendix B gives a socio-economic profile of the district in a comparative perspective with the state. Palakkad is very often described as the granary of Kerala state with the highest relative share of wet lands suitable for paddy cultivation. The district has the largest share of net irrigated area among all the districts. Recent statistics as given in the table show that Palakkad contributes 30 percent of paddy production, the highest among the districts of Kerala. It has a much higher proportion of rural population, 84 percent compared to about 74 percent for Kerala and over half the work force is engaged in agriculture against a state average of 37.8 percent. The district accounts for the largest number of agricultural labour households in the state.

Historically, Palakkad has had a small industrial base producing simple agricultural implements, cutlery and locks a also bell metal products, grass mats, beedi, handlooms and timber related products. Prior to the formation of Kerala state there were a few industrial units in the district, primarily metal based, which were concentrated in select locations. During the first two decades of the formation of the state there was a concerted effort by the government to set up a few large and medium scale enterprises in the district. Some large private industrialists mostly from outside the state, taking advantage of cheap land and power, set up units in the region connected to Coimbatore in the mid-sixties and then in the seventies. A few of these were electronics units while others were chemicals and metal based, the latter two being very power intensive. While this did result in the growth of small-scale units, primarily engineering in that area, (some in the nature of sub-contractors to the large and medium units), there was even otherwise an overall improvement in the industrial situation with manufacturing units being set up in different parts of the district (Palakkad Gazetteer 1976).

However, it was since the late eighties and early nineties that there was a spurt in the growth of small-scale enterprises in the district as revealed by a recent study on the industrial potential of Palakkad district. Over half the units surveyed in the study were set up after 1986 within which the larger proportion of units were set up since 1990 (KITCO 1994). The proportion of rurally located small-scale units is much higher in Palakkad. In another study by the Economic Intelligence Unit (The Economist 1995), on economic opportunities in India with its opening up, cited in Mathew (1996), the south (in particular Kerala and Tamil Nadu) has been ranked above the west (Gujarat and Maharashtra) as the future industrial destination of India. Kerala scores high due to its highest road density, highest literacy rate and adequate power supply. Despite the growing deficiency of the latter with increasing consumption, it still ranks second, next only to Tamil Nadu in power supply position. However, land being very scarce in the state, with traditional industrial centres like Ernakulam in central Kerala, facing problems, Palakkad has emerged as a potential area for industrial development.

The district consists of 13 blocks within which two, broadly on the eastern side, were selected for a more indepth study of linkages of rural small-scale units. The selection of the two blocks was purposive[4], guided by our desire to capture the recent growth in rural small-scale industries with apparently different types of linkages: one a dominantly agricultural block, Kollengode (K), in which we would expect the intensity of local linkages to be high; the second,

[4]The selection was done after a discussion with all the block officers in the district.

Malampuzha (M), a newly formed block,[5] which witnessed a spurt in the growth of small-scale enterprises in rural areas some of which have become part of the Palakkad urban agglomeration or lie in its hinterland and are also contiguous to the industrial city of Coimbatore. Such units would have stronger external linkages.[6] Our survey findings from these two blocks would also be used to explore the role of local capital and entrepreneurship in generating relatively higher developmental links with the rural sector. While we do not claim that this case study represents Kerala or India, it certainly throws up certain processes and pattern of relationships which have a wider relevance.

The agrarian character of Kollengode vis-a-vis Malampuzha is brought out in Table B.2 in Appendix B in terms of the industrial distribution of the workforce as also land utilistion figures. Parts of four panchayats[7] were declared as towns in the last Census, two in Kollengode and two in Malampuzha. These, primarily small towns,[8] have been included in our definition of "rural". Note that the average size of a panchayat in the two blocks is slightly larger than that of a **small** town defined as having a population between 5,000–20,000 persons. While a village in Kerala is on average large in terms of population size (about 17,000 persons compared to 911 persons at the all-India level)[9], our definition of "rural" and "local" in the context of linkages is considerably broad, covering the block and the small towns within it. Given the observed interaction, spatial and economic between small towns and the rural hinterland (Bagachwa and Stewart 1990), inclusion of such towns in "rural" is essential. The choice of a broader definition of rural, covering the block, was also dictated by our decision (to be explained later) to survey the more recent units, set up between 1990–95, whose numbers would be inadequate in a single panchayat. From the point of view of policy too, while local resources and local needs should play an important role in rural industrialisation, "local" could mean a panchayat or block or district depending on the type of industry and technology utilized.

However, from the point of view of development of a "micro region" and the devolution of financial resources, there is a virtue in keeping the concept of local-rural within narrower limits.

---

[5]There has been some reorganisation of blocks after the 1991 Census in view of the new decentralised administrative set up. A new block, Malampuzha was added to the existing 12 blocks in Palakkad carved out of Palakkad, Kuzhalmannam and Kollengode blocks. We have reconstituted the two blocks according to the current set up and hence the panchayats included in the two blocks differ from those given in the 1991 Census.

[6]It may be noted that parts of Koduvayur and Pudunagaram panchayats in Kollengode block and Marutharode and Puduppariyaram panchayats in Malampuzha block have been upgraded into census towns in 1991. While the latter two have been absorbed in the Palakkad urban agglomeration, the two towns in Kollengode block are part of a medium town urban agglomeration. However, the latter two are located at a much greater distance from the core medium town than the other two from the core city (see Table 6.7). Moreover, Kollengode block continues to be relatively more rural than Malampuzha as evident from Table A.2.

[7]Ibid.

[8]One of the new towns, Puduppariyaram, has a population slightly above that of a small town viz. 24,800 persons.

[9]As per the 1981 Census.

There could be a tendency otherwise, for a large part of the funds to find their way to larger towns as happened in the case of the Rural Industries Projects in India launched in the early sixties (Sigurdson 1978). Although the only city in the district, Palakkad falls within the spatial spread of the Malampuzha block and the medium-size town, Chittur-Tattamangalam, is in close proximity to the Kollengode block, we have excluded these two from our definition of "rural".

One of the panchayats in Malampuzha, Pudussery particularly the area known as Kanchikode, borders Coimbatore and has also been the focus of considerable Government initiative for promotion of industry which has had considerable impact on the structure of small-scale industries in that area. Growth in manufacturing has been the highest in Pudussery during the period 1971–91. The percentage of workers in manufacturing almost doubled, from about 15.3 in 1971 to 29.1 in 1991; for males the increase was from 20 percent to 36.6 percent and for females from 6 percent to 12 percent. There was a sharp decline in the proportion of agricultural workers in the panchayat during this period. However, since the absolute number of workers in agriculture registered a marginal increase, a large proportion of the additions to the work force during 1971–91 were absorbed in manufacturing.[10]

6.3 Pattern of Linkages Based on Secondary (DIC) Data

6.3.1 The DIC *Data on Small Scale Units*

An attempt was then made to obtain data on small-scale units in the two blocks under study. As pointed out in Chapter 5 it is very difficult to procure information on the universe of small- scale units, a large proportion of which fall outside the purview of official agencies. The closest that we could get to the units we wanted to capture in the study viz. relatively independent, private entrepreneurs in rural areas who operate manufacturing and processing units on a small scale, was through an examination of the DIC data. However, as pointed out earlier not all small-scale units register with the DIC and the number of unregistered units is not insignificant. This was brought out by the Economic Censuses of 1980 and 1990. We attempted a quick estimate of the likely magnitude of unregistered units in our area through a complete enumeration of all households in four randomly selected wards of a panchayat in Kollengode. In view of time and budgetary constraints it was not possible to do this for all panchayats in both the blocks.[11] Out

[10]The number of workers in Pudussery panchayat increased by about 6000 persons between 1971–91 of which manufacturing accounted for 3200 persons, that is, more than 50 percent.

[11]As stated in the text there are 5 panchayats in Kollengode and 8 in Malampuzha. A panchayat on average has 10 wards in M and 8 wards in K and each ward can have an average of 600 households. This would have meant surveying almost 70,000 households.

of a total of 2750 households surveyed (based on a brief questionnaire which elicited answers to questions like: name of head of household, whether owning a business or industrial unit, nature of activity and whether registered with the DIC), about 10 percent were found to be running an unregistered unit. However barely 5 percent of these units were manufacturing units; the overwhelming proportion were in the nature of small retail shops selling provisions, vegetables, medicine, stationery, flowers etc. or were engaged in repair, largely of two wheelers. To the extent that concerted drives for registration of units by the local DIC officials have netted in some of the very tiny enterprises, our sample does not entirely miss out this category in the manufacturing sector though in the personal services and repair sector this may not be correct.

Hence we confined ourselves to the units registered with the DIC which also covers the larger small-scale firms most of which are located on the industrial development areas in Pudussery panchayat.[12] There are three-mini industrial estates (MIE) in Kollengode and Malampuzha and two large industrial development areas (IDA) in M, which were set up to act as growth centres in industrially backward rural areas. A list of the newly registered units in rural areas, with a permanent registration[13] from the DIC between 1990 and 1995 was drawn up for the two blocks, giving information on location of unit, nature of activity, investment and employment. The decision to study **newly registered units** was prompted by (a) the perceived growth of the small-scale sector which had been rather impressive since the late eighties and early nineties (KITCO 1994); and (b) the possibility of capturing the linkages of rural industries with greater precision for the more recently set up units.

6.3.2 *Analysis of the Newly Registered Units*

Within the area selected for the field survey, there were about 315 units registered in the five panchayats of Kollengode block during 1990–5 and 342 units in the eight panchayats of Malampuzha block.[14] For the district as a whole about 2000 units are estimated[15] to have been set up

[12]For instance while about 10 percent of the modern units (excluding the IDA/MIE units) registered with the DIC in Malampuzha block between 1990–5 and less than 5 percent in Kollengode block had a capital investment above Rs. 500,000 in plant and machinery, the proportion was as high as 70 percent for the IDA units.

[13]Registration with the DIC is a two-stage process. Provisional registration is granted to enable an entrepreneur to set up his/her unit. It entitles a unit to approach different agencies for inputs at pre-production stage, that is land, industrial shed, raw materials, loan etc. Permanent registration is granted to the functioning units or those which are ready to start production. All those who take provisional registration need not necesarily set up the unit and hence estimates of DIC units based on provisional registration would overstate the figures.

[14]Since the survey was conducted in early 1996, some of the units in industrial development areas, old and, especially the new, in Malampuzha which were still in the process of being set up are not included.

[15]While the block wise figures of units registered during the period 1990–5 for the five panchayats in Kollengode and 8 in Malampuzha, were collected from the registers in the DIC office, Palakkad, the district wise information was taken from the Department of Industries, Thiruvananthapuram, which compiles the data from all the districts.Rural units in Palakkad constituted 78 percent of all the small-scale units registered with the DIC as on

in rural areas during this period. Hence the two blocks accounted for almost one third of the units recently registered in Palakkad. Although for purposes of administering assistance the DIC covers "modern" units, in recent years a number of traditional industrial units were also registered with it[16]. In Palakkad the traditional industries are handloom weaving, pottery making, bell metal products, cutlery, beedi making, and bamboo/grass weaving. And since the late seventies small-scale service and repair (industry related) enterprises were also made eligible for benefits available to tiny units and could register with the DIC. These were primarily in the nature of personal or industrial services (beauty parlour, dry cleaner, telephone booths, clinical laboratory, xerox, typing and computer centres) and repair of cycles and motor vehicles particularly two-wheelers, tractors, electrical goods etc. New units in the industrial development areas, primarily in Malampuzha, were dominated by chemicals, metals and machinery industry group and have been largely studied as a separate category.

Needless to state, in both the blocks "modern" industrial units dominated. This was partly due to the source of data used viz. DIC; but more so because relatively fewer new units in the traditional industrial sector would be set up. The data on workers, fixed capital invested in these units pertaining to the year of application for a license and location as given in Diagrams 1-3 reveal the following characteristics of small industry in these two blocks:

- The average size of a unit is smaller in Kollengode; almost 80 percent of the units fall in the category 1-4 workers and there is a much larger proportion of 1 person enterprises. In Malampuzha less than two thirds of the units fall in the 1-4 worker category and over one third employ more than 5 workers. Units on IDA are much larger; over one third employ more than 10 workers (Diagram 6.1).

- In terms of investment in plant and machinery (at historical cost) too, units in Kollengode are relatively smaller; over 60 percent of the units had an investment of Rs. 25,000 or less in K (less than 10 percent in Malampuzha) and barely 2 percent of the units had an investment of more than Rs. 500,000. In Malampuzha 12 percent of the units had an investment of Rs. 500,000 (7 percent if we excluded the IDA units). While the modal interval in Kollengode was upto Rs. 25,000, in Malampuzha it was between Rs. 100,000–Rs. 500,000 (Diagram 6.2) With respect to the IDA units the modal interval was more than Rs. 10,00,000 (not shown separately).

31.3.98 (DCSSI 1992). This was the percentage used on a total of about 2600 units newly registered in Palakkad district to estimate the number of rural units newly registered during the period 1990–5. It yielded a figure of about 2000 units.

[16]While those traditional industrial units organised as cooperatives can register with the DIC, very often it is the initiative and interest of individual block officers which draws in a number of such units motivating the entrepreneurs to avail of loans and upgrade the units.

Diagram 6.1. Distribution of units by size class of workers

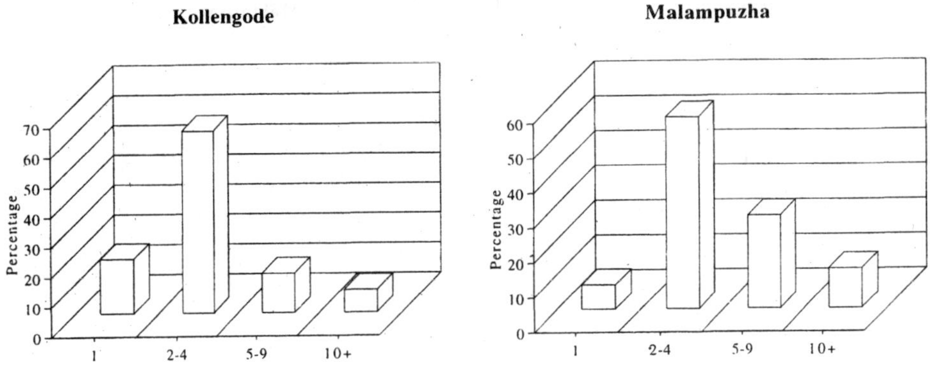

Diagram 6.2. Distribution of units by size class in terms of investment in plant & machinery (in Rupees thousands)

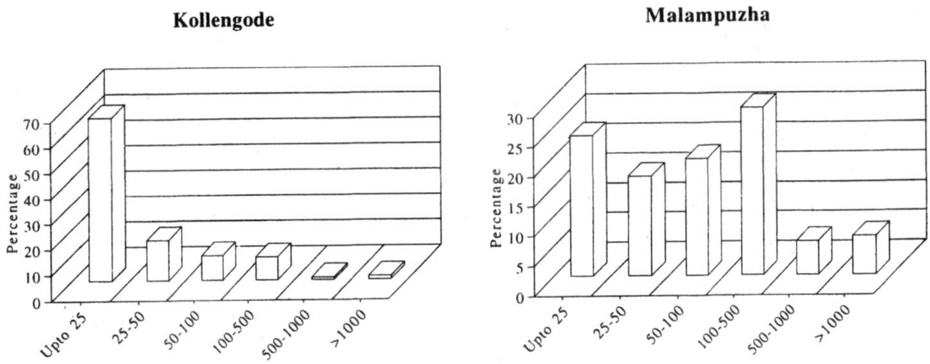

- The distribution of the units over the panchayats reveals that the spread is more even in Kollengode; albeit the larger proportion of units have come up in the new small towns, Koduvayur and Pudunagaram in the block. However, in Malampuzha there is considerable concentration of newly registered units in two of the eight panchayats - Pudussery and Marutharode, which account for 57 percent of these units. While part of the latter is now a town, the former with a population of a medium size town is still a panchayat. The other new town in this region, Puduppariyaram, accounted for a very marginal proportion (9 percent) of the new units (Diagram 6.3).

On the whole it may be noted that in both the blocks, the "tiny" units (viz. those with an investment of Rs. 500,000 or less) are dominant. However in Malampuzha, there was a

Diagram 6.3. Distribution of units by panchayat

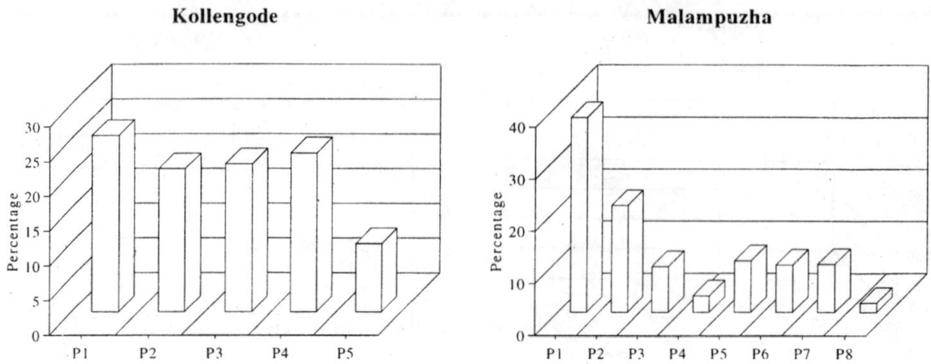

Diagram 6.4. Distribution of units by product group

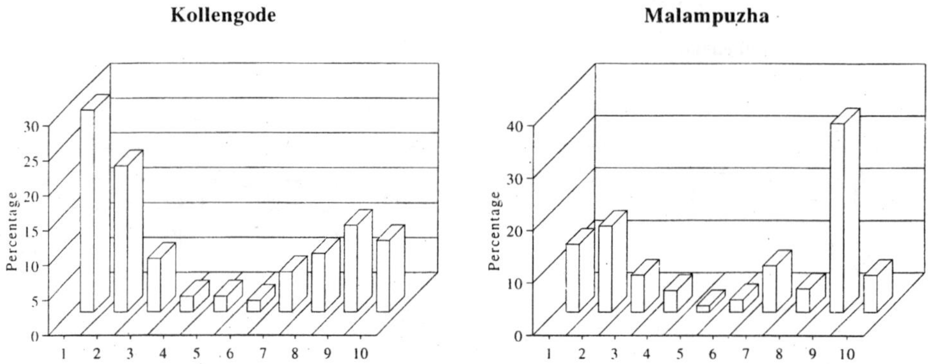

1 – Food; 2 – Clothing Textiles; 3 – Wood, Cane, Bamboo; 4 – Printing;
5 – Leather products; 6 – Rubber; 7 – Chemical and Plastics; 8 – Bricks, Cement;
9 – Metal products & Machinery; 10 – Service & Repair

much larger proportion of units at the upper end of the "tiny" limit while the incidence of the larger units was high in the IDAs. This dominance of tiny units is true for the state too, as the 1987–8 Census of the Small Scale Industrial Units reveals: units with investment in plant and machinery of Rs. 500,000 and less constituted almost 97 percent of the total units (DCSSI 1992). The irrelevance of an official upper limit of investment in plant and machinery as high as Rs. 65,00,000 (recently raised to Rs 3 million)[17] for inclusion as small-scale units, country wide, is brought out by this reality. Do such units really represent small, independent producers or are

[17]See the Economic Times (a leading financial paper of India) dated 8.2.97.

they owned and operated by entrepreneurs not independent of the large industrialists already in the field and are able to siphon off most of the benefits given to SSEs (Banerjee 1992).[18] Such sharp upward increases in investment limits to broaden the reach of the small sector confounds the definition of small by number of workers employed.[19]

6.3.3 *The Nature of Linkages with Agriculture*

A classification of the units for the two blocks by product group provides us with a broad idea of the nature of their linkage with agriculture according to whether the units comprise backward, forward or consumption links. The number of registered units in each category in relation to the total gives us a first impression of their quantitative significance (see Harriss 1987a).

In Kollengode (Diagram 6.4) the primary agro-processing industries such as rice and oil milling and food products dominate as also natural resource based industries like ready made garments, wooden furniture, bricks and tiles which suggest the possibiliy of strong backward production linkages with agriculture. They also constitute consumption linkages with agricultural and other rural incomes. A small proportion of units produce non-agricultural consumer goods, like plastic utility items, soap, PVC products (7 percent) and simple electrical equipment (2 percent). In Malampuzha it is the non-agricultural, engineering, machinery and (to some extent) chemicals goods industries which account for a larger share. The engineering units are largely linked to other industrial enterprises in the consumer electronics sector through subcontracting. However, the possibility of forward production linkages with agriculture does exist in terms of units producing pumpsets, ancillary equipment and parts of agricultural machinery. Approximately[20] 15 percent of the metal products and machinery units were engaged in some activity related to agricultural machinery or equipment. Consumption linkages too in terms of units producing food products and ready made garments (30 percent) existed in Malampuzha block; 10 percent of the newly registered units in the IDA were modern food products undertakings (data not shown separately). Although a large proportion of the firms in K and to some extent in M have obvious linkages with agriculture, to what extent these linkages are local or non local would be possible to gauge from our sample survey. Another obvious limitation of the above exercise is the inability to trace the linkages of RSSEs with other sectors of the rural economy in particular the service or tertiary sector.

---

[18]See (Nirmala Banerjee 1992). Policy appears to confuse between small producers and small-scale production.

[19]We found that the entrepreneurs of the larger small-scale enterprises try to play down the number of workers employed since more than 10–20 workers and using power would require them to register as a factory or with more than 50 workers and using power would be categorised as a medium size unit.One method is to report some workers as apprentices; another is to treat a certain number as workers engaged in loading/unloading.

[20]It was not always possible to discern the type of use from the information in the DIC registers on product to be manufactured by the unit.

Table 6.1: Distribution of Sample Units

	Product group	Sampling Frame				Sample			
		K (No.)	%	M (No.)	%	K (No.)	%	M (No.)	%
1.	Food products	91	28.9	44	12.9	20	32.2	8	11.8
2.	Textiles, readymades, coir, handlooms	66	20.9	56	16.3	10	16.1	7	10.3
3.	Wood, cane, leather, rubber products	36	11.4	36	10.5	6	9.7	7	10.3
4.	Printing, plastic, chemicals	25	7.9	44	12.9	10	16.1	8	11.8
5.	Bricks, tiles, cement	26	8.4	15	4.4	6	9.7	4	5.9
6.	Metal products, machinery	39	12.3	123	36.0	7	11.3	27	39.6
7.	Service and repair	32	10.2	23	7.0	3	4.9	7	10.3
8.	All units	315	100	342	100	62	100	68	100

Source: DIC data on each block, District Industries Centre, Directorate of Industries, Palakkad

Notes: K-Kollengode Block; M-Malampuzha Block; No - Number

6.3.4 The Survey Design

The above set of newly registered units stratified by product group, and arranged year wise from 1990–5, in the two blocks constituted the frame from which the sample was drawn (Table 6.1).

It was decided to take about 20 percent of the registered units from each block as the sample, using systematic sampling procedure. A total sample of 130 units was drawn up comprising of 62 units in Kollengode and 68 units in Malampuzha. The latter included 10 units operating in the IDAs which have been examined separately. It may be noted that the industrial distribution of the sample units is broadly similar to the distribution in the sampling frame. We would like to state here that our primary interest was to understand the pattern of linkages of these small-scale units with the rural sector rather than to derive rigorous quantitative estimates of the economic parameters for the underlying population. Hence in respect of the relationships that we discern and the inferences that can be drawn, our study has wider application.

Our findings for both the blocks have been reported separately to highlight the differences between them, except where it was deemed necessary to combine them. A single point in time procedure was adopted for collecting data from the sample producers on capital, labour and raw materials, their sources, location of the market as also on variables such as earnings, wages, costs and surplus on the basis of a detailed questionnaire (see Appendix C). Information on the socio-economic characteristics of the entrpreneurs, their problems and future plans, was also obtained.

6.4 Findings from the Survey: Primary Sources

6.4.1 A Profile of the Units

(a) By type

A number of studies have drawn our attention to the hetrogeniety in the organisational forms of rural small-scale units (Staley and Morse 1965; Anderson 1982; Liedholm and Mead 1986; Islam 1987; Mukhopadhyaya and Lim 1986; Saith 1987; Wickramanayake 1988; Berry 1987; Davies et al 1992). Given the size of our sample we have not attempted too fine a differentiation, following the most commonly adopted two-fold classification of units: the household form or Lipton's "family enterprise" units (FEs) and the non-household form or small-scale units (SSUs) which range from the smallest to more modern units organised along capialist lines. The distinction is made primarily on the basis of type of labour used - whether largely family or hired labour. While traditional industries are normally organised as household units and modern industries as non-household units, with the growing significance of self-employment[21], the family enterprise form has gained a certain ubiquity due perhaps to what Lipton (1984) terms as its central advantage viz. fungibility combined with self-provisioning. Its tenacity has also been observed in other regions (Tambunan 1994). Similarly traditional industries adapting to changing demand conditions can be organised as SSUs. Though we have used the terms "household" unit and "family enterprise" interchangeably, the latter encompasses a wider reach since location is not restricted to the household. However, even though located outside the house sometimes, the family should control by ownership or by hire, most of the land and capital to which its labour is applied (Lipton 1984). Our focus as noted earlier is on the modern small-scale sector which could be organised as FE units or SSUs. While modernisation includes the gradual transformation of traditional industries (Staley and Morse 1965), by "modern" we mean the non-traditional industries. The 10 units located in the Industrial Development Area (IDA) are treated as a separate category since IDA units are relatively "large" small-scale units; some may be registered as factories.

Table 6.2 classifies the sample RSSEs[22] by type of (a) organisation; and (b) ownership. There is a relatively large proportion of family enterprise (FE) units in Kollengode (40 percent) vis-a-vis Malampuzha (28 percent). However, in both the regions small-scale units (SSUs) dominate;

[21]This is brought out by the last two Rounds of the National Sample Survey Organisation (NSSO) surveys on Employment and Unemployment. While the proportion of self-employment among males was 42 percent in the state in 1987–8, it increased to 50 percent in 1992. For females the increase was higher in the casual worker category.

[22]It may be recalled that the acronym RSSEs refers to all rural small-scale enterprises which are classified into FEs and SSUs.

Table 6.2: Distribution of Samples RSSEs by Type of (a) Organisation and (b) Ownership

6.2 (a): Organisation

	Organisation	Block					
		Kollengode		Malampuzha		IDA	
		Number	Employ-ment	Number	Employ-ment	Number	Employ-ment
1.	Family enterprise	40.3	20.1	27.6	6.5	–	–
2.	Small-scale units	59.7	79.9	72.4	93.5	100	100
3.	All RSSEs	100	100	100	100	100	100
	Sample size	62	310	58	557	10	197

Note: 1. Figures indicate cell counts as percent of column totals

6.2 (b): Ownership

	Block	Ownership type					
		Proprietor-ship	Partner-ship	Co-opera-ative	Private Ltd. Co	All RSSEs	Sample size
1.	Kollengode	90.3	8.1	1.6	–	100	62
2.	Malampuzha	84.5	5.2	3.4	6.9	100	58
3.	IDA units	40.0	10.0	–	50.0	100	10
	Total	83.8	6.9	2.3	6.9	100	130

Source: Field Survey

Note: 1. Figures indicate cell counts as percent of row totals

in M they account for almost three fourths of the total. Hence that the units would be smaller and organised more along lines of petty commodity production in K is suggested by these data as was also observed in the earlier section.

While we may think that this is further confirmed by the distribution of these units by type of ownership, an overwhelming proportion (90 percent) being proprietory concerns in Kollengode, this observation is not entirely correct. In Malampuzha too, around 84 percent of the units are organised as proprietorships. In the course of our field survey we came across fairly large, though small- scale units, in both the blocks, a few in the IDAs too, organised as proprietorships. Hence the tiniest to the fairly large small-scale units tend to be organised as proprietorships and need not always reflect a family enterprise form. It has been noted in other developing regions too, that most rural small-scale enterprises are organised as proprietory concerns (Liedholm and Mead 1987).

(b) By Size

Whether one uses employment or capital invested in plant and machinery[23] as the measure of size, almost all studies on rural industries conclude that an overwhelming proportion of such enterprises are concentrated at the lower end of the small-scale spectrum. In terms of employment this is upto 10 workers (the range being from 1–50 workers); in fact the tiny or "dwarf" (Hoselitz 1959) units employing upto 4 or 5 workers constitute a significant proportion. With respect to capital, tiny units in the Indian context[24] are those in which investment in plant and machinery (at historical cost) does not exceed Rs. 500,000. Since size is most often defined in terms of workers, in Table 6.3 we give the distribution of the capital invested in plant and machinery by size class of workers. Small units in terms of workers (1–4) also appear to be small in terms of capital investment. The overall relationship between size in terms of number of workers and the size of investment is statistically significant[25]. There ia a greater tendency for units to be small both in terms of workers and capital invested in Kollengode: over 60 percent of the units are tiny in terms of both workers (upto 4) and investment in plant and machinery (upto Rs. 500,000). In Malampuzha this percentage is less than half (data not presented in the table). The IDA units are much larger in terms of workers and capital invested. For instance 66 percent of the units have an investment of Rs. 25,00,000 and fall in the 10 plus workers group. The above data also suggest that on average units in Kollengode would tend to be more labour intensive.

(c) Composition

Table 6.4 brings out the significant differences in the product structure across size classes of investment in plant and machinery in the two blocks. It enables us to see whether the type of product and the magnitude of capital invested is related. In Kollengode, units producing agriculture and natural resource based consumer products like rice and oil, bakery items, sweets and snacks, ready-made garments, wooden furniture and bricks dominate.

The rural character of K is brought out further by the fact that the largest units (in terms of capital) are agro-based units. The modern rice mills are located mostly in Kollengode. One of

[23]Size is measured in terms of fixed capital invested in plant and machinery excluding "land and buildings". The latter has not been included due to a tendency to over value it in the smaller units since the premises are usually used for residential purposes also (Ishikawa 1962).

[24]The earlier limit for "tiny" units was an investment in plant and machinery of Rs. 200,000 which was raised to Rs. 500,000 in the new industrial policy of 1991.

[25]The Chi-square test of independence was significant at 5 percent level for both Kollengode and Malampuzha based on the rows as given in the table; however, columns Rs. 500–2500 and >Rs. 2500 were combined into one column.

Table 6.3: Distribution of Sample RSSEs by Number of Workers and Investment in Plant and Machinery

Kollengode Block							
Workers	Investment in plant and machinery (Rs.000)						
	upto 25	25–100	100–500	500–2500	>2500	Total	Sample size
1 worker	70.0	30.0	–	–	–	100	10
2–4	53.6	35.7	10.7	–	–	100	28
5–9	64.3	28.6	7.1	–	–	100	14
10 and above	20.0	30.0	30.0	10.0	10.0	100	10
Total	53.2	32.2	12.9	1.6	–	100	62

Malampuzha Block										
	Investment in plant and machinery (Rs.000)									
Workers	upto	25–100	100–500	IDA	500–2500	IDA	>2500	IDA	Total	IDA
1 worker	25.0	25.0	50.0	–	–	–	–	–	100 (4)	–
2–4	47.6	38.1	14.3	100	–	–	–	–	100 (21)	(1)
5–9	25.0	25.0	45.0	66.7	5.0	–	–	33.3	100 (20)	100 (3)
10 and above	7.7	7.7	30.8	–	30.8	66.7	23.1	33.3	100 (13)	100 (6)
Total	29.3	25.9	31.0	30.0	8.6	40.0	5.1	30.0	100	100

Source: Field Survey

Notes: 1. Figures indicate cell counts as percent of row totals.
2. In Malampuzha, figures in brackets in the last column indicate sample size
3. Figures for the 10 IDA units in Malampuzha are given in the relevant cells.

the new small towns in Kollengode block-Koduvayur- is emerging as a centre for tailoring and readymade garments, accounting for almost one third of the 54 newly registered garment and tailoring units in the block. While the share of more "modern" industries such as metal, machinery products and chemicals, is not insignificant in Kollengode block, accounting for about a fifth of the sample units, the nature of activity is relatively simple using lower fixed capital equipment as can be seen from the table. In Malampuzha block over half the units (excluding the IDA units) come under the metals and machinery product group. A number of units are engaged in sub-contracting work for large electronics and machinery producing firms or doing some fabrication work. The difference between the two blocks in respect of fixed capital use is very striking in the metals and machinery group - over 80 percent of such units in Kollengode fall within the first two investment ranges, that is upto Rs. 100,000 while in Malampuzha over 50 percent of the units have an investment of more than Rs. 100,000. The small average size

Table 6.4: Distribution of Sample RSSEs by Product Group and Investment in Plant and Machinery

Kollengode & Malampuzha Blocks										
	Investment in plant and machinery in Rs.000									
Product group	upto 25		25–100		100–500		>500		Total	
	Koll	Mal	Koll	Mal	Koll	Mal	Koll	Mal	Koll	Mal
Food products	55.0	20.0	25.0	40.0	15.0	40.0	5.0	–	100(20)	100(5)
Textiles, readymaces, coir, hand-looms, wood, leather, rubber	56.2	53.8	25.0	15.4	2.5	15.4	6.3	15.4	100(16)	100(13)
Printing, plastic, chemicals	30.0	–	60.0	50.0	10.0	33.3	–	16.7	100(10)	100(6)
Bricks, tiles, cement	50.0	25.0	50.0	–	–	50.0	–	25.0	100(6)	100(4)
Metal products, machinery	57.1	17.4	28.6	30.4	14.3	34.8	–	17.4	100(7)	100(23)
Service and repair	100	57.1	–	14.3	–	28.6	–	–	100(3)	100(7)
Total	53.2	29.3	32.2	25.9	11.3	31.0	3.2	13.8	100(62)	100(58)

Source: Field Survey

Notes:
1. Figures indicate cell counts as percent of row totals; figures in brackets in the last column indicate sample size. Koll - Kollengode; Mal - Malampuzha
2. IDA units not shown here. Their distribution by product group and investment in plant and machinery is discussed in the text.

of a unit in Kollengode block, in terms of workers and fixed capital, appears to be on account of both the type of unit, family enterprise or small-scale unit, and product group. However, the relationhip between product group, classified broadly into agro-based and non agro-based industries and capital investment is not statistically significant suggesting that intra-industry differences at the two-digit level of industrial classification may have overwhelmed inter-industry differences[26] (Berry 1990). The IDA units were distributed between metals and machinery product group (40 percent), chemicals (30 percent) and food products (30 percent); 70 percent of the units fell in the over Rs. 500,000 capital slab (data not shown in the table).

(d) By Location

Given the preponderance of family enterprises and smaller SSUs in Kollengode and the fact that almost all the entrepreneurs are local (as we see later), it is not surprising that an overwhelming proportion of the units in Kollengode are located within the household (including sheds next to household). In Malampuzha, while 80 percent of the units are located in or near the house, almost one fifth (excluding IDA units) are located far from home. An overwhelming proportion of the IDA units are located far from home. This characteristic is strongly linked to the origin of the entrepreneurs, data for which are examined later.

In respect of the location of these units in terms of distance from the nearest town (Table 6.5) there is no doubt that the mean distance of most of the panchayats from the nearest town is higher in Kollengode block (16 kms) than those in Malampuzha (9 kms). The fact that a larger proportion of the units in Kollengode were tiny, and agro-based appears to support the presumption regarding RSSEs in a more isolated, rural environment vis-a-vis those nearer a big urban settlement (Tambunan 1994). We attempt to link this with the nature of linkages in the two blocks in the following chapter.

From the foregoing brief description of the sample RSSEs it is clear that as in most developing economies, in our region too, the units are concentrated at the lower end of the small-scale spectrum and the petty mode of production[27] plays a significant role, particularly in Kollengode. However, tiny units, defined by number of workers, constitute a smaller proportion in the two blocks as compared to other developing regions of the world. Their incidence was as high as 95 percent in most of Sub-Saharan Africa (Chuta and Leidholm 1985; Haggblade et al 1989). In Malaysia too, a larger majority were units with less than 5 workers (Saith 1989).

[26]The Chi-square test of independence was not significant. It was based on combining the first two and fourth rows that is, Food Products, Textiles, readymades etc. and Bricks/cement into the Agro-based group. The remaining three rows were combined into the Non agro-based group of industries/services.

[27]A distinguishing feature of the petty mode of production is that "the labourer is the private owner of his own means of labour set in motion by himself" (Marx, Capital, vol I)

Table 6.5: Distance of Panchayats from Nearest Town

Kollengode Block[1]			Malampuzha Block		
Panchayat	Nearest town	Distance (in kms)	Panchayat	Nearest town	Distance (in kms)
Muthalamada	Chittur-T*	24	Puduppariyaram	Palghat@	5
Kollengode	Chittur-T	16	Malampuzha	Palghat	10
Vadavannur	Chittur-T	11	Akathethara	Palghat	6
Koduvayur[2]	Chittur-T	12	Pudussery[3]	Palghat	11
			Elapully	Palghat	13
			Polpully	Chittur	6
			Peruvambu	Palghat	13
			Marutharode	Palghat	5
Mean Distance		15.8	Mean Distance		8.6

Source: Census of India 1971, Series 9, Kerala, District Census Handbook 1971, Palghat

Notes: * Chittur-T is Chittur-Tattamangalam; @erstwhile name of Palghat.

1. One panchayat, Pudunagaram, could not be traced in Kollengode in the above source.
2. For panchayats with more than one village the average distance has been taken. For instance Koduvayur I is 18 kms from Chittur-T and Koduvayur II is 14 kms from Nenmara; the average distance of 16 kms. has been taken.
3. Pudussery panchayat is divided into three and the distance of each from Palakkad is Pudussery West (6 kms) Central (13 kms) and East (15 kms); the average is 11 kms.

Most studies reveal an almost similar (to Kollengode) structure of small-scale rural manufacturing units, the dominance of "light" consumer goods industries, food, ready made garments and wood products (Leidholm and Mead 1987) and also metalworking including blacksmithing and welding (Anderson and Leiserson 1980; Haggblade et al 1989). However, the product structure in Malampuzha is relatively different, characterised by a higher incidence of "light" engineeing goods industries. What needs to be noted is that a significant proportion of these tiny enterprises are undertaken with "great ingenuity and entrepreneurial spirit" (Rakowski 1994). This raises the question of how much the RSSEs can contribute to the process of accumulation, employment and growth, issues we take up later.

6.5 Pattern of Linkages of Sample RSSEs

In this section we explore the linkages of these units emphasising the rural linkages.

Table 6.6: Distribution of Entrepreneurs by Place of Origin

Block	Origin of entrepreneur						
	Local panchayat and block	Non-local			Total non local*	Total	Sample size
		district	state	outside state			
1. Kollengode	100	–	–	–	–	100	62
2. Malampuzha	84.5	10.3	1.7	3.4	15.4	100	58
3. IDA units	–	60.0	30.0	10.0	100	100	10
4. Total	85.4	9.3	3.1	2.3	14.7	100	130

Source: Field Survey

Notes: 1. Figures indicate cell counts as percent of row totals

* Total non-local is the sum of district, state and outside state

6.5.1 Socio-Economic Characteristics of the Entrepreneurs

6.5.1.1 Place and Sector of Origin

To what extent do the rural entrepreneurs have genuine rural social origins? This question has important social and economic implications and we attempt to answer it by examining (a) whether the area of operation is place of birth of the owner; (b) whether father's occupation was farming or related activity; and (c) whether prior occupation of the owner-operator was agriculture. The first is perhaps the most significant indicator of rural origins of an entrepreneur and the latter two if positive, suggest an ongoing process of rural diversification.

(a) Area of Operation

This information is broadly similar to the response on location of the unit, but is more directly linked to the origins of the entrepreneur. While in Kollengode all the proprietors operated in the area where they were born, this proportion was not as high in Malampuzha (Table 6.6). About 15 percent of the entrepreneurs in Malampuzha were non-local, hailing from other parts of the district, primarily the city of Palakkad, other parts of the state or outside the state. All the entrepreneurs operating in the IDA came from outside the region; about 10 percent from outside the state.

While it is true that geographical mobility of small entrepreneurs is not very feasible, the fact that a substantial majority of the owner-producers operated in their area of birth in both the blocks, since it was their home, reflects the real subjective value which local entrepreneurs attribute to being in their own environment. This redresses to some extent the relative locational disadvantages of rural areas in setting up non-agro based industries. However, such

Table 6.7: Distribution of Sample RSSEs by Origin of Entrepreneur and Product Group: Malampuzha Block

Product group	Origin of Entrepreneur				
	Local	Non-local[2]	IDA	Total	IDA
Agro and natural resource based industries[1]	40.8	11.1	30.0	36.2	30.0
Printing, plastic and chemicals	8.2	33.3	30.0	12.1	30.0
Metal products and machinery	36.7	55.5	40.0	39.7	40.0
Service and repair	14.3	–	–	12.1	–
Total	100	100	100	100	100
Sample size	49	9	10	58	10

Source: Field Survey

Notes: 1. Agro and natural resource based industries include food products, clothing, wood and cane furniture, leather and rubber products, bricks, tiles and cement.

2. All three components of non-local viz. district, state and outside state have been combined due to the small number of non-local entrepreneurs.

3. Figures indicate cell counts as percent of column totals.

entrepreneurship is only slowly emerging in this area. An attempt to relate origin of the entrepreneur with product group in Malampuzha (in Kollengode all entrepreneurs are local) shows that the highest proportion of units owned and operated by local entrepreneurs are found in the agro-natural resource based industry groups such as food, clothing, furniture, leather and rubber products etc (Table 6.7).

The relationship between product group and origin of entrepreneur was found to be statistically significant.[28] Most of the non-local entrepreneurs were operating in the metals, machinery and chemicals group. (In the IDA even the food units in our sample were owned and operated by non-local producers). While the proportion of local entrepreneurship was also high in the metals and machinery group, the units run by non-local entrepreneurs were relatively higher-technology firms with a larger capital investment in plant and machinery. Similarly for the chemicals group, in which too the units run by non-local entrepreneurs had a higher capital investment. This is evident from Table 6.4 which gives a distribution of the sample RSSEs in Malampuzha by product group and size of fixed capital investment in plant and machinery: a high proportion of the largest units in Malampuzha, in terms of a capital investment of Rs. 500,000–25,00,000 and all the units with an investment above Rs. 25,00,000 were operated by non-local entrepreneurs.

[28]The Chi-square test of independence was significant at 5 percent level.

Table 6.8: Distribution of Sample RSSEs by Father's Occupation and Type of Units

	Father's Occupation	Kollengode Block			Malampuzha Block			
		FE	SSU	All	FE	SSU	All	IDA
1.	Agriculture	28.0	35.1	32.2	31.2	28.6	29.3	20.0
2.	Traditional Industry	16.0	–	6.4	12.5	4.8	6.8	–
3.	Employee/employer in similar/related SMLI	28.0	16.2	20.9	25.0	31.0	29.3	40.0
4.	Business	24.0	35.1	30.6	12.5	14.2	13.8	40.0
5.	Services	4.0	8.1	6.4	18.8	9.5	12.1	–
6.	Agriculture plus Business	–	5.4	3.2	–	11.9	8.6	–
7.	Total	100	100	100	100	100	100	100
	Samplesize	25	37	62	16	42	58	10

Source: Field survey

Notes: 1. Figures indicate cell counts as percent of column totals.

2. Father's occupation of the promoter of the two co-operative societies in Malampuzha and one in Kollengode has been taken.

* SMLI - small, medium and large scale industry

FE - Family enterprise; SSU - Small-scale unit

IDA - Industrial Development Area

(b) Father's Occupation

Almost one-third of the sample entrepreneurs in Kollengode and a little less in Malampuzha came from agricultural households: father is/was a cultivator or an agricultural labourer (Table 6.8). Approximately 60 percent of the rural households in Palakkad were agricultural households (CRD 1995). Evidently a much larger proportion of entrepreneurs in our region came from non-agricultural households. In Kollengode the most dominant non-agricultural occupation of the father was business (30 percent of the units) followed by employee or employer in similar or other small/medium/large industry (SMLI). In Malampuzha it was the other way round, that is, employee or employer in similar or other SMLI was the more dominant father's occupation, accounting for over a quarter of the entrepreneurs followed by business and services, primarily Government service.

About 3 percent of the units in Kollengode and 9 percent in Malampuzha reported father's occupation as both agriculture and business. These related largely to the better off cultivator households. An interesting inference can be drawn from this observation: a large cultivator household diversifies first into business, generally trade and then into industry. The interconnections between agriculture, trade and industry among rural capitalist entrepreneurs has been highlighted by Rutten for a Gujarat region (1991). The entry of big farmers into non-agriculture related industry is only emerging in our area of study; those who have invested in industry have done so primarily in modern rice and flour mills, hosiery, cement, hollow bricks and printing with investments in the first three touching the outer limit for small-scale units.

The percentage of entrepreneurs with an agricultural background is somewhat lower in our survey area in comparison with some of the studies cited earlier; the proportion of proprietors with fathers engaged in agriculture and related activities was almost two thirds in Sierra Leone (Chuta and Liedholm 1985) as also for Jamaica (Liedholm and Mead 1987); over half for Malaysia (Saith 1989) and a little less than half for West Java (Tambunan 1994). However Wickramanayake's field survey threw up an even lower percentage for southern Sri Lanka, 28 percent.

(c) Prior Occupation of Entrepreneur

Very few of the entrepreneurs, less than 15 percent in Kollengode[29] and a marginal proportion in Malampuzha, were themselves engaged in agricultural activity before starting the enterprise unlike Saith's findings for Malaysia, though more in keeping with the Liedholm and Mead study. This implies that a high proportion of the rural households had already diversified at the time of our survey. Nor did the entrepreneurs directly move into the enterprise. A large proportion of them worked elsewhere to gain experience or accumulate funds before setting up the unit, a finding similar to Wickramanayake's study (1988).This prior work experience appears to have been guided by family background, in terms of father's occupation for the non-agricultural households and is revealed by a cross tabulation of entrepreneur's prior occupation with father's occupation (Table 6.9). Over two-thirds of the entrepreneurs engaged in similar or other small/medium and large industry and a little under two-thirds of those doing some business in Kollengode (the proportions are three fourths and a quarter in Malampuzha respectively) before starting the enterprise came from families with the same background. It may be noted that the options for those with a traditional industry background appeared to be fewer with considerable mobility between agricultural work and traditional industry. An overwhelming proportion of the entrepreneurs in both the blocks were first generation entrepreneurs. Having worked as wage or salaried workers in industrial units or business prior to setting up the enterprise and gaining some familiarity with the trade is perhaps the most prevalent method of skill formation and resource generation for small scale enterpreneurs (see Liedholm and Mead 1987; Bagachwa and Stewart 1990; Tambunan 1994). About 45 percent of the entrepreneurs in Kollengode and 55 percent in Malampuzha stated having the necessary skill and experience as the major reason for starting the enterprise. This relationship between father's occupation and prior occupation of the entrepreneur was found to be statistically significant.[30]

---

[29]However, as a proportion of the agricultural households in the sample, these entrepreneurs constituted about one third of such households.

[30]The Chi-square test of independence was found to be significant at 5 percent level based on the following to achieve adequate cell frequency for the purpose of test:

Table 6.9: Cross Tabulation of Prior Occupation of Entrepreneur by Father's Occupation

	Prior occupation of entrepreneur	Father's occupation													
		Agriculture		Traditional industry		Employee/ employer in SMLI		Business		Services		Agriculture and business		Total	
		K	M	K	M	K	M	K	M	K	M	K	M	K	M
1.	Agriculture	35.0	10.0	25.0	25.0	7.7	–	–	–	–	–	–	–	14.5	4.4
2.	Traditional industry	–	–	50.0	75.0	–	–	–	–	–	–	–	–	3.2	4.4
3.	Employee/employer in SMLI	35.0	85.0	–	–	69.2	75.0	10.5	33.3	25.0	28.6	–	80.0	30.6	61.8
4.	Business	10.0	–	–	–	7.7	–	63.2	25.0	–	14.3	50.0	–	25.8	5.9
5.	Service	–	–	–	–	–	10.0	5.3	25.0	25.0	14.3	–	–	3.2	10.3
6.	Student, housewife,unemployed	20.0	–	25.0	–	15.4	15.0	21.1		50.0			20.0	22.6	13.2
7.	Total	100	100	100	100	100	100	100	–	100		100	100	100	100
	Sample size	20	20	4	4	13	20	19	–	4	–	2	5	62	68

Source: Field Survey

Notes: 1. Figures indicate cell counts as percent of column totals.

2. IDA units are included in Malampuzha Block

K - Kollengode Block; M - Malampuzha Block; SMLI - Small, medium, large-scale industry

The close connections between business and industry comes out in this table too. Some entrepreneurs with a business family background but themselves engaged in industry prior to setting up their own unit, followed an activity related to the business: for instance tailoring or making ready-made garments in a cloth merchant's household; trading of some food item by father leading to the son acquiring the know-how in respect of its processing; trade in hardware, machines and electrical equipment helping the next generation entrepreneurs to familiarise themselves with some engineering activity etc. In respect of the agricultural households, the extent of inter-generational diversification was quite considerable, 65 percent of the agricultural households in Kollengode and 90 percent in M had diversified into non-agricultural activities. A major reason stated by entrepreneurs from agricultural households for setting up the enterprise was the need to supplement household income. Most of these entrepreneurs were engaged in industry or business, the nature of which appeared to depend on the type of agricultural household they came from - agricultural labourer, small, medium or large farmer households.

To sum up: while the vast majority of proprietors were rural in terms of operating in (rural) area of birth except in the IDA and to some extent in the rest of Malampuzha block, less than one third came from agricultural households and an even lower proportion were agriculturists themselves prior to setting up the enterprise. What are the implications of the origins of the entrepreneur on the nature of activity undertaken and linkages of the RSSEs? Entrepreneurs coming from non-agricultural households started enterprises that reflected a strong correlation between family background and choice of industry. It appears that entrepreneurs originating from outside the local region, primarily in Malampuzha block tended to set up larger units in the more modern sectors. These units as we will see, generate lower rural linkages. There was considerable diversification among the agricultural households and the nature of activity was not necessarily agro-based. The type of activity that was set up is to some extent mediated also by the level of education of the entrepreneur besides his/her socio-economic background which we examine below. Education broadens the horizon within which the choice is made, cutting across the obvious resource/caste constraint imposed by the family background. Its modernising influence which makes the younger work seekers averse to agricultural work is another factor inducing diversification in most classes of agricultural households.

---

rows: 2 and 3, viz.	Traditional industry and Employee/employer in SMLI were combined into a single row;
4 and 5, viz.	Business and Services were combined into a single row
columns: 1 and 6, viz.	Agriculture and Agriculture plus business were combined into a single column.
2 and 3 viz.	Traditional industry and Employee/employer in SMLI were combined into a single column; and
4 and 5 viz.	Business and Services were combined into a single column.

Table 6.10: Distribution of the Entrepreneurs by Level of Education

	Level of education	Block						
		Kollengode			Malampuzha			IDA
		FE	SSU	All	FE	SSU	All	
1.	No formal education	12.0	10.8	11.3	18.8	–	5.2	–
2.	Below matric	60.0	32.4	43.5	37.5	11.9	19.0	–
3.	Matric	12.0	37.8	27.4	25.0	21.4	22.4	–
4.	Matric plus*	12.0	16.3	14.5	18.8	30.9	27.6	20.0
5.	Graduate and above	–	2.7	1.6	–	26.2	19.0	40.0
6.	Technical degree	–	2.7	1.6	–	9.5	6.9	40.0
7.	Total	100	100	100	100	100	100	100
	Sample size	25	37	62	16	42	58	10

Source: Field Survey

Notes: 1. Figures indicate cell counts as percent of column totals. No education refers to no formal education; however most of the entrepreneurs had practical experience.

* matric plus refers to additional short term diploma/certificate technical courses in Industrial Training Institutes (ITI) and polytechnics or two more years of schooling

FE - family enterprise; SSU - small-scale unit

IDA - industrial development area

6.5.1.2 *Educational Level of the Entrepreneur*

The level of education of the entrepreneurs was lower in Kollengode. Over half the entrepreneurs in Kollengode were below matriculation (10 years of schooling) compared to only about a quarter in Malampuzha (Table 6.10). At the higher level too, almost a quarter were graduates or with technical degree in M while in K the proportion was small.

Not unexpectedly the level of education of those running family enterprises was low. However, almost a quarter of such entrepreneurs in Kollengode and a higher proporion in Malampuzha were educated that is, matriculates or with some lower (than degree) level of technical training imparted by polytechnics and industrial training institutes (ITIS).[31] This reflects the attempts of the educated at self-employment. In Kollengode the percentage of those with no formal education was not very different for family enterprises and small-scale units. The difference was sharper with respect to matriculation and above. We found that the association between education of the entrepreneur and type of enterprise was not statistically significant in Kollengode but in Malampuzha it was significant.[32]

[31]This type of technical training can be done before matriculation with respect to certain trades but more generally after matriculation.In our sample all the entrepreneurs with such a qualification were matriculates and in a few cases with two more years of schooling or even graduation.

[32]For Malampuzha, the Chi-square test of independence was significant at 5 percent level.

The incidence of ITI trained entrepreneurs was much higher in Malampuzha. While our results, suggesting a difference in the level of owner's education between FEs and SSUs in Malampuzha is broadly similar to the Sri Lankan study (Wickramanayake 1988) our findings for Kollengode were more similar to the study by Tambunan who found no difference in the level of formal education between cottage and small scale industries (Tambunan 1994). A cross-tabulation of the owner's level of education with product group (see Table 6.11) shows certain interesting patterns.

There is no doubt that no formal education limits the sphere of activity to simple food and other consumer goods industries. The real difference is made by matriculation and matriculation with some technical training. (A number of the matriculates also reported that they had aquired practical experience if not any formal training).[33] The larger proportion of entrepreneurs with this or higher level of education have set up units in chemicals, metals and machinery product groups. However, there are interesting outliers too. For instance the entrepreneur with the highest level of education in the Kollengode sample, a technical degree, came from an agricultural household and was engaged in rice milling, a highly mechanised, modern rice mill. Similarly in Malampuzha and in our sample of the IDA units. About 6 percent of the entrepreneurs in Kollengode and even more in Malampuzha, originating from low income households viz. agricltural labour, small cultivator or petty business households, who managed to complete matriculation and undergo some formal technical training were able to set up units in plastic, printing, metals and machinery group. To some extent education, particularly of a technical nature does cut across socio-economic barriers to setting up relatively modern units. From our study of the sample units we observed that while working in similar trades and gaining some experience was an important source of acquiring skills for modern types of activities, some technical training also seemed essential for widening the choice on the type of activity and technology to adopt. Hence from the policy point of view imparting some type of technical training is important for the growth of small- scale units.

6.5.2 *Sources of Initial Capital*

In our survey area, besides some units which reported negligible use of plant and equipment, the range of invested capital was quite high not only between different types of product groups but also within the same product group. It is often stated that the initial capital requirements of a small enterprise are small which certainly creates ease of entry and the danger of crowding in select sectors. However, given the evidence regarding the hetrogeniety of the small-scale sector,

[33] A number of entrepreneurs with lower levels of eduction had also reported practical experience in the activity undertaken.

Table 6.11: Cross Tabulation of Educational Level of Entrepreneur and Product Group

	Level of education	Food products		Clothing, furniture, leather rubber,bricks		Printing, plastic, chemicals		Metal products & machinery		Repair and services		Total	
		K	M	K	M	K	M	K	M	K	M	K	M
1.	No education	28.6	–	71.4	100	–	–	–	–	–	–	100 (7)	100 (3)
2.	< matric	44.4	27.3	33.3	36.4	3.7	–	7.4	9.1	11.1	27.3	100 (27)	100 (11)
3	Matric	23.5	–	29.4	23.1	35.2	7.7	11.8	53.8	–	15.4	100 (17)	100 (13)
4	Matric plus	11.1	12.5	22.2	25.0	33.3	18.8	33.3	31.2	–	12.5	100 (9)	100 (16)
5	Graduate and >	–	9.1	*	9.1	–	18.2	–	63.6	–	–	100 (1)	100 (11)
6	Technical degree	*	–	–	25.0	–	–	–	75.0	–	–	100 (1)	100 (4)
7	Total	32.2	10.3	35.4	27.6	14.7	10.3	11.3	39.6	4.8	12.1	100 (62)	100 (58)

Source: Field Survey

Notes: 1. Figures indicate cell counts as percent of row totals. Figures in brackets in the last column indicate sample size

@ matric plus refers to additional short term diploma certificate technical courses in ITI and polytechnics or two more years of schooling.

* Sample size is too small; K - Kollengode; M - Malampuzha

2. IDA units are not shown here. Their distribution by level of education of the entrepreneur and product group is discussed in the text

Table 6.12: Distribution of Units by Main Source of Initial Funds

	Source of initial fund	Block						
		Kollengode			Malampuzha			IDA
		FE	SSU	All	FE	SSU	All	
1.	Internal sources	20.0	43.2	33.9	43.7	16.7	24.1	10.0
	i. Own savings	20.0	37.8	30.6	37.5	16.7	22.4	10.0
	ii. Friends and relations	–	5.4	3.2	6.2	–	1.7	–
2.	External sources	28.0	10.8	17.7	18.8	11.9	13.8	50.0
	i. Banks, govt institutions*	20.0	8.1	12.9	18.8	11.9	13.8	50.0
	ii. Money lenders/traders	8.0	2.7	4.8	–	–	–	–
3.	Both internal & external sources	52.0	45.9	48.4	37.5	71.4	62.1	40.0
4.	Total	100	100	100	100	100	100	100
	Sample size	25	37	62	16	42	58	10

Source: Field Survey

Notes: * Relates to state financial institutions which gives loans to the larger small-scale units

IDA - Industrial development area

1. Figures indicate cell counts as percent of column totals.

one must beware of such generalisations; invested capital in SSUs close to the upper end of the range of small, is exceedingly high in relation to the resources of the overwhelming majority of small investors. This also cautions us, very importantly, against a highly aggregative support policy regime for the small- scale sector, emphasising the need for specific approaches to the problems of the different constituents of this sector.

Only about one third of the units in Kollengode and a quarter in Malampuzha identified own savings (internal funds) as the main source of initial funds; the larger proportion that is, almost half in K and about two thirds in M, depended both on own savings and external funds for setting up the unit (Table 6.12, see also Diagram 6.12). About 50 percent of the IDA units depended mainly on external funds. Interestingly, almost the entire amount from outside came from the formal credit market, primarily the commercial banks and to some extent the State Financial Corporations (SFCs).

While loans from the SFCs are generally given for fixed capital investment (that is plant and machinery) to the larger of the small-scale units, banks provide both long-term (for fixed capital) and short-term credit as working capital. Use of other external sources, like moneylender or trader was in the aggregate negligible; however three entrepreneurs had taken a loan from a moneylender two of whom were among the smallest family enterprises. Evidence from some of the earlier studies on small-scale enterprises cited above revealed an almost complete reliance on own savings (and funds from relatives or friends in some countries) as initial source of capital for starting the firm (Ho 1980; Chuta and Liedholm 1985; Little et al 1987; Liedholm

Diagram 6.12.

Kollengode

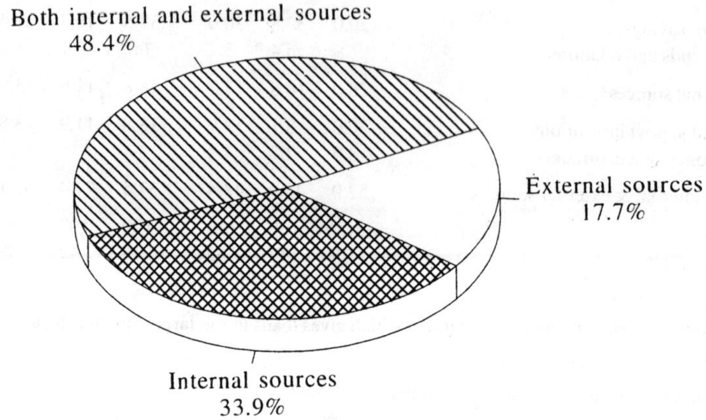

Malampuzha

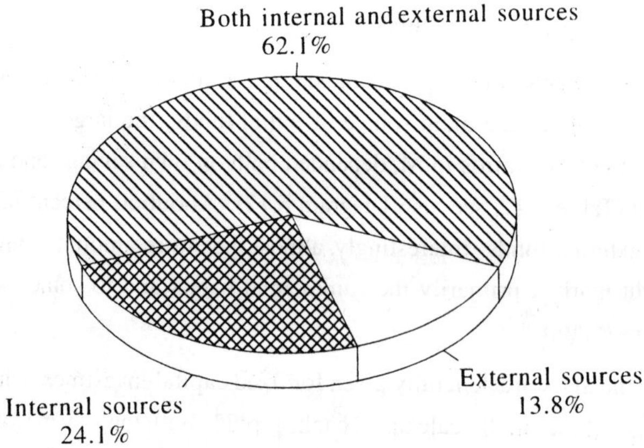

and Mead 1987; Wickramanayake 1988). The later study for Indonesia shows, however, that almost 60 percent of the enterprises relied on external sources (Tambunan 1994). However all these studies find an almost negligible contribution of the formal credit market to the initial capital requirements. No more than one percent of the initial funds in the countries surveyed by Liedholm and Mead was contributed by either the commercial banks or Government; as few as 2 percent of proprietors secured start up funds from banks in Wickramanayake's study; 9 percent in Korea (Ho 1980), while the proportion was about 14 percent in Tambunan's study on Indonesia. Most of the external funds in the case of the latter came from informal sources viz. the urban based wholesalers. The relatively minor role played by "indigenous" bankers has been noted in the other studies too.

Do our findings imply a greater integration of the small sector, including the smallest, with the organised credit market? We may note that a country wide study on bank credit to small-scale units in India (urban and rural) in the late seventies, revealed a much higher degree of commercial bank penetration, than in other developing economies cited earlier, though a very small proportion (3 percent) of the tiniest units availed of it. India has made greater efforts, unlike other developing economies, to channel institutional finance, mainly from banks, to small enterprises (Little et al 1987). In the case of our region the much higher penetration of institutional credit into the rural small-scale sector could to some extent be a part of the overall Kerala scenario of low disparities between achievements in the urban and rural areas. This is reflected in the much higher levels of infrastructure availability (including formal credit) in rural Kerala relative to the all India situation (Franke and Chassin 1991). This was also a period which witnessed a spurt in State Government's efforts to promote small-scale industries by providing concessional finance from the formal credit institutions and granting fiscal concessions.[34] However, we must not overlook the fact that the nature of our sample of firms, largely constituting "new" firms, that is those established in the recent past and registered with the DIC (one of the reasons for registration being the possibility of availing of concessions to the small-scale sector), could have influenced our findings.

Further probing of the data (not shown here) however, brings out certain well known features of the operation of the capital market in respect of small producers, more specifically in rural areas:

- the proportion of those who did not borrow was overwhelmingly high for the smallest of the small units. In Kollengode, 48 percent of the units who did not borrow fell in the smallest size class viz.upto Rs. 10,000 (in terms of capital invested in plant and machinery) which cumulates to over 80 percent if we include units with capital investment less than Rs. 50,000. In Malampuzha, 78 percent of the units who did not borrow came within this category;

[34]This was evident from the numerous policy statements made by the officials of the Ministry of Industries in Kerala and was incorporated in the 1991 industrial policy of the Government of Kerala (see GOK Economic Review 1992).

- a little less than 10 percent of the amount sanctioned by banks was for loans below Rs. 25,000 in K even though 45 percent of the total number of loans disbursed were in this range. The distribution was even more skewed in M: less than one percent of the total amount of bank loans was in this category while accounting for over 20 percent of the number of loans sanctioned. At the other extreme, 18 percent of the number of loans in Kollengode accounted for almost 62 percent of the total amount disbursed; in Malampuzha, 9 percent of the larger loans accounted for a similar proportion; the larger loans were at least five times higher in M;
- smaller borrowers encountered greater difficulties in finalising the loan sanction[35]; and
- provision of working capital needs to the small units (both "big" and small) was highly unsatisfactory as reported by the entrepreneurs themselves; most of them had to use internally generated surpluses to meet part of the working capital requirement.

Since almost all entrepreneurs expressed the need for more finance as a major problem they face, in particular working capital finance and were critical of the stringent lending conditions of the banks, there is obviously an urgent need to review and restructure banking finance. This is also compelled by the fact that at times concessional finance, by making entry easy without a proper market appraisal, may tend to be "wasted" through "crowding in" in certain sectors. This appeared to be the case in respect of the flour, oil milling and ready made garment units in Kollengode and hollow bricks, machining and engineering units in Malampuzha.[36] The issue of wastage was highlighted in Sandesara's study (1988) on evaluating institutional assistance for small scale units, emphasising the need for much greater sensitivity in the designing of assistance programmes for the very small units. We now examine how rural or local are the sources of funds used for investment.

6.5.2.1 *Place and Sector of Origin of Initial Sources of Finance*

In keeping with our interest in the role of local capital, an important question is how local are the funds invested in small enterprises and what is their sector of origin (Table 6.13). We focussed on the sector of origin of the initial funds of those enterprises which either wholly (33 percent in Kollengode and 24 percent in Malampuzha) or partially (48 percent in K and 62 percent in M) used own savings as start up capital.

[35]It was reported by some entrepreneurs, that the number of times they had to visit the DIC office prior to setting up the unit was at times very frustrating.

[36]Wastage could also occur through a tendency to overcapitalise due to easy availability of capital. It is used more excessively, sometimes as a substitute for labour, which ofcourse runs counter to the argument favouring small-scale enterprises for generating employment. However, we did not probe this issue.

Table 6.13: Distribution of Units Wholly or Partially dependent on Own Savings by Sector of Origin of Initial of Funds

	Sector of origin	Block						
		Kollengode			Malampuzha			IDA
		FE	SSU	All	FE	SSU	All	SSU
1.	Agriculture[1]	33.3	36.4	35.3	7.7	35.1	28.0	20.0
2.	Small/medium/large industry	33.3	18.2	23.5	53.8	35.1	40.0	60.0
3.	Trade and Business	27.8	39.4	35.3	–	8.1	6.0	–
4.	Others[2]	5.6	6.1	5.9	38.5	21.6	26.0	20.0
5.	Total	100	100	100	100	100	100	100
	Sample size	18	33	51	13	37	50	5

Source: Field Survey

Notes: 1. Also includes those households in which father's occupation is reported as agriculture and business.

2. Includes sale of property, gold or Gulf remittance and in particular employment in "Services" in Malampuzha as a means of mobilising initial funds.

3. Figures indicate cell counts as percent of column totals.

IDA - Industrial development area

The two together accounted for over 75 percent of the units in both Kollengode and Malampuzha. From the table we see that agricultural savings provided the initial source of capital for over one-third of the units in Kollengode and less than 30 percent in Malampuzha (see Diagram 6.13). The larger proportion of initial capital within each block in our survey area, came from non-agricultural sources within which business was the most important source in Kollengode and industry in Malampuzha. We could to some extent trace the origins of these sources: almost 75 percent of such savings were local in Kollengode, since the entrepreneurs engaged earlier in business were operating from own home and those in SMLIs were employed in small local units; a few had worked in large units outside the state. However, the proportion of non-local funds was higher in M since a larger number had worked outside the region to acquire skill and initial capital. In the IDA units too, the non-local industrial sector was the dominant source of accumulating initial funds. However, comparing the above data with the prior occupation of the entrepreneurs from agricultural households, very few of whom were themselves engaged in agriculture, suggests a higher contribution of agricultural savings towards the setting up of small-scale industries in our area.

Most of the external sources of funds which were in the nature of bank finance also appear to be local in nature, since almost all loans were disbursed from local banks. Palakkad has almost 232 rural and semi-urban branches of commercial banks and on average a branch covers

Diagram 6.13.

Kollengode

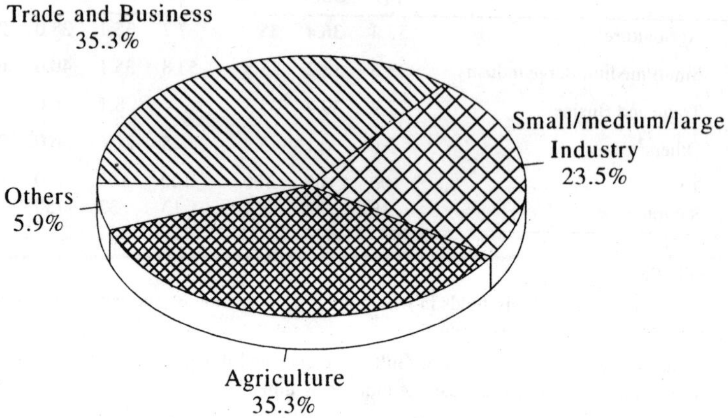

Malampuzha

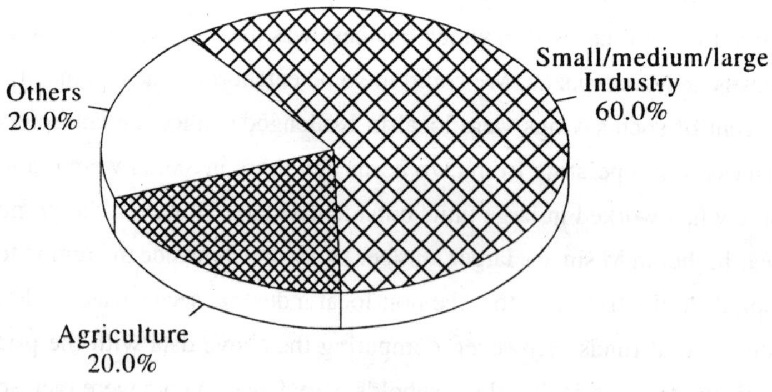

a village (NABARD 1995). However, loans from developmental financial institutions routed through the local banks, may not always be local.

6.5.2.2 *Role of Agricultural Surplus in Financing Industry*

The use of agricultural surplus for financing industry has been a controversial issue in development debates. Historically, accepting Mendels' thesis, proto-industries had created adequate capital in the hands of merchant entrepreneurs, some of whom emerged from the ranks of peasant-craftsmen, to make possible the adoption of machine industry. This helped in the formation of an entrepreneurial class which played an important role in the initial stages of modern industrialisation. A large proportion of the first English textile factory builders were former merchants (Mendels 1972). Large agricultural savings going into rural industry did not appear to have occurred; the more prosperous farmers invested in more land moving into positions of squires and engaged in trade during this period (Habib 1995). It was later in the phase of the Industrial Revolution that structural changes in agriculture viz. the transition from feudalism to capitalism enabled the "primary accumulation" of capital as described in the context of the English experience. This as we stated earlier, enabled enormous concentration of capital in the hands of the landlords through the displacement of small peasants and craftsmen which constituted a major contribution to industrial capital located primarily in urban areas.

In the context of most developing economies, while rural industry of the traditional type was destroyed under the colonial regimes, its remanants or new forms, did show similar financial control by urban or rural based merchant capital in some regions. Interestingly, Tambunan's study on Indonesia (1994), even in the contemporary context appears to lend support to Mendels' observations: one third of the total sample of units, not necessarily of the craft type, or almost two thirds of the units who depended on external sources of funds were financed (and controlled) by urban wholesaler merchants. However, more generally, with the emergence of rural industries of diverse types in the recent past, either in conjunction with seasonal agricultural work or as the sole occupation, and the emphasis on the development of an industrial sector in the countryside, the focus is more on an endogenous process of rural industrial growth. To what extent do rural savings, in particular from agriculture, provide the initial source of finance for rural small-scale industries, given the relatively greater importance of agriculture in rural areas.

Mellor in his framework of an agriculture led strategy of growth, placed considerable emphasis on increased agricultural savings (out of increasing agricultural incomes) being used for investment in labour intensive, small-scale rural industries. Some of the empirical studies inspired by Mellor, assumed an elastic supply response from local non-farm production, without in fact actually tracing the investment behaviour of large surplus owning farmers. To substantiate his position, Mellor cited the instance of Taiwan which had achieved such a net resource transfer (Mellor 1976). However, as argued by Saith and others, such rural industrialisation occurred in very special circumstances in Taiwan, China and Japan (Ho 1979; Saith 1992).

In an attempt to test the veracity of this key premise of Mellor's thesis, viz. the propensity of successful farmers in diversifying their investments into manufacturing, Dunham exmined the evidence in a "classic" Green Revolution area, the Punjab, as we discussed in Chapter 2. Though admitting that it was difficult to gauge the extent to which profits from agriculture flow into rural industry, some direct evidence on ownership of small-scale enterprises or indirect evidence such as credit-deposit ratio of banks (to assess the channeling of agricultural savings via the banks), in the region of study, offered little support to the above expectation. Harriss (1987) found some enterprises in North Arcot district being set up with agricultural profits but this source was not dominant. However, there is some evidence from other regions of India and elsewhere of an emerging class of capitalist farmers diversifying into trading, processing and transport, and even manufacturing (Rutten 1991).

Some of the other empirical work based on small enterprise surveys, which we have cited earlier, did address this question of the origin of the initial source of funds, since it implies a strong developmental linkage with the rural sector. The findings were not very different from the above: the direct transfer of savings from agriculture to investment in small-scale rural industry was limited, less than 15 percent of the entrepreneurs who used own savings derived it from agriculture (Wickramanayake 1988). In the study by Tambunan (1994) while the proportion of entrepreneurs using own savings as initial capitl was less than half, within this category, almost 36 percent had mobilised the initial capital from agricultural earnings.

To sum up our findings, small enterprises do appear to have played an important role in mobilising own savings or local capital that may have otherwise remained idle, although the contribution from agriculture did not appear to be dominant. This was supplemented by institutional finance in varying proportions. The greater penetration of institutional credit is not an unmixed blessing; that banks have to be very innovative to cater to the hetrogeniety of the small-scale sector is perhaps a critical component of future policy. Our findings also suggest a considerable amount of entrepreneurial aspirations even from the poorest of households. What was very striking was the high level of awareness regarding small industry schemes among all categories of entrepreneurs as reflected in the involvement of family enterprises in concessional finance. The credit for this should go to the block level functionaries some of whom had made very sincere attempts to popularise the various Government programmes.[37] In a situation

[37]In fact that a significant number has been drawn in is to the credit of the efforts of the DIC Extension Officers. While it is partly induced to fulfil targets, there is also a sincere desire to create awareness among small producers of the benefits to be availed through registration through seminars and training programmes.We were witness to one such activity in Kollengode block.

where non-agricultural employment opportunities are not growing fast enough, first generation entrepreneurs are emerging from agricultural and non-agricultural households, after familiarising themselves with the activity they would establish. A larger proportion of the initial savings emanate from these (primarily) non-agricultural activities. The contribution of agricultural surpluses though not dominant in our survey region, is not small.

6.5.3 *Place of Origin of the Workers*

6.5.3.1 *Main Categories of Labour Employed in* RSSEs

One of the major concerns of rural industrialisation is the generation of employment opportunities for the local work force, be they underemployed labourers or small cultivators or the rural unemployed seeking work. It is this rural linkage which has a direct bearing on levels of living of the rural poor. The two main categories of workers employed in small-scale enterprises in our sample were family labour and hired labour; the proportion of apprentice labour was marginal in both the blocks. This is not very surprising in the Asian (see also Tambunan 1994) or Latin American context; however in regions of West and Central Africa it was found to be as high as 30- 40 percent and sometimes as high as over 50 percent, for instance in Nigeria and Ghana (Liedholm and Mead 1987; Bagachwa and Stewart 1990).[38] There were 310 persons employed in Kollengode, 557 in Malampuzha and 197 in the IDA units (Table 6.14).

Hired workers or wage labour dominated in both the blocks, accounting for almost two thirds of the workers in Kollengode and over 80 percent in Malampuzha. That wage labour constitued the larger segment of the work force employed in RSSEs is further reiterated by the fact that the largest category was of units using hired labour only; almost 50 percent in Malampuzha and about 46 percent in Kollengode (right hand side of the table). The workers in these units accounted for about 60 percent of total employment. This was in contrast to the study by Liedholm and Mead (1987) who observed that hired workers typically form the smallest segment of small enterprise employment in most developing economies. While by and large the proportion of hired workers was higher in the larger of the small-scale units, we came across a number of firms in the modern small-scale sector (for instance bakery, oil mill, readymade garments, printing and engineering units in Kollengode and to a smaller extent in Malampuzha), with the propietor and very often one or at times two hired workers. This high incidence of wage labour even in very small units could be a characteristic of the Kerala

---

[38]While it is true that working in other units, small and big, is the most prevalent method of acquiring experience and skill among the entrepreneurs before they set up their own units, it appears, based on informal discussions with some employers, that there was no formal system of apprenticeship. This was perhaps because the remuneration was too low. Workers gained experience while working at a wage and some would leave after acquiring the skill.

Table 6.14: Distribution of Main Categories of Persons Employed and Units Distributed by Main Type of Labour Used

	Block/ Region	Workers				Units				
		Propr-ietor	Family labour	Hired labour@	Total Persons employed	One person units	Units with Mainly family labour	Units with Mainly hired labour	Units Using both	Total units
1.	K	21.6	16.1	62.3	100 (310)	16.1	24.2	46.8	12.9	100 (62)
2.	M	11.1	7.2	81.7	100 (557)	6.9	20.7	46.5	25.9	100 (58)
3.	IDA	11.2	2.0	86.8	100 (197)	–	–	70.0	30.0	100 (10)
4.	Total	14.2	8.8	77.0	100 (1064)	10.8	20.8	48.5	20.0	100 (130)

Source: Field Survey

Notes: 1. Figures in both parts of the table indicate cell counts as percent of row totals; figures in brackets indicate sample size.

K–Kollengode; M–Malampuzha; IDA–Industrial development area.

@ includes apprentice labour which is less than 5 percent of all persons employed in the blocks.

economy since even on the smallest farms, wage labour employment is not uncommon (Jose 1990).

Women constituted an important segment of the workforce not only as family workers, but also as wage workers employed outside the home. Over one third of those working in the RSSEs in Kollengode were women, while in Malampuzha it was just over half (data not shown here). While it is true that women are still concentrated in the food and textiles group, with the entry of sophisticated engineering industries, like telephone assembly, printed circuit board and other precision equipment, particularly in Malampuzha, their "nimble hands" and acceptance of low wages, offers a vast potential supply of labour for rural industries. Women account for a substantial proportion of rural non-farm and manufacturing employment in most developing economies. In fact differences in the perspective on women's work and their inclusion in the work force contributes significantly to the wide range of manufacturing employment (or total non-farm employment) in different countries (Haggblade et al 1989).

Whether maximising employment in small-scale enterprises, conflicts with maximisation of output and incomes in the long run continues to be a much debated issue (Bar-el 1984). It had drawn considerble attention in the context of India's Second Five Year Plan (Raj 1956). Research, particularly on the "modern" as opposed to traditional small industries, yielded results which appeared to go counter to the conventional view regarding small-scale industry: it was neither employment generating nor capital saving (Sandesara 1981; Goldar 1988). Though there was an early critique of Sandesara's findings in which it was argued on the basis of Ishikawa's observation that the higher capital intensity in smaller units could be a data problem due to overvaluation of land and buildings in fixed capital investment, it appears to have gone unnoticed (Nagraj 1985a). Hence it appeared that the case for small-scale units could be argued only on social grounds. However, this view has changed in recent years with new empirical evidence contesting its relative inferiority to large-scale units. More importantly, it is necessary to view the issue not merely from a scalar problematic but as a valid policy subject in itself (Thomas et al 1991). It is within this broader perspective that we study the linkages of this sector:to what extent has the growth of rural industries, in particular of the non-traditional type, drawn in local labour, an issue which is an important aspect of rural developmental linkages.

6.5.3.2 Place of Origin of Workers Employed

While in Kollengode the overwhelming majority of the units (over 90 percent), employed local labour only, in Malampuzha it was 70 percent. About 30 percent of the units in M also hired workers who commuted from other parts of the district or neighbouring district; in 3 units workers from outside the state were hired on a contract basis, which does not render them

Table 6.15: Distribution of Sample RSSEs[1] by Place of Origin of Workers Employed

	Block	Place of origin					
		Local[2]	Non-local[3]		Total	Total	Sample
			District/State[4]	Outside State	non-local		size
1.	Kollengode	98.0	–	1.9	1.9	100	52
2.	Malampuzha	70.3	14.8	9.3	24.1	100	54
3.	IDA	30.0	30.0	40.0	70.0	100	10
4.	Total	79.3	9.5	8.6	9.5	100	116

Source: Field Survey

Notes: Figures indicate cell counts as percent of row totals.

1. One person units numbering 10 in Kollengode and 4 in Malampuzha have been excluded.
2. Referes to panchayat and block.
3. No unit was using only non-local labour. We could not obtain information on the proportion of non-local labour to local labour. The figures given above indicate those units which are using some non-local labour categorised by whether it originates from other parts of the district or state or from outside the state. If workers come from two non-local destinations, the unit is classified by the higher degree of non-localness. For instance if a unit reported the use of non-local labour from other parts of the district or state and outside the state, it was classified under "outside state".
4. Total non-local includes district, state and outside state.

permanent settlers in the region. In the IDA over 40 percent of the units used labour from outside the state[39] (Table 6.15).

What is interesting to note is that non-local labour[40] in Malampuzha block was largely employed by the units whose proprietors were non-local (Table 6.16). Of the nine entrepreneurs who originated from outside the block, eight of them employed labour from other parts of district/state and outside state. At the same time a little less than one fifth of the local entrepreneurs also hired non-local labour. Of these at least three units had strong links with the non-local region, in particular the neighbouring state of Tamil Nadu, or other parts of Kerala, either through marriage or related industrial and business interests and hence continued to maintain those connections. The close association between non-local entrepreneurs and non-local labour is statistically significant.[41]

With respect to the IDA units, all the entrepreneurs were non-local and 70 percent of them employed non-local labour. Since most of these units are in the chemicals, metal products and machinery group as also modern food products in the IDA, it is not surprising that the incidence

[39] A large proportion of the younger non-local workers who are not married live on the premises of the unit itself.

[40] We were unable to procure the exact break up between local and non-local labour for units using both, since entrepreneurs did not appear very keen to give actual numbers of outside labour employed.

[41] The Chi-square test of independence is significant at 5 percent level.

Table 6.16: Distribution of Units by Place of Origin of Workers and Place of Origin of Enterepreneurs: Malampuzha Block

	Place of origin of Workers	Place of origin of Entrepreneurs					
		Local[1]		Non-local[2]		Total[3]	
		M	IDA	M	IDA	M	IDA
1.	Local	82.2	-	11.1	30.0	70.4	30.0
2.	Non-local	17.8	-	88.9	70.0	29.6	70.0
3.	Total	100	-	100	100	100	100
	Sample size	45	-	9	10	54	10

Source: Field Survey

Notes: Figures indicate cell counts as percent of column totals.

1. Local refers to panchayat and block.
2. Due to the small number of non-local entrepreneurs we have given only the broad category non-local which includes district, state and outside state. Also see Note 3 in Table 6.15.
3. Four one-person units in Malampuzha are excluded.

M–Malampuzha; IDA–Industrial development area.

of non-local labour is high in these product groups. However, the relationship between nature of entrepreneurship and type of product manufactured was not statistically significant.[42]

The employment of non-local labour by non-local entrepreneurs should not appear surprising in the context of an underdeveloped labour market, particularly for the small, unorganised sector, where personal knowledge and contacts still play a significant role in securing employment. A study on small-scale entrepreneurs from Kerala who have set up units in Karnataka and Tamil Nadu reveals a similar situation: all the units employed workers from Kerala particularly the newer ones; almost half the units in Karnataka recruited more than 50 percent of their workers from Kerala (Oommen 1981). Perhaps the entrepreneur is keen to have a core of loyal workers from his/her own region and create a more conducive environment of work. While lack of requisite skill locally was very often stated as the rationale for employing non-local labour by the entrepreneurs, evidence on it did not appear very convincing in some cases. Nonetheless to the extent that a large proportion of the units employing non-local labour are concentrated in the larger, more capital using industries as mentioned above, viz.metal products,machinery, chemicals and plastic, the use of skilled labour not available locally may be warranted. However, this has to be probed further. It appears therefore, that in terms of generating employment for local labour it is necessary to encourage "indigenous" entrepreneurs to set up rural industries. We now examine the production and consumption linkages in the following chapter.

[42]However, the study by Tambunan (1994) showed that there was a statistically significant relationship between labour used by place of origin and the industry group.

7

Production and Consumption Linkages of RSSEs: Evidence from Primary Data

7.1 Introduction

One of the most often cited advantages of rural industry is its use of locally available materials, agricultural and natural resource based, constituting a backward production linkage (BPL) with agriculture. A lot of processing activity is involved in the transformation of local agricultural and natural resources. However, evidence on whether the activity gets located locally is very mixed and it is emphasised that supplies of raw material do not always determine location of a rural industry; one has to consider the agricultural and social situation prevailing in a region. It needs to be pointed out that in the current context of considerable policy emphasis on rural industrialisation in developing economies, the need to go beyond the narrow activities in which the rural areas have some advantage, is also recognised (Bar-el and Felsenstein 1990).

Historically, the type of agricultural community, the nature of agricultural activity, pastoral or corn growing and employment situation were far more important determinants of rural industry in England (Thirsk 1961). And as has been pointed out in recent work on developing economies, when one goes beyond the grain processing and brick, pottery, basket making activities the assumed flexibility in the use of raw materials is not always supported by empirical evidence. Particularly in the case of clothing, footwear and printing, evidence from some countries revealed that extra-regional sources of raw materials were being used despite local availability (Uribe-Echavarria 1991). The agrarian structure in terms of size distribution of holdings, the crop mix, its perishability and transportability, the fairly large range of available technology for transforming these materials and market location, as also the trading networks in respect of raw material supplies, are factors which impact on this agriculture-industry linkage spatially. Most of the studies have pointed out that a more egalitarian rural structure and a preponderance of food crops generally favours local small-scale production.

It may be noted that backward production linkages overlap with consumption linkages since those natural resource based products processed or produced locally and consumed locally fall in both categories (Bagachwa and Stewart 1990). On the other hand forward production linkages (FPL) of SSEs with agriculture in terms of supply of inputs which also depend on the agrarian structure, and nature of agricultural technology used, are generally found to be weak (Liedholm and Mead 1987; Haggblade et al 1989; Bagachwa and Stewart 1990; Hazell and Hojjati 1995).

This chapter is organised in six sections. In Section 7.2 we examine backward production linkages of the surveyed RSSEs with agriculture and the rest of the rural sector. Forward production linkages are analysed in Section 7.3 which, as our evidence reveals, offers considerably greater potential than has hitherto been assumed, particularly with the non-agricultural sectors of the rural economy. Consumption linkages are dealt with in Section 7.4. The latter, as a number of studies have shown, appear to be the more significant source of generating rural economic activity. We conclude the analysis on linkages of RSSEs, based on the two sets of field samples, with a discussion on the roles of the spatial factor (in terms of distance from nearest town) and local entrepreneurship in explaining the observed differences in the relative strength of rural linkages as between the two blocks. Section 7.5 is devoted to a broad evaluation of the sample RSSEs, based on quantitative and impressionistic data, to throw some light on their income and employment generating role and growth potential. Can RSSEs contribute to the advance of modern industry in Kerala and benefit the rural poor? Other issues such as wage rates in small-scale units, how these compare with the agricultural wage rate which is generally assumed to act as a floor[1], and with the earnings of self employed, as also the impact of education on wage rates in a literate state, are discussed in Section 7. 6.. The results of this chapter are again based on the primary data of our own field survey.

7.2 Backward Production Linkages

7.2.1 Sources of Raw Materials/Intermediate Goods (BPL)

Besides labour, other inputs of RSSEs comprise primarily of raw materials, producer and intermediate goods. Almost all capital equipment for the units was procured from outside the blocks.

[1]It is generally argued that the agricultural wage rate (in the slack season) defines an approximate floor below which an occupation is considered a residual category. A number of studies have shown that wage rates in some cottage and household industries would fall in that category (Islam 1987). However, in our view, as has been argued elsewhere (see Schmitz 1990) the floor for wages is set by the rural subsistence economy which mostly offers only a precarious alternative.

There were hardly any local producer goods industries whose output was being used as major capital equipment by the sample enterprises; however, some industrial units in Malampuzha block were producing intermediate goods like yarn, certain components and chemical products which could be used by RSSEs. While we give market location of sources of raw materials and/or intermediate goods for all the sample units, our focus is on the (direct and indirect) use of agricultural and natural resource based raw material inputs which could generate a local linkage and has been the subject of discussion in the literature. We discuss first the market location of raw material supplies in terms of number of units (Table 7.1).

The table shows that 35 percent of the units in Kollengode purchased or procured their raw materials locally[2], that is, from within the panchayat and/or block, which is a very high proportion compared to that in the study by Tambunan (1994). On the other hand 48 percent of the units procured them from outside and about 11 percent reported the use of both local and non-local sources of raw materials.

However if local is defined as including the district, then the proportion rises to almost two thirds, somewhat lower than in Tambunan's study (1994)[3] at the district level. About 16 percent of the units are most strongly outward oriented, depending on purchases from the big towns and cities outside the state. "Within district" relates primarily to a neighbouring town as also to the biggest town, Palakkad in the district. Contrary to what one might have expected, a larger proportion of SSUs rather than FEs, use local resources exclusively which is true in Malampuzha also as will be seen in Table 7.2. This could of course be due to a higher incidence of FEs in service and repair units whose input requirements are different.[4]

Some interesting features of this table need to be pointed out:

- Clearly, the broader the definition of local that we use, the higher is the degree of local linkage (see Tambunan 1994). However, the inadequacy of the availability of non-agriculture based raw materials in Kerala is brought out by the fact that even if local is defined upto the state level, more than 16 percent of the units still rely largely on supplies from outside the state. In Tambunan's study defining local upto the "province" level (which appears broadly equivalent to our state), raises the degree of local linkages to 100 percent;

[2]It may be recalled that as in the preceding chapter "mostly local" refers to panchayat and block, while "mostly non-local" covers all locations beyond the block. The categorisation in respect of production and consumption linkages is based on where more than 70 percent of the raw materials are bought or output sold. In case the percentage is less than 70, say 65:35 the category "local and non-local" is used. Within non-local, the same principle holds and in fact we elicited the dominant practice in case more than one non-local location was stated. Needless to state these limits are arbitrary and used as broad guidelines.

[3]In Tambunan's study (1994 p. 161), sub-district is broadly comparable to block in our study, district to our district and province to state.

[4]The service and repair units have been shown as not using raw materials. Taking into account their other input needs it is most likely that they are procured non-locally.

Table 7.1: Distribution of RSSEs by Location of Market for Raw Materials

	Kollengode Block								
	Location								
Type of Unit	Not using raw material	Mostly local panchayat and block	Mostly non-local district	Mostly non-local outside state	Mostly non-local state	Total non-local	Local & non-local	All locations	Sample size
FE	12.0	32.0	32.0	8.0	12.0	52.0	12.0	100	25
SSU	–	37.8	21.6	10.8	18.9	51.4	10.8	100	37
All RSSEs	4.8	35.5	25.8	9.7	16.1	51.6	8.1	100	62

Source: Field Survey

Notes:
1. For definition of "local", "non-local" see footnote 2.
2. Figures indicate cell counts as percent of row totals.
3. Total non-local includes district, state and outside state.

FE - family enterprise; SSU - small scale unit

- in this context it is also necessary to distinguish between place of purchase and place of production (Harris 1987b). For instance, cement or steel or yarn which may be purchased in Palakkad or even within the panchayat is not necessarily being produced there and hence the degree of localness within regional boundaries is exaggerated if one looks only at the place of purchase. However, for convenience we too have classified location in terms of place of purchase.

We now look at similar data for Malampuzha (Table 7.2). A very small proportion of the units had local backward production linkages in this block. Even if one includes the district and state within the definition of local, the proportion of units procuring raw materials locally increases to a little over one-third of the units. This is due to:

- the nearness of Coimbatore to the panchayat which has the largest number of industrial units in Malampuzha block. This region, through which runs the highway connecting the town of Palakkad with the even larger city of Coimbatore is well placed for importation of materials from Coimbatore. Hence a significant proportion of the units are strongly linked through raw material purchases to Coimbatore (which accounts for most of the purchases "outside the state"). An overwhelming proportion of the IDA units purchase raw materials from Coimbatore; and
- differences in the raw materials or intermediate goods consumed between Kollengode and Malampuzha given the difference in product structures. Not only does Kollengode have a greater proportion of agro-based units as noted earlier; within the latter almost one third of the units process food crops, paddy and coconut, which increases the degree of local linkages in Kollengode. The difference between the two blocks becomes more understandable if we look at raw material use and its degree of localness by product groups.

7.2.2 *Location of Market for Raw Materials by Product Group*

Our blocks present an interesting contrast.

While in Kollengode over two-thirds of the SSEs are agriculture or natural resource based (42 as percent of 62, see Table 7.3), in Malampuzha about 40 percent of the sampled SSEs are of that kind (23 as percent of 58, see Table 7.4). Backward production linkages with agriculture are certainly high in K but in terms of sourcing of materials, the percentage of units depending on local sources is smaller, 52 percent. Looking at Table 7.3 for Kollengode we find that within

Table 7.2: Distribution of RSSEs by Location of Market for Raw Materials

Malampuzha Block									
	Location								
Type of unit	Not using raw material	Mostly local panchayat and block	Mostly non-local district	Mostly non-local outside state	Mostly non-local state	Total non-local	Local & non-local	All locations	Sample size
FE	50.0	12.5	31.2	–	–	31.2	6.3	100	16
SSU	11.9	4.8	26.2	4.8	45.2	76.2	7.1	100	42
All RSSEs	22.4	6.9	27.6	3.4	32.8	63.8	6.9	100	58
IDA	–	–	–	30.0	70.0	100	–	100	10

Source: Field Survey

Notes:
1. For definition of "local", "non-local" see footnote 2.
2. Figures indicate cell counts as percent of row totals.
3. Total non-local includes district, state and outside state.

FE - family enterprise; SSU - small scale unit; IDA - industrial development area

food products, indeed the major crop grown in the region, paddy is almost entirely processed locally in small-scale units though this is a misnomer for some of the "modern" rice mills functioning in this region. These mills use fairly advanced technology, and operate on a much larger scale than the more conventional mills, but manage to remain small at the upper end of the cut-off limit.[5] The rice mills are owned and run by the bigger farmers and the modern ones depend to a large extent on paddy from other states too. Oil milling is another activity which utilises locally available copra, that is, dried coconut, and is undertaken on a small scale. We did not come across any large-scale oil extraction plants in the region. Other food products such as bakery, sweets and savoury items using wheat flour and its variants, a crop not grown in the state, depend largely on local sources of supply. These are the two medium-scale flour roller mills in the block which themselves import wheat from other states and Koduvayur, a small town in the block.

Within the other agro and natural resource based industries, units producing ready made garments,[6] handlooms, rubber products and cane furniture depend almost entirely on raw materials from outside the state while wooden furniture, basket and mat weaving[7] and brick making, used local resources. It is interesting to note an instance which also brings out the problem with respect to defining "local" in terms of place of purchase versus place of production: the purchase of yarn by the handloom unit in our sample is recorded as a "local" purchase of yarn. It is in fact purchased from the local cooperative society which procures the yarn from outside the state.[8] The remaining units which fall in the chemicals group like soap making, plastic furniture, toys, buckets and components,or the engineering group making simple equipment, purchased their materials from Palakkad or from outside the state. While Koduvayur, the local, small town caters to the simple raw material needs of primarily food units, more sophisticated items like metal supplies or chemicals are procured from Palakkad by the units.

From the similar data for Malampuzha given in Table 7.4, it can be observed that even within food the intensity of local raw material use is low since the bakeries, or units making sweets and snacks depend on Palakkad for materials like wheat flour, sugar etc. As in the case of Kollengode, most garment and tailoring units procured their materials from outside the state. While the wooden furniture unit depended on other parts of the district to procure the required wood, the unit making cane furniture depended largely on supplies from outside the state. A unit making baskets and other utility items from bamboo used the bamboo grown

[5]The definition of "small" in terms of investment in plant and machinery at book value, excludes the cost of certain items of fixed equipment which are more in the nature of support systems like power generators. This provides some flexibility to the limit.

[6]The fact that non-cotton cloth is also used for making garments, this industry is not strictly agro-based.

[7]Palakkad grass mats have traditionally been very well-known.

[8]On enquiring why yarn from the local (if defined upto the district level) mill was not used, we were told that the spinning mill produced very superfine yarn while the handlooms in that area used the coarser varieties.

Table 7.3: Location of Market for Raw Materials by Product Group

Product Group	Kollengode Block								
	Location								
	Not using raw material	Mostly local panchyayat and block	Mostly non-local: District	Mostly non-local: state	Mostly non-local: Outside state	Total non-local	Local & non-local	All locations	Sample size
1. Agro and natural resource based industries	–	52.3	21.4	4.8	14.3	40.5	7.1	100	42
a. food products	–	70.0	20.0	–	–	20.0	10.0	100	20
b. clothing, coir, wood, cane, leather, rubber, bricks	–	36.4	22.7	9.1	27.3	59.1	4.5	100	22
2. Printing, plastic, chemicals	–	–	40.0	20.0	20.0	80.0	20.0	100	10
3. Metal products and machinery	–	–	42.8	28.6	28.6	100	–	100	7
4. Service and repair	100	–	–	–	–	–	–	100	3
Total	4.8	35.5	25.8	9.7	16.1	51.6	8.1	100	62

Source: Field Survey

Note: 1. Figures indicate cell counts as percent of row totals.

2. Total non-local includes district, state and outside state.

* Clothing refers to textiles, readymades and handlooms.

locally. Raw material supplies coming from outside the state for brick making units is due to one of the hollow concrete brick making units (of which there are a few in this region) procuring rock powder and cement from Coimbatore. Similarly the small-scale cement unit in our sample needed to purchase clinker and gypsum from outside the state. However, it needs to be noted that the hollow brick making unit was getting cement from outside despite the fact that two cement making units, one large and the other small-scale, operated within this particular panchayat.

It appears then, that almost 52 percent of the agro, natural resource based units had local backward production linkages in Kollengode, processing and using locally produced paddy, copra, wood, bamboo, grass and clay compared to less than 20 percent in Malampuzha. The relationship between location of raw material supplies and nature of product is statistically significant [9] for both the blocks but with an interesting difference. While in Kollengode it is due to the agro-based product structure, generating strong local linkages, in Malampuzha, it is strongly outward oriented based on the high proportion of non-agro based industrial units.

The interesting feature in Malampuzha block was the overwhelming dependence of the non-agriculture based SSEs on supply of raw materials from the neighbouring state of Tamilnadu. Two units in the metal and machinery group were producing pumpsets while more than half were sub-contracting units[10] to three local large electronic units, one in the public sector and the other two in the private sector, as also a large public sector unit producing instruments and another, agricultural machinery. Half of these units were merely transforming the entire raw material supplied by the mother company (which procured it from outside the state) into a specified product and should really be included under forward production linkages. However, the other half had slowly started to fabricate some small machine part or component independently. The raw materials came largely from Coimbatore or even Bombay. Almost 33 percent of the units in Malampuzha, excluding the IDA units (compared to 16 percent in Kollengode), were strongly outward oriented in raw material purchase. But what surprised us, despite a large number of small-scale engineering units on both sides of the highway, was the rather primitive conditions in which some of these units operated. The level of technology in the individual firms and the division of labour between firms appeared to be rudimentary.[11] It reflected perhaps the attempts of first generation entrepreneurs to minimise costs as much as possible and once established, to

[9]The Chi-square test of independence was significant at 5 percent level and was based on the following to achieve adequate cell frequency for the purpose of test:
The product groups were collapsed into two broad groups- agro-based and non agro-based industry groups the latter including printing, plastic,metals and machinery, service and repair.
Similarly the columns were collapsed into two- mostly local and mostly non-local(including district,state and outside state). The column, local and non-local was combined with local.

[10]Sub-contracting refers to an arrangement whereby the parent firm (usually a large manufacturer, wholesaler or retailer) formally requests another independent enterprise, generally small-scale (the sub-contractor) to manufacture or process parts or the whole of the product it sells as its own (Liedholm and Mead 1987).

[11]This cluster of firms certainly did not conform to what is envisaged under the flexible specialisation paradigm.

Table 7.4: Location of Market for Raw Materials by Product Group

	Malampuzha Block									
Product Group	Not using raw material	Mostly local panchayat and block	Mostly non-local			Total non-local	Local & non-local	All locations	Sample size	IDA
			district	state	outside state					
1. Agro and natural resource based industries	–	17.4	34.8	8.7	30.4	73.9	8.7	100	23	(3)
a. food products	–	28.6	42.8	–	14.3	57.1	14.3	100	7	(3)
b. Clothing, @ coir, wood, cane, leather, rubber, bricks,cement	–	12.5	31.2	12.5	37.5	81.2	6.2	100	16	–
2. Printing, plastic, chemicals	–	–	60.0	–	40.0	100	–	100	5	(2)
3. Metal products	26.0	–	21.7	–	43.5	65.2	8.7	100	23	(5)
4. Service and repair	100	–	–	–	–	–	–	100	7	–
5. Total	22.4	6.9	27.6	3.4	32.8	63.8	6.9	100	58	(10)

Source: Field urvey

Notes: * IDA units have been given in brackets by product group in the last column. Their market location of raw materials is entirely non local

1. Figures indicate cell counts as percent of row totals.
2. Total non-local includes district, state and outside state

@ clothing refers to textiles, readymades and handlooms

improve working conditions. This was suggested by the fact that some of them who were doing well had plans to move to better premises and expand production.

The units surveyed in the IDA/MIE were located in the new industrial development area in Pudussery panchayat which was coming up at the time of the survey, as also the old industrial development area and a mini-industrial estate in the same panchayat. Three of the sample units were agro-based food products while the rest produced intermediate goods. The pattern of sourcing raw material purchase was almost entirely from outside the state, primarily Coimbatore, even in respect of the units producing food products. Hence the spread effect of these units in terms of raw material sourcing was nil; in the previous chapter we have noted their weak labour linkages also.

Before we conclude our discussion on backward production linkages we would like to state emphatically that the existence of some rural enterprises not using local resources is not a problem. In fact a major problem for rural industrialisation lies in attracting non-agriculture based industries to a rural area which is at a relative disadvantage compared to the urban in terms of location factors. The real issue is whether such units are able to generate at least other than raw material linkages or spread effects with the rural sector either in terms of labour or market. And our survey revealed, specifically in respect of the IDA units, and a few other units in Malampuzha, that they failed to create local labour linkages in adequate measure. It may be recalled that most of these units were set up by outside capital or those with strong links with outside capital. This suggests that in respect of small-scale units the nature of entrepreneurship is an important determinant of the type of linkages they would generate. SSEs set up by local entrepreneurs even if procuring their raw materials entirely from non-local sources would display other linkages with the rural sector, certainly in terms of labour as we observed among the units in Kollengode and perhaps also in respect of rural demand which we examine later in this chapter.

Another fact to be noted is that, while in our region of survey, in particular the more agrarian block, viz. Kollengode, most of the agricultural produce was being processed locally upto the last stage, there is substantial leakage in respect of a major crop of Kerala, rubber, which has drawn considerable attention in discussions of industrialisation of the state. The initial processing is done primarily into sheet rubber or to a smaller extent into crepe rubber, centrifuged latex and crumb rubber, mostly in rural areas itself. However, these activities generate minimal backward and forward production linkages. There are a large number of rubber manufacturing units in Kerala, with an overwhelming dominance of small units producing a variety of simple industrial and consumer products, classified as footwear and other rubber products group, and three tyre and tube manufacturing units which account for almost 70 percent of the rubber consumption. However, data on the large-scale sector show that the rubber based industries in

Kerala constitute only 15 percent of value added, 12 percent of the value of output and less than 10 percent of employment generated in the rubber industry in India dominated by the automotive tyres and tubes sector. Hence we find that, although the state accounts for 93 percent of natural rubber production in the country, its estimated share in consumption of rubber is only 13 percent (George and Kumar 1996). That there is considerable potential for the growth of small-scale rubber based industries in the "other rubber products" group (tread rubber, moulded rubber and latex based products) is highlighted in the study by George and Kumar (1996). The leakage is not intra spatial, from the rural to urban areas of the state but to other states.

7.3 Forward Production Linkages

Most studies find that forward linkages in terms of industrial inputs into agriculture are relatively less important than backward production linkages. Since fertilizers, followed by agricultural equipment and then building materials are identified as major production inputs into agriculture, and pumpsets in irrigated areas (Johnston and Kilby 1975), this is not surprising. The first two are generally urban and/or import based while building materials like bricks and tiles provide some local linkage though cement might not. Of course with the growth of irrigation, the production of pumpsets is a commonly found rural small scale industry (Cartillier 1975) as also units producing simple farm equipments. Studies have shown the capacity of small-scale production of farm machinery for idiosyncratic design adaptation which implies a strong potential linkage (Liedholm and Mead 1987). Besides, repair services, for instance for tractors, pumpsets or other equipment would also represent a forward linkage; however these perhaps do not always add upto a very significant proportion of farm investments.

On the whole we feel that this linkage has considerable potential but has been underemphasised given the major concern of the rural growth linkage literature to explore forward production linkages with agriculture which tend to be primarily non-local in nature. There can be linkages with other sectors of the rural economy like services such as trade and commerce, hotels, transport, education and health; industry, especially in terms of a sub-contracting relationship (which has drawn considerable attention especially in the context of Japanese industrialisation)[12] and construction, which can induce the setting up of diverse local small-scale industries. We try to elaborate this in the discussion of our own evidence, placing special emphasis on linkages with the service sector.

[12]Liedholm and Mead 1987; Odaka 1980; Watanabe 1983.

Table 7.5: Distribution of Sample RSSEs with Forward Production Linkages by Sector

	Block	Sector					
		Agriculture	Industry	Construction	Services	Total	Sample@ size
1.	Kollengode	8.7	21.7	39.1	30.4	100	23
2.	Malampuzha	11.1	58.3	19.4	17.4	100	36
3.	IDA	14.3	57.1	–	28.6	100	7

Source: Field Survey

Notes: 1. Figures indicate cell counts as percent of row totals.

@ Only those sample units with Forward Production Linkages have been taken.

IDA - Industrial devleopment area.

7.3.1 *Forward Production Linkages of the Surveyed* RSSEs

Of the 62 units in K, about 37 percent had forward production linkages with other sectors in the rural economy[13]; however, less than 10 percent of these units were linked to agriculture. In Malampuzha, a little less than two-thirds of the units had forward production linkages of which over 10 percent had linkages with agriculture. We have defined FPL rather broadly, not in terms of the supply of some critical producer or intermediate good but as including any auxiliary item also which facilitates the production process in the purchasing sector. Our attempt is to emphasise the point that there are potential forward linkages for RSSEs which can be exploited (see Table 7.5). We highlight in particular the linkages with the tertiary sector, albeit few, for in an economy where this sector is growing rapidly, its demand for a number of essential industrial products can form an important element of a rural industrialisation policy based on small-scale enterprises. The fact that demand for most services increases with increasing incomes and services are largely insulated from urban competition, with barely any consumption leakages (Haggblade et al 1989), the potential for local linkages (of the RSSEs) with this sector is high.

While one of the units linked to agriculture in Kollengode produced and repaired a part of the pumpsets used for irrigation purposes, the other made gunny bags for supplying organic manure and livestock feed to the farms as also for transporting paddy to the mills. A significant linkage in rural areas was with construction and building activity, reflected in the fairly large number of brick making units, engineering units producing gates and grills, a saw milling unit and a unit producing PVC pipes and fittings. While the unit producing transfer bobbins was doing sub-contracting work for one of the large industrial undertakings in the other block, four other units were linked to industry in simple ways. These were producing plastic granules and

[13]Of course inter sectoral use is not always clear cut and a unit may have links with more than one sector depending on the nature of the product. We have taken the more dominant usage as reported by the entrepreneur.

components, steel brushes for cleaning machines and one of the coir units produced yarn for the weaving sector. We noted some interesting forward production linkages with the service sector, for instance with:

- "trade": printing units making letter heads, receipt books and other stationery for shops and companies and another coir unit making yarn for packaging;
- "education": creating a demand for copy books from the printing units;
- "health": a rubberised coir unit making mattresses for institutions including hospitals; and
- "petrol and service stations": with a unit making distilled water for them[14].

In Malampuzha given the large number of sub-contracting units, the forward production linkages with industry were important. Over half the units were linked to other industries. However, not all were exclusively sub-contracting units; some were making machine parts. A unit was producing an automotive component, another, rubber fittings and products and another, an item for the textile industry. A relatively "large" small-scale unit was producing power transformers while another unit was doing anodising work, the output being used primarily in the industrial machinery sector. There was a unit producing chemicals for the match industry. The larger proportion of units linked to agriculture in M was due to the units producing pumpsets and a part of the pumpset and two units engaged in tractor repair. As in Kollengode, the brick, gate and grill making units had forward links with the construction sector. There was also a unit producing cement and another making barbed wire for fencing. The interesting links were again with the service sector; the printing units were linked with trade and education. One unit which was doing very well was producing gas stoves for hotels and other institutions; another was making trailers for light commercial vehicles for transporting small loads.

If we compare Kollengode with Malampuzha, it appears that while backward production linkages with agriculture are higher in the former, in the latter, the forward production linkages with agriculture are relatively higher. Overall, the forward production linkages are higher in M. However, our interest lies in examining these linkages in terms of location of demand, or in other words how local are the forward production linkages, which we discuss below.

[14]It is interesting to note that this unit was set up on the advice of a friend in the local petrol station who perceived the potential demand for distilled water.

Table 7.6: Market Location of Units with Forward Production Linkages by Sector

	Block	Location								
		Mostly local[1]	Mostly Non-local			Total non local	Local & non local	All locations	Sample size	
			district	state	outside state					
		Kollengode								
1.	Agriculture	100	–	–		–	–	100	2	
2.	Industry	20.0	40.0	–	20.0	60.0	20.0	100	5	
3.	Construction	66.7	22.2	11.1	33.3	–	100	100	9	
4.	Service	42.9	14.3	–	–	14.3	42.9	100	7	
	Total	52.2	21.7	4.3	4.3	30.4	17.4	100	23	
		Malampuzha								
1.	Agriculture	75.0	–	–	25.0	25.0	–	100	5	1*
2.	Industry	47.6	–	19.0	9.5	28.5	23.8	100	21	4*
3.	Construction	28.6	42.8	14.3	–	14.3	14.3	100	7	–
4.	Service	75.0	–	–	–	–	25.0	100	4	2*
	Total	50.0	8.3	13.9	8.3	30.5	19.4	100	36	7*

Source: Field Survey

Notes:
1. Refers to Panchayat and block.
2. Figures indicate cell counts as percent of row totals.
3. Total non-local includes district, state & outside state.

* IDA units are shown separately in the last column. While the one unit linked to agriculture and two linked to services had a local and non-local market, two units in the industry group, had a non-local market and two had a local and non-local market.

7.3.2 Market Location of Forward Production Linkages

For over half the units in Kollengode which had forward production linkages, the market was largely local. The proportion rose to almost three-fourths of the units if district was included in local; only 4 percent had a demand outside the state (Table 7.6).

While in Malampuzha the proportion of locally oriented units was marginally lower than in Kollengode, those with a strong outward orientation was higher at 8 percent. Of the units located in the IDA, one third were linked to external demand (data not shown here). With respect to units having forward production linkages with agriculture, the two units in K were very closely linked to local agriculture while in M one of the units producing pumpsets had its major market outside the state. It may be noted that of the 13 units in both Kollengode and Malampuzha (including the IDA) with links to the service sector, little less than half catered largely to local demand and a similar proportion to both local and non-local demand.

While the attempt above is not to make a virtue out of the extent of local forward production linkages, we would like to emphasise that their existence implies a greater cognisance of local rural demand in investment decision making. Naturally the spread effects of such activities with the rural sector would be higher. While the entrepreneur does think beyond the immediate market, a local perspective would influence the nature of activity undertaken and enhance the possibility of larger local linkages. From the above evidence it appears that local forward production linkages in terms of number of units, are not insignificant in our survey region.

In this context, we would like to reiterate the potential role of small-scale industry - service sector linkage in generating rural manufacturing activity since a fairly high proportion of the market for such units would be local given the relatively localised nature of the demand for services itself. Kerala is a state in which the service sector has been growing out of proportion to the other two sectors (Krishnan 1994). While it is not denied that the disproportionate growth of this sector also reflects an excess supply of labour, there is within it a large component which is a function of the high expenditure elasticity of demand for services. And it is the growth of such services which should provide an inducement for the manufacture of industrial goods required by them.

7.4 Consumption or Expenditure Linkages

7.4.1 Introduction

In this section we examine the location of market for consumer goods being produced by the remaining units in both the blocks. Products which fall under the investment demand of households, example for housing, in terms of bricks, cement, gate and grill etc have been considered as intermediate inputs for the construction sector; their market location was found to be largely local. The products covered in this section are consumer goods, primarily food products, oil, beverages, clothing, furniture, leather products, consumer plastics, toys, soap and other miscellaneous household articles. Consumption linkages were found to be quantitatively the most important in the rural growth linkages literature. The results from our own survey confirm this finding, though in a somewhat weak manner.

Consumption linkages or, the demand (for industrial goods) generating role of the agricultural sector, as we discussed in Chapter 2, is an agriculture-industry linkage which was not explicitly incorporated in the industrialisation led development strategies of the fifties. Given the initial low levels of demand in most developing economies, lack of demand was not perceived as a constraint on the development process. However, the consequences of ignoring this linkage in the context of predominantly agrarian economies, became apparent in the inadequate growth of the home market, acting as a constraint on the industrialisation process. Mellor's emphasis on the rural households' consumption links to the non farm economy, as the prime source of generating employment and incomes in the local economy, drew considerable appeal. It appeared to bypass the need for a politically unpalatable land reforms policy since what needed to be done was somehow to increase agricultural productivity, for example, via increases in physical inputs or technology change, which would result in larger agricultural incomes. The latter would increase demand in rural areas and thereby encourage decentralisation of production to those areas. Savings from the higher incomes would provide the resources for investment in local small-scale industries (Mellor 1976). However, the strength of this linkage, particularly in terms of rurally manufactured goods was not found to be strong empirically. It has been argued that this was more due to the non-egalitarian nature of agricultural growth in most developing economies, which encouraged the consumption of urban and/or import based consumer goods and hence discouraged local production of manufactured goods. Given a relatively more egalitarian rural set up, and in the context of Kerala we have been arguing that it is so, the potential for local consumption linkages and the growth of rurally produced goods would be higher. Well developed transportation networks and a greater rural-urban mix, are also conditions favourable to the growth of rural manufacturing activity (Haggblade *et al* 1989) although it also results in a substitution of some rurally produced goods by urban manufactures. We now examine consumption linkages (CL) and their spatial location in the light of our own data.

7.4.2 *Consumption Linkages of Surveyed* RSSEs

It is evident from our preceding discussion that more units in Kollengode as compared to Malampuzha would be engaged in the production of consumer goods: over 60 percent produce goods for household consumption in K and in M such units account for a little over one third of the sample units. However it is the market location of the output of these units in each region which is of interest to us (Table 7.7). The table shows that about 59 percent of these units cater to local markets in K while in M the proportion is (surprisingly) higher. However, the proportion of externally oriented units is also higher in Malampuzha.

The degree of local linkage seems to be closely related to type of enterprise. Over two-thirds of the units (taking the two blocks together)[15] catering to demand within the panchayat and block are organised as FEs; those units whose market lies beyond the local region, particularly beyond the district are largely organised as SSUs. Over two-thirds of the FEs catering to local demand, market their output directly to the consumer; however the marketing network is

[15]Since the total population of small-scale units was not very different between the two blocks and the sampling proportion was the same for both the blocks, we can combine the units.

Table 7.7: Distribution of Sample RSSEs Producing Consumer Goods/Services by Market Location of Output

Block	Location							
	Mostly Local panchayat & block	Mostly Non Local district	state	outside state	Total Non local	Local & non local	All loca-tions	Sample@ size
1. Kollengode: All RSSEs	58.9	23.1	5.1	–	28.2	12.8	100	39
FE	75.0	15.0	–	–	15.0	10.0	100	21
SSU	38.9	33.3	11.1	–	44.4	16.7	100	18
2. Malampuzha: All RSSEs	63.6	27.3	9.1	–	36.4	–	100	22
FE	100	–	–	–	–	–	100	11
SSU	27.3	54.5	18.2	–	72.7	–	100	11
3. IDA	–	–	*	*	100	–	100	3
4. K & M & IDA: All RSSEs	57.8	23.4	9.4	1.6	34.4	7.8	100	64
FE	83.9	9.7	–	–	9.7	6.4	100	32
SSU	31.2	37.5	18.8	3.1	59.4	9.4	100	32

Source: 1. Field Survey

Notes: 1. Figures indicate cell counts as percent of row totals.

2. Total non-local includes district, state and outside state.

@ Only those units with consumption linkages have been taken.

FE - family enterprise; SSU - small-scale unit;

K - Kollengode; M - Malampuzha; IDA - Industrial development area

more varied for the SSUs. While some market their product directly to consumers, a larger number sell it to a local wholesale or retail dealer while a few market it through non-local dealers or (as for instance in the case of a rice mill and two food related units in the IDA) through their own dealers. The above analysis certainly suggests the petty nature of FE production, supplying simple consumer goods and services. Certain modern services however, like photostat or computer services, organised as FEs, can be fairly capital using.

7.4.3 *Market Location of Output of Consumer Goods and Services by Product Group*

We now look into the market location of the output of these units by the type of consumer goods and services being produced (Table 7.8). Clearly the food group within which the products with a shorter shelf life (bakery items, sweets, juice) or convenience of transporting (milling of copra or flour) and which therefore cater to small, dispersed markets, are the most locally oriented in both the blocks. This is followed by furniture units and units producing other household articles like mats, bamboo baskets, brushes, pottery and incense which too cater largely to the local market.

Table 7.8: Distribution of Units by Market Location of Output of Consumer Goods by Product Group

	Location	Product group: Food products		Clothing handlooms bags, toys buckets		Furniture baskets, mats		Service and repair	
		K	M	K	M	K	M	K	M
1	Mostly local	50.0	50.0	57.1	33.3	66.7	50.0	100	100
2	Mostly non-local	25.0	50.0	42.9	66.7	33.3	50.0	–	–
	district	15.0	–	42.9	50.0	33.3	50.0	–	–
	state	10.0	37.5	–	16.7	–	–	–	–
	outside state	–	12.5	–	–	–	–	–	–
3	Local & non-local	25.0	–	–	–	–	–	–	–
4	All locations	100	100	100	100	100	100	–	–
	Sample size	20	8	7	6	9	6	3	5

Source: Field Survey

Note: 1. Figures indicate cell counts as percent of column totals.

2. IDA units are included under Malampuzha block

Food - includes, rice mill, flour/oil mills, bakery, halwa, snacks, processed food and beverages.

Within the chemicals group too, units in Kollengode produced simple consumer goods like plastic chairs, toys and washing soap. It is interesting to note that while the readymade garments units were outward oriented in Malampuzha, depending for their market largely on Palakkad city[16], those in Kollengode were dependent largely on the small town of Koduvayur within the block and hence their market was "local". There has been in fact a mushroom growth of readymade garment units in Kollengode, particularly in and around Koduvayur. While a number of these units sold their output in this town, some had started doing job works for a few larger units situated in it. The artisanal tailoring units in both K and M catered to the local market, while handloom cloth was sold outside the panchayat through the cooperative society. Within the other outward oriented units in Kollengode were those producing washing soap and bell metal products (traditional ironing boxes and ornamental decorations), which sold their product largely to a local and non-local dealer respectively. Plastic toys, buckets and pitchers were marketed directly all over the district. Interestingly, within the food group itself, some of the larger units had a strong outward orientation.[17] The three food units located in the IDA, catered almost exclusively to non-local demand, reaching out beyond the state. Units engaged in service

[16] A hosiery unit in Malampuzha marketed its products mostly to other parts of the state.

[17] A processed food unit in Kollengode which sold its output largely to wholesale dealers in Palakkad had started exporting its products in a small way.

and repair both in Kollengode and Malampuzha largely served the local market. The proportion of such units was higher in Malampuzha which explains the higher degree of local consumption linkages in M. The relationship between market location of consumer goods and type of product was not statistically significant suggesting that most units, irrespective of product group, were outward oriented though the degrees varied.

7.4.4 Consumption Linkages versus Production Linkages

Summing up our analysis of production and consumption linkages, we find that local linkages of rural SSEs, in terms of the proportion of units catering largely to local demand, are not insignificant in our region. Particularly consumption linkages are indeed high in both Kollengode and Malampuzha. While about 60 percent of the units in K and 56 percent in M, which produce consumer goods and services derive their demand primarily from the local region, these proportions were 52 percent and 17 percent for units with local BPL and about 52 percent and 42 percent for units with local FPL respectively. Backward production linkages are very weak in Malampuzha. The data on the three types of linkages are presented in Table 7.9. The percentages under the different types of linkages indicate the number of units (and employment) with a local orientation for each type of linkage to the total number of units displaying that linkage. IDA units are included in Malampuzha block.

The relative importance of local FPL (in fact higher than BPL in Malampuzha) in both the blocks is brought out by the table, within which we had already noted the higher incidence of such linkages with non-agricultural sectors of the rural economy. Our findings are at variance with Tambunan's results for the region in West Java; none of the linkages in his study, BPL, FPL and CL, are locally (at the village or sub-district level) oriented. Even with respect to simple food processing units, the majority of the sample producers were highly non-localised in their market orientation.[18] It may also be noted that the majority of the sample producers in the study were entirely outward oriented for their capital requirements (Tambunan 1994). This appears to support our findings that use of external capital to set up rural enterprises tends to generate largely non-local linkages.

A very striking feature of the table is the data on employment. If we look at the proportion of employment accounted for by the units which have strong consumption linkages, it is much lower than their proportionate numerical strength. This is primarily because most of these units are family enterprises or smaller SSUs (2–4 workers) carrying on productive activity in the household either as single member enterprises or helped by one or two family or hired

[18] However, if the district which included a city was defined as local, then the external dependence of the producers was significantly reduced.

Table 7.9: Percentages of Units with BPL, FPL and CL[1] which are Locally Oriented and Employment therein

Block	Type of Linkage					
	BPL		FPL		CL	
	Units	Employment	Units	Employment	Units	Employment
1. Kollengode All RSSEs	52.3	53.5	52.2	37.6	59.0	37.6
FE	53.3	54.3	75.0	86.7	80.0	56.6
SSU	51.8	53.4	47.4	32.1	36.8	28.6
2. Malampuzha All RSSEs	15.4*	4.8	41.9	40.3	56.0	15.4
FE	33.3	29.4	100*	100*	100*	100
SSU	10.5	3.2	34.2	38.9	21.4*	6.0

Source: Field Survey

Note: 1. For each type of linkage, all units which displayed such linkages were identified and the percentages refer to those units within each category which were locally oriented.

2. BPL - backward production linkage; FPL - forward production linkage; CL - consumption linkage.

3. IDA units are included under Malampuzha.

FE - Family enterprise; SSU - Small scale unit

* The number of units is very small, 5 and below.

workers. In terms of employment then, production linkages are more important in Kollengode and in Malampuzha it is the forward production linkages which generate a higher percentage of employment. It is in this sense that consumption linkages are weak. We now sum up our findings on the linkages focussing on the differences between the two blocks in respect of the relative importance of local rural linkages.

7.4.5 *All Linkages: Summing up of Findings*

Our emphasis throughout the discussion on linkages has been on trying to assess the strength of rural linkages. An overwhelming proportion of the entrepreneurs in both the blocks were first generation entrepreneurs. While almost all the proprietors in Kollengode were rural in terms of operating in (rural) area of birth, in Malampuzha at least one fifth were non-local, the larger majority being from the city of Palakkad followed by the state of Tamil Nadu. The entrepreneurs operating from the IDA were almost entirely non-local, about half of them hailing from Palakkad and 10 percent from the neighbouring district of Coimbatore. However, less than one third of the entrepreneurs in both the blocks came from agricultural households and an even lower proportion were agriculturists themselves prior to setting up the enterprise. In terms of the initial source of start-up capital, a larger proportion of units were dependent on own and borrowed funds than on own funds alone. About one third of the own funds originated in agriculture, the rest being savings from prior non-agricultural occupations of the entrepreneurs, which were primarily local in nature in Kollengode but non-local in Malampuzha since a larger number of entrepreneurs had worked outside the region to gain skill and savings. However, what appeared important to us in terms of the development of rural linkages, which became clearer in the course of our findings on the different linkages, was the local origin of the entrepreneur rather than his/her agricultural background.

The units in Kollengode were using local labour only. While there were no units in Malampuzha, even in the IDA, which used only non-local labour, over one-third of the units did employ some workers from outside the block, largely from other parts of the district and to a small extent from Tamil Nadu. The proportion of units using non-local labour is higher than the proportion of non-local entrepreneurs, since some entrepreneurs although settled locally, maintained strong links with industry/business outside the state.[19] In the preceding chapter we observed that the association between non-local entrepreneurs and use of non-local labour in Malampuzha was statistically significant. However, while both capital and labour linkage can be very strongly local for rural units, this need not be the case in respect of the raw material input (backward production linkage) as also the market for their output (consumption and forward production linkages) as our findings revealed.

While a little over one-third of the units in Kollengode purchased the raw materials locally this proportion was less than one-tenth in Malampuzha. It was mostly the agro-processing units which were strongly local in procuring raw materials in both the blocks though the larger rice mills had to import paddy from other states. Among the small bakery and sweets/snacks making units in Kollengode purchase of wheat flour, sugar etc was relatively more "local" compared to Malampuzha since the units depended largely on the small town within the block rather than on Palakkad. Even in some of the natural resource based units in Malampuzha there was a tendency to depend much more on Coimbatore for purchases: small metal and rock powder in the production of hollow bricks, yarn for a handloom unit despite the existence of spinning mills in the Malampuzha block or liquid glucose in the case of two confectionery units in the IDA. Non-agriculture based raw materials like metals and products, plastic and chemicals were procured almost entirely non-locally. For a larger proportion of the units in Malampuzha block, Coimbatore was the source of purchase while in Kollengode block Palakkad played a more important role in the purchase of such materials. As pointed out earlier, the existence of rural enterprises not using local resources per se is not a problem; the problem arises if available local resources are not being used for lack of entrepreneurial capital or due to preference for non-local

[19]This was normally through marriage. The "local" resident of the family would be engaged in the production of a similar (to parent family enterprise) or related complementary item.

sources. The major problem for rural industrialisation lies in attracting non-agriculture based industries to a rural area which is at a relative disadvantage compared to the urban in terms of location factors. Hence the real issue is whether such units are able to generate at least other than raw material linkages or spread effects with the rural sector either in terms of labour or the market. Our findings revealed, primarily in respect of the IDA units in Malampuzha and the other units whose entrepreneurs originated from outside the local rural area, that they failed to create labour linkages in adequate measure. What about the market linkage of units producing non-consumer goods (forward production linkages) and consumer goods?

Forward production linkages with agriculture could be locally oriented; however only a small proportion of units in the two blocks were producing goods and services which constituted inputs into local agriculture. It was primarily with the non-agricultural sectors of the rural economy that the larger proportion of units had forward production linkages. A little over 50 percent of these units in Kollengode were locally oriented, the highest proportion being in construction. In Malampuzha while a larger proportion of units had forward production linkages, primarily with the industrial sector, due to the high incidence of sub-contracting firms, those with mostly a local market was lower. In both the blocks we highlighted the potential for growth of rural small-scale enterprises linked to the tertiary sector through the production of simple intermediate goods. About 42 percent of the units linked to services were locally oriented in both the blocks. While almost 70 percent of the units in the IDA had forward production linkages, all of them catered largely to a non-local market; 42 percent were strongly outward oriented, that is their market was outside the state. What is of interest in respect of some of the IDA units is the fact that their entire raw material comes from outside the state and almost the entire output is transported outside the district.[20] Coupled with lower local labour linkages, as was the case with a substantial proportion of the IDA units which were operated by non-local entrepreneurs, these units generated low developmental links with the rural sector. As argued earlier, the existence of local forward production linkages implies a greater cognisance of the rural economic environment in investment decision making. While the entrepreneur does think beyond the immediate local market, a local perspective would influence the nature of activity undertaken and enhance the possibility of larger local linkages. Similar is the case of consumption linkages. A high proportion of units producing consumer goods with a local orientation implies a greater response to rural demand, its pattern and changes over time.

The market location of almost all units in the food group was local in both the blocks; the bigger rice mills also catered to other parts of the state. In respect of other non-food consumer

[20]As in the case of the newly set up hosiery exporting complex, TeakTex, for which land and water was provided by the Kerala government in another part of Pudussery. In the old development area of Pudussery panchayat, we came across a unit not included in our sample, which had been set up earlier and was in the nature of a backward integrated plant of a chemical unit in Coimbatore. The raw material came from the latter and the entire output was sent back to it.

goods also the units were catering largely to local demand. In fact newer household articles of plastic, like buckets, pitchers and chairs, cane furniture and other goods like leather bags were being produced by some of the units. While the readymade garment units in Malampuzha block were considerably influenced by the nearby city of Palakkad, and a hosiery unit sold its output primarily to other parts of the state, in Kollengode their market was relatively local due to the links with the small town of Koduvayur. On the whole, local consumption linkages were higher (than production linkages) in both K and M; and much higher in K. The three food related units in IDA, one owned by an entrepreneur from Palakkad and the other two from other parts of the state, marketed their output almost entirely outside the block.

In the preceding chapter we had shown that the average distance of a panchayat from a big town in Kollengode was much higher than of a panchayat in Malampuzha block from Palakkad, the nearest city. The emergence of two types of spatial formations in the Kerala economy, according to whether the rural areas are distant from larger urban centres but contiguous with small independent towns or, as peripheral urban areas become part of urban agglomerations including its hinterland, seems to imply a duality in the pattern of rural industrialisation. The nature of industrial activity undertaken as also its linkages tend to differ between these two types of settlements. In the former the process of growth of rural industry is largely in response to extant rural conditions. This was brought out in our analysis of the process of diversification in Chapter 4 based on a study of villages which became urban in 1991. Those which grew into independent towns and were at a distance from larger urban settlements, showed stronger rural linkages. However, since "rural prosperity" was dealt with primarily in terms of agricultural factors, we were not able to capture the impact of non-agricultural incomes. Our survey findings appear to support this premise. The product structure of units in Kollengode is along this pattern, displaying considerable local linkages, particularly in terms of local entrepreneurship and labour. On the other hand, growth and nature of units located within urban agglomerations tends to be determined exogenously with fewer local linkages. Large industrial undertakings in Coimbatore and in the small towns and rural hinterland of the Palakkad agglomeration appear to have considerably induced the growth of small-scale units in that region. While the market linkage of some of these RSSEs is hence "local", most units have strong external links with Coimbatore, other parts of the district and rest of state in terms of raw material supplies and the market. A major finding of our survey of RSSEs was that agriculture need not be the main sector with which the units have linkages in terms of capital or demand for intermediate products even in case of units located in the more "rural" block. However, consumption demand as also the raw material linkage with agriculture was higher in the latter.

What also emerged from the discussion on linkages based on our findings, was that units operated by non-local entrepreneurs, tended to display weak local linkages, particularly in terms of utilising local labour and catering to rural demand. On the other hand local entrepreneurship tended to ensure greater local linkages on all accounts. This implied that local capital was perhaps the most important rural linkage. Relatively "isolated" rural areas like Kollengode had a high percentage of local entrepreneurs; non-local entrepreneurs operated in the IDAs and to some extent in the panchayats close to Palakkad. The latter displayed low local linkages in terms of labour and market. It should be noted that the nature of activity set up by small entrepreneurs was also relatively different between the two types of spatial structures: in Kollengode it was smaller, less capital using and concentrated in food-clothing-wood products groups. While there were some modern food units and units producing newer products are emerging viz. PVC pipes and fittings, soap, plastic moulded toys and household goods and simple electrical equipment, which are organised along more modern lines, these are still relatively small in number. On the other hand in the Malampuzha block, the average size of a unit was larger both in terms of workers and investment in plant and machinery and the incidence of engineering and chemicals based units was much higher.

However, in both the blocks an overwhelmingly large proportion of the units were "tiny" in nature. The petty nature of such activities, particularly in Kollengode does raise a rather critical question regarding the earnings they generate for the household, its adequacy and potential for growth. Firstly, in terms of the objective of creating employment for the rural poor, does this imply a neglect of the level of earnings? In other words is there a conflict between these two objectives. Secondly, can we identify certain correlates of economic efficiency, in terms of size, education of the entrepreneur and surpluses generated, which would make it possible for such enterprises to contribute to the advance of modern industry in the state?

7.5 Broad Evaluation of the Sample RSSEs

There has been a growing interest in small unregistered and micro-enterprises, evoked in the context of the urban informal sector first conceptualised in the early seventies. Many scholars view it as playing an important role in providing a livelihood to very many poor people over a long period of the development process. The interest has also spread to the rural small-scale sector with the increasing recognition of its growth potential. An alternative view, deriving from the hetrogeniety in the micro-enterprise sector, has focussed on these enterprises as a possible source of industrialisation. While Berry (1987) has discussed this issue in the context of rural industry, Grosh and Somolekae (1996) appear to discuss the potential in terms of the urban informal sector. From being labelled as marginal, many informal activities are recognised as being valuable economic endeavours (Rakowski 1994). They can contribute to the evolution of manufacturing in two ways: First, these micro-enterprises could grow into medium or large sized firms and hence foster the growth of an industrial sector. In the context of rural industry, they are to play the role of a proto-industrial sector. Second, despite the fact that few or none of them might grow into large firms, micro-enterprises could lay the basis for the growth of medium enterprises later if they foster adequate savings. The entrepreneur can then use the accumulated capital but with different technology or a different location and labour force to operate a bigger enterprise (Berry 1987). Or, second generation entrepreneurs who would presumably be more educated than the original entrepreneur could then set up bigger firms with the savings generated (Grosh and Somolekae 1996). This of course does not imply that micro-enterprises provide the only group of potential entrepreneurs. It has also been argued elsewhere, by classifying rural industry into modern, traditional and primitive on the basis of technology used, that mobility occurs primarily within the classes: modern small to large industry; traditional small workshops to large traditional industry and primitive self-employed to extended home industry (Weijland 1989). The possibility of the primitive self-employed category graduating to the modern small is not visualised.

Related to the above is also the employment and income implications of fostering small enterprises and whether employment as a development objective would conflict with raising the standard of living of the poor (Bar-el 1984). We attempt to assess the growth potential of the RSSEs we have surveyed broadly in terms of the two mechanisms outlined above. As noted earlier, we were unable to elicit the relevant information on earnings, and reinvestment behaviour from all the units and hence the analysis is based on scanty data supported by our own impressions and interviews with the entrepreneurs.

7.5.1 Expansion of Small Enterprises

Since most entrepreneurs in our sample were first generation entrepreneurs and we had considered only those units which were set up in the last five years, it is perhaps too early to observe the first mechanism (small becoming large). However, some information was obtained on whether the unit had expanded and the entrepreneur's own perceptions regarding future growth, which were quite revealing. We continue to distinguish between the two blocks and type of unit, family enterprises and small-scale units (in most tables), which do vary in a number of ways in their economic behaviour.

The entrepreneurs were asked the following questions:

- Has the demand for your product increased in the last 2–3 years?
- What are the possible reasons?

Table 7.10: Distribution of Units Reporting Increase/Decrease in Demand for Product by Unit Type

	Block	Change in Demand				
		Yes, demand has increased	No, it has declined	Has been steady/ do not know	Total	Sample size
1.	Kollengode	59.6	17.7	22.6	100	62
	FE	60.0	16.0	24.0	100	25
	SSU	59.4	18.9	21.6	100	37
2.	Malampuzha	85.3	5.9	8.8	100	68
	FE	75.0	6.2	18.8	100	16
	SSU	88.1	4.8	7.1	100	42
3.	IDA	90.0	10.0	–	100	10

Source: Field Survey

Notes: 1. Figures indicate cell counts as percent of row totals.
FE - Family enterprise; SSU - Small scale unit
IDA - Industrial development area

- What are your future plans? and,
- How do you intend to achieve your plans?

The question of demand is critical to the long term growth of RSSEs and has evoked considerable controversy in terms of the inferior goods argument. A number of studies have presented empirical evidence against the general validity of the latter (Saith 1992). While there is no doubt that the answers to the above questions addressed to the sample producers would to some extent be subjective and tend towards over-optimism, the tabular presentations below suggest considerable entrepreneurial ingenuity and dynamism. The responses to the question of increased demand are given in Table 7.10. A majority of the producers, which was overwhelming in Malampuzha, reported an increase in demand for their product or service.

That this was not entirely credible is suggested by the information volunteered by the units on whether their product faced competition. Over 90 percent of the units in Kollengode reported competition for their product almost entirely from other local small-scale units, while in Malampuzha, 75 percent of the units faced competition from a more varied source: a little over 60 percent of these units reported competition from local SSEs and the rest competed with non-local (that is beyond the block) SSEs and non-local big units. Five of the IDA units fall in the latter category, while two of them competed with local SSEs (the data on competition are not shown here). With so much local competition the response of the entrepreneurs on expansion in demand appears surprising. Perhaps the question was understood in terms of their perception of a general growth in demand at the aggregate level, which at their own enterprise level reflects

Table 7.11: Future Expansion Plans of Producers by Mode of Expansion: Block-wise

	Block	Mode of Expansion		Sample size
		With existing labour and capital	By increase in both	
		% of total no. of units	% of total no. of units	size
1.	Kollengode			
	i to expand	29.0	37.1	62
2.	Malampuzha			
	i. to expand	13.2	55.9	68
	ii. to start another unit		8.8	68

Source: Field Survey

really a marketing issue. Particularly, in the Kerala context, with the sharp and broad based increase in rural consumer expenditure in the post-Gulf migration period there is a considerable amount of "consumerism" in the economy. This has created a general feeling of a continuing growth in expenditures while it is possible that most units individually may have experienced only a small increase in demand. A little over a quarter of the producers in both Kollengode and Malampuzha were not very specific regarding the source of increase in demand. However, almost 75 percent attributed it to increase in purchasing power and business and industrial activity (consumption and production linkages), the proportion being higher in favour of growth in consumption.

It may be noted that the table also revealed that a little less than one-fifth of the units in Kollengode and about 6 percent in Malampuzha were of the opinion that demand for their product or service had declined. A further probing into the nature of these units revealed however, that they were not concentrated in any particular product group nor especially (data not shown separately) in the FEs.

On their future plans, the majority of the producers were very optimistic. Almost two-thirds of the units in Kollengode and over three-fourths in Malampuzha wanted to expand production or diversify or (a very small number) to start another unit (Table 7.11). However, 34 percent of the units in K and 22 percent in M reported being satisfied with the status quo. The incidence of FEs is high among these units (in Kollengode); however, a larger percentage of FEs have expressed a desire to expand (data not shown here).

A distribution of the units by plans for expansion with the mode to be adopted shows that more than half the units in M would like to expand by increasing the input of both labour and capital. This proportion is high in K too, 37 percent; however an almost equal proportion expressed preference for the status quo, and a little over a quarter of the units in K planned to increase production with existing equipment and labour. A small number of producers in M wanted to start another unit. However, all these producers were quite certain that they wanted to keep well within the limits of small. Even the entrepreneurs who wanted to start another unit stated their preference for a small-scale unit, preferably with less than 10 workers. We observed that this was reported even by units who were doing well suggesting the preference for small-scale units in order to evade labour and tax legislation. There is no doubt, as our observation also confirmed that a number of these units would graduate into slightly larger units though certainly not into medium or large sized enterprises. This is feasible since we saw in the preceding chapter that an overwhelming proportion of the units in both Kollengode and Malampuzha (excluding the IDA units) are still much below the upper limit of small-scale in terms of investment in plant and machinery. Most of the small-scale units in the IDA were larger than the other units and at least four of them were set up by entrepreneurs who already had other small-scale units in similar or different activities. In our discussions with the owners we got the impression that they would like these units too to grow upto the outer limit for inclusion in the small-scale sector or set up another SSE.[21]

We now analyse certain correlates of economic efficiency such as, (a) size and (b) education of the entrepreneur which affect their performance and growth potential (Berry 1990; Grosh and Somolekae 1996).

(a) By Size

Table 7.12 gives the distribution of the units according to their future plans by size class for the two blocks together. The striking features of the table are:

- units in all size groups wanted to expand;
- However, those who wanted to expand production with existing capacity were higher in the smaller group (2–4 workers) and largest size group. Very few of the largest units wanted to increase size. This was more evident in Malampuzha;
- the percentage of units planning for expansion through increases in both labour and capital and hence size was highest within the "middle" group, that is 5–9 workers;
- most of the larger small-scale units preferred to set up another small-scale unit, suggesting a disinclination among the producers who already had achieved near upper end limits of small-scale to grow out of "small";

[21]A number of small-scale entrepreneurs told us that the problems were much less in remaining small. Of course for the very small producers setting up a small-scale unit was not free of problems, since the initial period of application, registering etc. could be quite protracted.

Table 7.12: Future Plans of Units and Mode to be Adopted by Size Class (in terms of workers) of Sample RSSEs: Kollengode and Malampuzha combined @

Size class of workers	Mode of expansion				
	To expand with existing capital and labour	To expand by increasing both	To start another small scale unit*	Status quo	Total
1	1.5	5.4	–	6.2	13.1
2–4	6.9	13.8	0.8	14.6	36.2
5–9	5.4	17.7	1.5	4.6	29.2
10–19	2.3	8.5	–	0.8	11.5
20 and above	4.6	1.5	2.3	1.5	10.0
Total	20.8	46.9	4.6	27.7	100
Sample size	27	61	6	36	130

Source: Field Survey

Note: 1. Figures indicate cell counts as percentage of total counts (=130).

* All these units are located in Malampuzha.

@ Since the total population of small-scale units was not very different between the blocks and the sampling proportion was the same for both the blocks, we can combine the units.

- among the units reporting status quo as their future plan, the percentage was high for the 1 worker and 2–4 workers enterprises as also the largest size group;

- the desire of a large number of 1 worker enterprises to expand by increasing both capital and labour was in fact a wish for higher subsidised capital. This would enable them to increase efficiency either through purchase of some simple capital equipment to replace a time consuming manual operation or through bulk purchases of raw materials and hence reducing costs; and

- most of the units operating in the IDA/MIE reported a preference for expanding production with the existing capacity or to start another unit.

(b) Education of the Entrepreneur

It has been discussed in the literature that lack of education can be a barrier to expansion; those with the lowest levels of education are found predominantly in the smallest enterprise (Grosh and Somolekae 1996). Modern entrepreneurs start from a higher schooling level than can be found in traditional enterprises; they have better access to credit facilities and essential public services (UNCP 1988). To function on a bigger scale with machinery and employing a few labourers involves planning ahead and a lot of paper work to be done. Without education it becomes difficult to make the transition unless other informal help is rendered to the entrepreneur.

Table 7.13: Level of Education of the Entrepreneur and their Future plans: Kollengode and Malampuzha Combined*

Level of education	Future Plans					
	To expand with existing capital and labour	To expand by increasing capital and labour	To start another small scale unit	Status quo	Total	Sample size
No formal education	30.0	20.0	–	50.0	100	10
Below matric	22.2	44.4	–	33.3	100	36
Matric	5.6	63.9	2.8	27.8	100	36
Matric plus@	31.8	45.4	9.1	13.6	100	22
Graduate & above	29.4	57.1	17.6	14.3	100	7
Technical degree	28.6	57.1	–	14.3	100	7
Total	20.8	46.9	4.6	27.7	100	130

Source: Field Survey

Note: 1. Figures in brackets indicate cell counts as percentage of row totals.

* Since the total population of small-scale units was not very different between the two blocks and the sampling proportion was the same for both the blocks, we can combine the units.

@ Includes two more years of schooling and ITI/polytechnic training.

By education we refer to formal education. Skills are also acquired through practical experience by working in a similar activity which helps, to some extent, in overcoming the disadvantages of lower education.[22] Our own evidence in the previous chapter revealed that the higher the level of education of the owner the larger tended to be the size of the unit. To what extent is this relationship observed in a cross section analysis applicable over time? Is it the more educated entrepreneurs who plan to make the transition to a slightly larger size? We examine the relationship between education of the entrepreneur and their future plans (Table 7.13). It can be seen from the table that the largest percentage of entrepreneurs who wanted to expand by increasing capital and labour fall in the education group matriculation and above. Similarly in respect of those entrepreneurs who wanted to start another small-scale enterprise. On the other hand those who reported status quo were predominantly those who either had no formal education or those with less than matriculation. However, not all those with a technical degree wanted to expand production with increased capital and labour, a few preferred to utilise existing capacity or maintaining status quo.

The above findings appear to confirm the observations made earlier that it does not seem likely that these small units would grow into large-scale firms. However, we would expect considerable mobility to slightly larger firms; the most dynamic appear to be the enterprises

[22] A number of entrepreneurs in our sample with an education level of less than matriculation or even matriculation, supplemented it with practical experience or "learning by doing".

with 5–9 workers. While the traditional industrial units in our survey appeared to be keen on "modernising" primarily with some product diversification and additional capital equipment, the self-employed certainly showed a dynamism which could move them into the modern small category. Hence there is considerable scope for growth of the small units. And given the changing upper limit of small-scale units in terms of investment in plant and machinery, there is adequate scope to grow while still remaining "small"

7.6 Wages and Earnings

7.6.1 Wage Earnings

The wage data relate largely to average wage earnings of unskilled workers in units hiring labour, viz. 37 units in Kollengode, 42 units in Malampuzha and the 10 IDA units. Producers in both the blocks responded differently on the question of wages: some reported it in terms of the daily wage rate paid to the workers and specified the approximate average monthly earnings. Others gave a monthly figure. The payment was generally made on a monthly basis. However, almost all workers were employed on a casual basis and got a wage only for the days worked; only the more skilled workers in some of the larger units were employed on a regular basis. Our data for the two blocks show that very few workers were illiterate; however, in almost 70 percent of the units in Kollengode and 40 percent in Malampuzha, workers were below matriculation level.

(a) Wage Rates in Kollengode

The average wage of an unskilled male worker in Kollengode varied between Rs. 40-50 and for a female from Rs. 15-35. On average in a month the wages earned were around Rs. 450-550 for males and Rs. 350-400 for females. Industries which involved relatively heavy work like saw milling and gate and grill making, without any particular need for a higher level of education, carried a higher daily wage, between Rs. 60-70. We found that the years of schooling upto matriculation did not appear to make a difference to the wage paid. However, the least paid among the workers, particularly female workers, had been reported as having no formal education. Being a matriculate or with some level of technical training made it possible to earn a higher wage on average, in the more modern (chemical and metal based) units as also the larger units. It varied between Rs. 700-750 per month. However, we did not probe into how long they had to wait to secure such employment. What was somewhat surprising was the much lower wage earned in printing units in which the workers were matriculates; all the units reported Rs. 600 as the average wage, for both men and women. The most striking finding was the inevitable lower (than male) wage rate for females in almost every unit which appeared to be a very normal, well accepted fact. It could be as low as Rs. 15 a day in certain food units.

The daily off-season agricultural wage rate in that region was reported as Rs. 45-50 for males and Rs. 30-35 for females. This implies that while the wage rate in the small-scale units did not appear to be below the agricultural wage rate on average for males, in respect of females it could be lower. The small-scale units also guaranteed more regular employment which implied higher monthly earnings.

(b) Wage Rates in Malampuzha

Examining the evidence for Malampuzha, we were surprised to find that the average wage for unskilled workers was not very different, varying betweem Rs. 500-600 for male workers and Rs. 350-400 for females. At the same time in the larger modern chemicals/metal based units the wage could be higher than in Kollengode but still between Rs. 1000-1500. This, despite the fact that a larger proportion of units are "modern" in Malampuzha and the workers relatively more educated. There could be two possible reasons for this:

- The large female work force which dominates the electronics sub-contracting units tends to pull down the average wage. About 48 percent of the workers in the sample units in Malampuzha were females. We found that most of these young, female workers were matriculates and were working for a wage of Rs. 350-400.
- There could be a problem of too many small engineering/subcontracting units squeezing into the sector. This oversupply has resulted in lack of orders for individual firms and competition among them has taken the form of keeping wages low (see Schmitz 1990).

Quite a few firms had admiited that the number of small

engineering units had been growing without a commensurate growth in orders from the parent firms. However, it may be noted that we are discussing general tendencies which do not preclude the possibility of innovation among these small frims. As mentioned earlier many sub-contracting units had started producing certain components independently.

Although it might appear that in Malampuzha, being educated did not matter due to the not so different (from Kollengode) initial wage, the level of literacy played an important role (in both the blocks) in another way. It improved the longer-term prospects of the worker, enabling him/her to procure larger increments or move up to better positions or move out to better paid employment when possible. The chances improved with some technical training together with matriculation.

Another striking finding from the survey was that the starting wage in most of the IDA units was not very different either, from the other units: around Rs. 500-650 for males and Rs. 400-450 for females. However, the increment was higher and at times other subsidised or free facilities like tea, food and lodging were also provided. It was stated by some of the entrepreneurs that the male workers could start earning Rs. 1000 within a year. Moreover, work was more regular and hence workers would prefer to be employed even at a lower wage. Forty percent of the units in our IDA sample employed women who earned on average Rs. 100-150 less than the men. All the workers were at least matriculates.

Most of the producers in both the blocks agreed that the wages paid to a worker were not adequate to support a family. It was rationalised by the argument that the bulk of these workers were young and their earnings were more in the nature of a supplementary income for the households, particularly in the case of the women.

7.6.2 *Earnings from Self-employment*

Self-employed units have been taken to include the single worker enterprises as also those using mainly family labour, that is family enterprises. It may be recalled that in Kollengode there were 25 such units and 16 in Malampuzha. There is no doubt that in both the blocks, a small entrepreneur earned more than a wage worker. That it most often involved using unpaid family labour or putting in long hours of work did not appear to matter. However, the question here was the adequacy of the amount for maintaining a family. In Kollengode over a quarter of the self-employed entrepreneurs reported the enterprise as a supplementary source of income, agriculture being the main source of income. In Malampuzha however, it was the main source of income for almost all the entrepreneurs.

The lowest monthly earning in a self-employment unit in both Kollengode and Malampuzha (reported by a little over 10-20 percent of the enterprises) was in the range Rs. 700-1000. This is just about the poverty line defined for the state which is estimated at an annual income of Rs. 11,000 for a family at 1991–2 prices. Most of the units in Kollengode earned between Rs. 2000-4000 per month and about 10 percent of the units earned Rs. 5,000. In Malampuzha the larger proportion of units earned a lower monthly amount of Rs. 1500-3000. Over 40 percent of the units were service and repair units in Malampuzha. It was rather surprising that even the modern service facilities like photo-stat units, clinical laboratories reported monthly earnings within the range of Rs. 2000-3000.[23] While in Kollengode the highest earning was reported for a traditional metal based unit, in Malampuzha it was for a food unit. However, the former had to support a large family of almost eight members. Overall the family enterprises appeared to have done better in Kollengode and the earnings helped to supplement incomes of at least a quarter of the households.

On the question of the ability of such enterprises to generate a surplus for re-investment, our findings were revealing. Of the 25 units in Kollengode, only five units reported to have generated an internal surplus which was ploughed back into the unit. While four were simple machinery/metal based units (including the traditional unit mentioned above), the fifth was a food unit. Our own observation too, confirmed their growth potential. In Malampuzha too, three units had reported expansion in terms of fixed capital investment. However, only one was through internal savings; the other two had taken a loan to do so.

7.6.3 Earnings of Small-scale Units (SSUs)

On average the earnings of SSUs vis-a-vis the family enterprises were higher. Earnings were defined as net of all costs, including interest and depreciation. Almost all the units in both Kollengode and Malampuzha, reported an earning above Rs. 1000 per month. About 46 percent of the units in Kollengode earned more than Rs. 4000 per month on average. This proportion was marginally higher in Malampuzha. In addition, over a quarter of the units in Malampuzha earned a monthly income above Rs. 10,000; in Kollengode it was much lower (15 percent). The SSUs appear to have performed relatively better in Malampuzha.

There was a quantum difference in the earnings of the IDA units, which varied from a low of Rs. 20,000 per month in our sample to Rs. 10,00,000. But what was striking was the fact that while the IDA units did pay a marginally higher amount as average wage to men and women when compared to other SSUs in Malampuzha, the enterprise earnings were in fact much higher. This seems to suggest that even among those small-scale entrepreneurs who have successfully embarked on the high-tech (proxied by investment in plant and machinery) route, the terms on which they employ workers are not very much better than those in other enterprises (see Schmitz 1990). However, as noted earlier work is generally more regular and longer term prospects are better in such organisations. This also suggests that so long as the surplus labour situation continues, wage ernings will tend to remain low.

---

[23]There is no doubt that there is a tendency to under-report earnings in SSEs for fear of tax legislation. However, it is not known whether this was more so in Malampuzha and why.

About 20 percent of the SSUs in Kollengode and one third in Malampuzha had undertaken some expansion largely from internal funds generated. Half the IDA units reported some expansion. While in Malampuzha more than half were in the engineering group, in Kollengode the spread was wider.

7.6.4 *Summing Up*

From the above it appears that indeed the rural small-scale sector presents a certain duality in terms of its character. While the majority of family enterprises and a sizable proportion of the small-scale units represent a strategy of survival for the households, there is a dynamic segment within it. Internally generated surpluses are ploughed back for further expansion. However, this seems possible without the firms necessarily growing into large-scale enterprises.

Insofar as the rural wage workers are concerned the majority of whom would be employed as unskilled or low skilled workers, we find that wage rates (and earnings) in the sample RSSEs are low; certainly not adequate to maintain a family even at the poverty line. They can only supplement household incomes. However, the wage rates fall below the agricultural wage rate only in some enterprises for females. The male-female difference in wages appears to be firmly entrenched and female earnings could be as low as Rs. 350 per month. While the majority of small-scale enterprises, particularly in Kollengode, utilises very little of educated labour, the more modern and larger units do provide such employment. The impact of education on earnings is more pertinent in a long-run sense and that is what creates the urge for improving literacy levels despite relatively little immediate benefit from it.

It is important to note however, that though a large segment of the enterprises appear to have a limited growth potential, they play a critical role in the process of development. They provide a vital source of employment and incomes to such a large number of rural households. The desire of the entrepreneurs to grow is reflected in their efforts to overcome their constraints and improve their situation. Our findings in the earlier section on future expansion plans bears this out.

8

Main Findings, Conclusions and Some Policy Suggestions

8.1 Introduction

Rural diversification and rural industrialisation are major areas of interest in large agrarian economies given the continued dependence of high proportions of the population on agriculture as a means of precarious livelihood. Our study was undertaken against the background of a felt need for greater autonomy to the rural sector in evolving its own development priorities. The major objectives of our study were:

- to examine the role of rural linkages in sustaining a process of rural industrialisation; and
- to what extent can the rural industrial sector contribute to the process of industrialisation in an industrially backward state.

We view rural industrialisation as a constituent of an industrialisation strategy placing particular emphasis on rural linkages for the generation of rural employment and incomes. The study was taken up for Kerala state, which is unique in many respects among the states of India. Historically, it was characterised by a high incidence of rural industries given its rich natural resource base, the products of which could be processed into industrial goods and were linked to the external markets. However, an area of major concern in its transformation process has been the declining fortunes of the traditional industrial production base and the inability of the state to develop and diversify its industrial sector. Since the latter half of the eighties however, there has been a fairly rapid growth of the non-factory, modern, small-scale manufacturing sector in the state, located largely in the rural areas which was the focus of our enquiry.

The concluding Chapter is organised in four sections. In Section 8.2 we review our main findings. The conclusions that can be drawn in answer to the questions addressed in the study are formulated in Section 8.3. Some policy implications which emerge from our analysis are discussed in Section 8.4.

8.2 Review of Findings

In our discussion of the importance of agriculture-industry linkages in the process of rural tranformation (Chapter 2), we highlighted the neglect of the rural industrial sector in early industrial history of England as also the development strategies of the 1950s which had largely drawn on the experience of the latter. Mendels' construct of proto-industrialisation, despite its limitations, did help in revising the perspective on rural industries. While there was very little evidence that rural industries in developing countries could grow into large modern firms, it was possible for them to contribute to the advance of modern industry in other ways. The sector need not be viewed as being transitional in nature. In addition, the role of small-scale enterprises in long-term economic development was being reassessed in view of its growing relative importance in industrialised countries (Acs et al 1996) and new emerging paradigms on industrial development - flexible specialisation.

In the restructured development strategies of the seventies, given the failure of the industrialisation led development strategies to "trickle down" to the rural poor, the rural sector was perceived as having greater flexibility in generating employment and incomes. It was in this context that rural industrialisation, based on small-scale manufacturing and induced primarily through intra-spatial linkages between rural manufacturing and the agricultural-rural sector, assumed importance. The emphasis was on consumption linkages (though production linkages were not to be ignored) to tap the large rural market. It was a linkage virtually unemphasised in the earlier development models. We focussed on Mellor's rural growth linkage model (Mellor 1976), the most complete version of an agriculture-led strategy of growth to understand the mechanism of linkages generally identified as of three types:

- consumption linkages;
- backward production linkages; and
- forward production linkages.

The critique of this model based largely on its near-exclusive emphasis on an agriculture-induced process of rural diversification, targeted at the more prosperous farmers and neglect of labour supply side factors opened up wider perspectives on the linkages between rural demand - both consumption and production - and generation of small-scale manufacturing activity. We attempted to draw up a framework of analysis for studying rural transformation within an environment of greater rural autonomy and focussing on certain aspects which had either not drawn adequate attention or had been underemphasised. An excessive concentration on agriculture induced linkages resulted in an underestimation of the potential of rural linkages. This was especially so in respect of rurally manufactured goods. The role of the fast growing service sector whose demand for simple intermediate goods could offer a vast potential for the growth of RSSEs needed to be highlighted. At the same time the impact of location of the rural areas in terms of distance from nearest town on the nature of linkages, though emphasised in the study by Tambunan (1994) has not received much attention. The relative importance of agricultural linkages very often tends to be swamped out by urban related indicators of rural diversification. The former could play a more dominant role in generating non-agricultural employment in relatively isolated rural areas. This implies that linkages that promote occupational diversification vary across villages.

Insofar as the rural industrial sector is to be included in the national economic and industrial trends, there is need to go beyond the narrow set of activities in which the rural areas have some advantage. It is in this context that local capital linkage or indigenous entrepreneurship, assumes importance. Local investment had been emphasised by Mellor, since larger farmers had to invest in rural small-scale industries out of the savings from the increaed incomes to sustain the process. However, it was found to be weak empirically since it had weak links with agricultural surpluses and hence tended to remain under-emphasised. A larger part of the initial capital for investment in small industries appears to come largely from non-agricultural households. Local capital and entrepreneurship needs to be emphasised since there is a real (psychic) advantage for local entrepreneurs operating in a local environment which redresses to some extent the relative place-specific disadvantages of rural locations. The goal of rural industrialisation can be realised through the stimulation of local initiative.

Within such a broad perspective we focussed on our region (Chapter 3) presenting certain macro economic and structural characteristics of the Kerala economy which serve as a backdrop to the study. The state has undergone a broad-based process of growth in which equity considerations have played a more important role rather than aggregate economic growth. While it displays high social development its economic performance has been relatively poor, particularly on the industrial front. This is most starkly manifested in high(est) rates of unemployment in the state, in particular educated unemployment. The broad-basing of its economy has also implied a small size of capital in the region. Coupled with its settlement pattern the state is characterised by a dispersed (and small-scale) pattern of industrial growth. While we noted the emergence of the small-scale sector as potentially dynamic in the long-run, what has been a cause for major concern in the Kerala context is its product structure (of the large sector too) which acts as a constraint on growth of output and value added in manufacturing. There is a concentration of agro and natural-resource based industries which are less capital using and display lower levels of productivity. Although a major objective of the rural industrialisation strategy is to maximise employment, it is difficult to achieve it without any consideration of capital intensity (Bar-el 1984). The state tends to remain industrially backward compared to all-India as also the other southern states.

The nature of its settlement pattern and dispersed industrial growth had a tremendous impact on Kerala's urbanisation process, which is marked by a relative absence of a dominant mode and a much higher incidence of smaller urban settlements. Urbanisation has occurred to a larger (than all-India) extent through the transformation of rural areas. This prompted us to examine the structural transformation of the work force in terms of rural and size class of towns during 1971–91 (Chapter 4) using the "continuous" method of estimating spatial growth rates (that is, defining rural and urban settlements by size of population at a point of time and including the same set of settlements in each spatial category over time). While the share of manufacturing employment in the total work force had been stagnant for the state as a whole, in terms of its rural-urban spread we found that growth had been faster in small towns and rural areas. However, there has been a substantial growth of agriculture related activities in the small towns (primarily livestock production, horticulture etc) resulting in a "ruralisation" of small towns. There has not been much further diversification in the large urban settlements (including urban agglomerations). However, within non-agricultural employment the share of the tertiary sector has increased while that of manufacturing has declined. While the dispersed pattern of growth of industry continues in the more recent period (1971–91), the evidence suggests that two spatial formations may be emerging in the state as revealed by changes in the occupational structure: on the one hand is a rural-small town nexus evident in the narrowing down of the occupational structures between the two, where possibly rural linkages will be more important. On the other hand are the larger urban settlements with a growing importance of urban agglomerations drawing in parts of the erstwhile rural areas as new towns. Linkages of rural small-scale industries in this case are more likely to flow from urban to rural areas.

By focussing on the villages which became urban by 1991 whether as extensions to urban agglomerations or as isolated/independent villages, we hoped to capture the process of diversification by relating it to certain socio-economic characteristics of the villages, data for which are available for 1971. Some of these characteristics could be used as proxies for the presence of certain linkages we discussed earlier. We could identify certain land based characteristics like extent of cultivated area, proportion of area irrigated and cultivated area per male agricultural worker as rural linkages. Estimates of income at the village level are not available. However, high values of each of the land based characteristics reflect rural prosperity and hence were used as proxy for consumption linkages. Information on distance from the nearest town was used to approximate urban linkages. Distress diversification was captured by the proportion of male agricultural labour to male agricultural workers representing a surplus labour situation. Cultivated area per male agricultural worker (being the land-man ratio) could also be a reflection of distress since a very low ratio would imply a "push" out of agriculture. The estimates on literacy, both male and female, represented accumulation of human capital and the availability of labour for employment in non- agricultural activities.

The results of the matrix on inter-correlations among the proportion of male non- agricultural employment and the charateristics described above for all the villages together revealed that the proximity to urban centres had the highest correlation followed by the literacy variables and the extent of irrigated area. It was also noted that most of the determinant variables were correlated with proximity to urban centre. In order to see whether villages which are relatively isolated have different determinants of non-agricultural employment we examined the village data classified by extensions and independent/isolated towns. However, in terms of proximity to urban centres the isolated villages as a category do not necessarily represent the most distant villages. For this reason we further classified the isolatd villages into two groups- those nearer an urban centre and those far off on the basis of a median distance of 14 kms. Then the villages with a high level of occupational diversification (<= 75 percent) in all the three categories, viz. extensions, isolated villages near an urban centre and isolated villages far off were identified. Linkages were then examined based on a comparison of the averages of the various indicators between the less and more diversified villages across the three categories. Of particular interest was the comparison between the far off villages and the extensions. The results showed that averages for all three rural indicators were much higher for the far off villages between the less and more diversified villages while they were very similar in the case of extended villages. However, literacy levels do not appear to be associated with diversifiction in the far off isolated villages. Nor are the distress induced indicators very different between the less and more diversified far off villages. The findings indicate that higher rural linked indicators are associated with the highly diversified far off isolated villages and not so with the extended villages.

A major limitation of this analysis, given the nature of existing data, is that rural has been defined in a narrow sense, covering only agriculture. It is not possible to capture the linkages of non-agricultural employment with, for instance the rural service sector, which we had regarded as an underemphasised linkage. However, it does bring out the important fact that factors affecting occupational diversification vary across villages.

An examination of changes in the industrial structure across space defined in terms of the three regions, north, central and south Kerala (broadly corresponding to its three erstwhile political constituents), suggests that growth in rural manufacturing has been the most rapid in the north followed by central Kerala. The former at the time of integration was less industrialised than the other two. However, the pattern of change over the two decades does not seem to have closed the gap between north and central Kerala, while that between the south and central has widened. Based on the regional differences in the growth of rural manufacturing we selected a district in the north of Kerala, Palakkad, to carry out our field survey on small-scale enterprises.

Having observed the spread of manufacturing across space, we then examined the size structure of manufacturing activity in Kerala focussing on the small-scale enterpries (Chapter 5). The limitations of data were highlighted given the existence of a large unorganised (non- factory) sector. The latter was found to be the fastest growing segment of the manufacturing sector. Changes in the size structure of manufacturing in Kerala suggest that the state is perhaps in the second stage as defined by Anderson (1982) in which small workshops dominate with a substantial decline in the household sector. However, there does not appear to be any emerging tendency towards a growing relative importance of the large-scale factory sector which would displace a large share of the small workshop and small factory production by the end of the second phase. After an initial increase in its share in manufacturing employment between 1961–81, the share of the factory sector, large and small, is stagnant around 20 percent in 1991. The share of the non-factory, non-household manufacturing sector has grown from 35 percent to 55 percent and in the more recent period to 60 percent. Together with the household sector, the small-scale manufacturing sector accounts for about 80 percent of total employment in manufacturing.

A more detailed examination of the small-scale sector was attempted in terms of value added, output, investment in plant and machinery and product structure using primarily the two major data sources on unorganised manufacturing, the National Sample Survey Organisation (NSSO) and the Small Industries Development Organisation (SIDO). This was done to highlight the weaknesses of the small sector and focus on its relatively poor performance vis-a-vis India in the period 1972–3 to 1987–8. In terms of numbers, the rate of growth in registered SIDO units was not very different in Kerala from all-India. Smaller units, in terms of workers, are on average larger in Kerala than their counterparts at the all-India level. However, the units use much less of capital equipment resulting in a larger share of "tiny" units in Kerala.

Our focus was on the product structure of the small-scale sector. In terms of output, more than three-fourths of the total output in 1987–8 in Kerala was accounted for by 5 two- digit industry groups, viz. (1) food products (2) wood products (3) rubber and plastics (4) chemicals and (5) metal products. These same 5 industry groups had also shared more than 75 percent of the total output in 1972–3 although the inter se shares were slightly different. The all- India product structure was much less concentrated in 1972–3: More than 75 percent of the output was shared by 9 industry groups the top three being metal products, chemicals and basic metals. While for India too, the pattern did not alter much by 1987–8, it was already more diversified.

In terms of employment in 1987–8, the product structure of the small-scale sector was almost as concentrated in Kerala as in India. About 70 percent of the employment was shared by 5 industry groups in Kerala (food products, wood products, non-metallic mineral products, metals and products and rubber/plastic products) and 6 at the all-India level (metals and products, food products, machinery and parts, non-metallic mineral products, chemicals and products and wood products). However, what distinguishes the Kerala structure is the heavy concentration within these groups of agro and natural resource based industries. About 60 percent of employment was accounted for by the latter while the proportion was about one- third for all-India. The latter tend to use much less fixed capital (plant and machinery) on average. While the above is not to deny that some diversification of the small-scale sector in favour of modern industries has occurred in Kerala, the pace of change is rather slow.

In Chapters 6 and 7 we presented our findings from the field survey which was an attempt to examine the nature of linkages, structure and performance of the small-scale sector on the basis of primary sources of information. Spread over six months in the first half of 1996, surveys were carried out covering 130 units in two blocks of Palakkad purposively selected to study the impact of location (in terms of proximity to urban centres) on the nature of linkages. The sample was drawn from the units registered with the District Industries Centre (administered nationally by the SIDO) which largely covers modern, small-time, relatively independent entrepreneurs engaged in manufacturing, processing and repair activity. However, very often some of the larger small-scale units organised as factories and those in industrial development areas also get included. More recently its scope has been widening to include industry-related small service units as also the co-operativised traditional industrial units. The survey was designed to generate data on the socio-economic characteristics of the entrepreneurs, linkages of the RSSEs with the rural economy in terms of:

- labour employed and initial source of start-up funds;
- production and consumption linkages; and
- wage earnings of hired labour, earnings of the household or family enterprises and of the small-scale undertakings.

While in both the blocks the "tiny" units dominated, Malampuzha had a higher proportion of the larger units; the difference in terms of investment in plant and machinery was sharper. The differences between the two was rather sharp in terms of product structure: simple consumption goods industries based on agro and natural resources in Kollengode and "light" engineering goods industries in Malampuzha, a large number in the nature of sub- contracting units .

In terms of origin, most of the entrepreneurs were local-rural by place of birth; however in Malampuzha there was a small proportion of non-local entrepreneurs and the proportion was fairly high in the IDA units (largely from the neighbouring state of Tamil Nadu). The larger proportion of entrepreneurs came from a non-agricultural background, primarily business in Kollengode and industry in Malampuzha; the nature of activity undertaken was significantly related to the family background. In respect of the agricultural households, both the large and small cultivator households, there was a tendency to diversify into agriculture related activity. However, with growing levels of education both at the top and bottom of the agrarian structure, entry into non-agriculture related activities was also emerging. Education did broaden the horizon within which the choice of activity was made cutting across the obvious resource/caste constraint. There is certainly a potential for an inter-generational improvement in quality of entrepreneurship with a higher level of education.

A much smaller (than in a number of other empirical studies) proportion of our units in both the blocks depended almost entirely on own funds as initial capital. The larger proportion of the units were dependent both on own and borrowed funds, the latter being primarily from the formal credit market. Given the more rural character of Kollengode block, it was not surprising to find a much higher proportion of initial capital originating from agricultural surpluses, over one third compared to a little over a quarter in Malampuzha. While most of the non-agricultural source of funds was locally generated in Kollengode, earned from prior occupation in some local business (normally trading) activity, in Malampuzha it was saved and brought home by working in other similar or related industrial activity outside the region, even outside the state.

Hired workers or wage labour dominated in both the blocks. Family labour constituted less than one fifth of the workers, much lower in Malampuzha. Women workers constituted almost 48 percent of the work force in Malampuzha. All the units in Kollengode used local labour from the panchayat itself or neighbouring panchayats in the block. While this was true for the large majority of units in Malampuzha, all the units set up by non-local entrepreneurs used a certain proportion of non-local labour and this relationship between nature of entrepreneurship and use of non-local labour was statistically significant. Even a few entrpreneurs who were local in terms of origin but had some non-local connections either through marriage or business/industrial interests tended to employ non-local labour. Most of the workers in Kollengode were less than matriculates while the incidence of matriculates and those with some formal technical training was higher in Malampuzha.

The type of product and location of raw material supplies (backward production linkages) were strongly related in both Kollengode and Malampuzha despite the difference in product structure. However, while in the case of the former it was locally oriented for the latter it was strongly outward oriented given the heavy dependence of the engineering units on external sources of supply of non-agricultural raw materials. In the literature forward production linkages of RSSEs with the rural (defined as agricultural) sector (or the backward production linkages flowing from agriculture to small-scale industries) are generally found to be weak due to the urban and/or import intensiveness of most of the inputs used by agriculture. However, an interesting finding from our study was the linkages of the small industrial units with the rural service sector, like trade, hotels, educational, health and transport services. While it is not denied that the disproportionate growth of this sector reflects also an excess supply of labour, there is within it a large component which is a function of the high expenditure elasticity of demand for services and could be tapped for the purpose.

Although the proportion of units with local consumption linkages is high in both Kollengode and Malampuzha (the latter due to the larger number of service and repair units) the relationship is not statistically significant. This suggests that most units are outward oriented though the degree varies.

Our findings reveal that consumption linkages were indeed higher than production linkages as argued by Mellor in both the blocks. However, in terms of employment generated, those consumer goods units which displayed a high local orientation contributed a much smaller proportion of the employment in all such units. This was primarily because most of these units were family enterprises or smaller SSUs (2–4 workers). In terms of employment then, production linkages appeared to be more important.

However, while Kollengode was characterised by a more rural and isolated location, with predominantly agro-based enterprises set up by local, small entrepreneurs using entirely local labour, differences between the two blocks in terms of wages and earnings, growth and expansion possibilities were much lower than expected. We attempted to assess the growth potential of the RSSEs surveyed broadly in terms of (a) whether these enterprises could grow into medium or large, modern firms; and (b) by fostering adequate savings enable the entreprenur to operate a bigger unit with a better technology. This could also be achieved inter-generationally, the more educated second generation entrepreneurs setting up better organised firms with the savings generated.

Whether the first had occurred was perhaps too early to observe since our sample constituted firms set up between 1990–5. However, based on questions regarding expansion, past and future, we found considerable dynamism among the units. Though not many had expanded, less so among the family enterprises and in Kollengode, a large majority had plans to expand since they felt that the demand outlook was very positive. They were of the view that there was an increase in the purchasing power of the rural population as also an increase in business activity.

Almost two thirds of the units in Kollengode and three fourths in Malampuzha expressed a desire to expand, a very small proportion (in M) also planned to start another unit. Relating this response to the size of unit and the educational level of the entrepreneur, we found that the middle size units, 5–9 workers and matriculates and above appeared to be the most dynamic in terms of planning to expand by increasing both capital and labour. However, the general preference was for remaining within the limits of "small".

Wage rates for hired workers were indeed low in both the blocks, Rs. 40–50 for men and Rs. 15–35 for women. On average in a month the wages earned were around Rs. 450–550 for males and Rs. 350–400 for females. These figures were only slightly higher in Malampuzha though we found that a much larger proportion of workers were educated (that is matriculates). It appeared that the large female work force tended to depress the wage rate as also a crowding of small engineering units with inadequate orders and inadequate work for hired labour. Nevertheless, the level of literacy played an important role (in both the blocks) in another way. It improved the longer-term prospects of the worker, enabling him/her to procure larger increments or move up to better positions or move out to better paid employment when possible. The chances improved with some technical training together with matriculation. However, on the whole given the fact that work is certainly more regular in the small-scale units, the earnings compare favourably with the agricultural wage rate which was about the same for men but could be higher for females.

Another striking finding from the survey was that the starting wage in most of the IDA units was not very different either, from the other units: around Rs. 500–650 for males and Rs. 400–450 for females with some additional benefits. It was also stated by some of the entrepreneurs that the male workers could start earning Rs. 1000 within a year.

Earnings from self employment, that is family enterprises were certainly higher than from wage employment; the latter was primarily in the nature of a supplementary source of income while the proprietor could at least generate an income adequate to maintain a family just above the poverty line (roughly Rs.1000 a month). However, about one fifth of such enterprises in both the blocks had managed to generate a surplus or taken a loan to expand capital investment.

Those small-scale units hiring labour earned on average more than the self-employed units. While the family enterprises appear to have performed better in terms of earnings in Kollengode, small-scale units had larger surpluses after meeting all costs in Malampuzha. There was a quantum difference in the earnings of the IDA units. But what was striking was the fact that while the IDA units did pay a marginally higher amount as average wage to men and women when compared to other SSUs in Malampuzha, the enterprise earnings were in fact much higher.

8.3 Main Conclusions and Answers to the Questions Addressed in the Study

From the above we conclude that:

- the socio-economic background of the entrepreneur in terms of father's occupation does play a significant role in the decision to diversify and the choice of activity undertaken. Some familiarity with the activity in terms of experience acquired either through familial contacts or working in a related unit appears to be an essential first step in setting up a small-scale enterprise. The relative "shyness" of agricultural capital to venture into manufacturing activity has, to some extent, be understood in this context. However, the imperative for diversification does compel investment of agricultural surpluses into non-agricultural occupations which initially occurs in agriculture related activities but inter-generationally seeks wider opportunities.

- Such decisions of course are also influenced by a changing environment and emerging opportunities. Location plays an important role in determining the type of diversification and the nature of linkages generated. The emerging duality in spatial structures with the rural-small town nexus on the one hand and the urban agglomeration-rural hinterland combine on the other, implies differences in the character of rural industry and its linkages. In the former the process of growth of rural industries is relatively endogenous responding largely to extant rural conditions in which agriculture induced linkages play an important role. On the other hand in villages which become part of an urban agglomeration, the growth of small-scale enterprises tends to respond more to exogenous factors. Large urban based units often sub-contract work to small enterprises located in peripheral urban areas. Or entrepreneurs from nearby urban areas in search of cheaper land and labour set up small-scale units catering primarily to urban demand. Local manufacturing activity by independent rural producers is also generated as a spin-off from an environment of increased industrial activity. However, perhaps due to better infrastructure available in such rural areas due to proximity to big towns or the type of trading networks operating, linkages in terms of raw materials and output tend to be more outward oriented.

- As seen from the above, agricultural linkages do play a relatively more important role in inducing the growth of non-agricultural employment in far off rural areas, while urban linkages most often dominate the diversification process in contiguous rural areas However, the potential offered by the non-agricultural rural sector, in particular the fast growing tertiary sector and its demand for simple intermediate goods, needs to be given greater emphasis in respect of all rural areas. In other words there is scope for increasing the strength of local-rural linkages even in locations close to urban settlements. This does not imply viewing villages or panchayats as closed or isolated economies since Government expenditures on services, infrastructure and the agricultural sector, all of which generate rural incomes, are externally determined. Even the technological change in Mellor's agriculture-led growth strategy which is required to keep the process going is exogenously given. Rather, they should be seen as having greater flexibility in generating productive employment opportunities in the context of their own development priorities through a broader spread of interaction.

- Very few units are completely locally oriented nor does it appear necessary to be so. Indeed the well-cited advantage of rural small-scale enterprises utilising local raw materials is not so critical. If the rural industrial sector is not be excluded from the national industrial trends, there is need to go beyond the narrow set of activities in which rural areas have an advantage. It is in this context that local capital or entrepreneurship assumes importance. For in instances in which few other locational advantages exist, the psychic advantage of operating in one's own environment in the development of local economic activity beyond what is feasible with local advantages,largely redresses the place-specific disadvantages. As our survey revealed such entrepreneurship was not entirely lacking. However, the numbers of such entrepreneurs was stillv ery small. Local entrepreneurship tends to ensure higher local labour absorption as also a greater cognisance of rural demand conditions in investment decision making. In this sense perhaps it can be identified as having the strongest developmental linkage with the rural sector. Units operated by non-local entrepreneurs, for instance in industrial developmental areas, display negligible local linkages. While their raw material supplies are procured almost entirely from outside, the market location of their output is similarly outward oriented sometimes completely exported. These are also the units which tend to use non-local labour.

- On the whole the proportion of "tiny" units (that is with an investment in plant and machinery less than Rs. 500,000) is much higher in Kerala compared to all-India. However, there is considerable hetrogeniety within the small sector. The nature of activity of SSEs in terms of size and product group varies depending on location of rural areas. It tends to be smaller, particularly in terms of investment in plant and machinery and concentrated in the food-clothing-wood-bricks product groups with a higher incidence of family enterprises in the isolated rural areas. The level of education of the entrepreneur and also of the hired workers is relatively lower. In the urban periphery, there is a tendency for units to be larger, more capitalised and with a higher proportion of chemicals and engineering based industries. Levels of education among the entrepreneurs and workers are also higher. However, while units may be larger and the earnings on average higher in the latter type of location, wages paid to workers do not vary very much between the different locations. This seems to suggest that even among those small-scale entrepreneurs who have successfully embarked on the high-tech, high-quality route (proxied by investment in plant and machinery), the terms on which they employ workers are not very much better than those in other enterprises. The impact of education on earnings is more qualitative (enhancing the possibility of being employed in a more modern enterprise) and is higher in a long-run sense (improving chances of higher increments and superior status). That is what creates the urge for improving literacy levels despite relatively little immediate benefit from it.

- While the broad picture suggests that the majority of rural small-scale enterprises are of the survival type, the field survey serves to throw much greater insights into the potential sources of dynamism within it: accumulation even within family enterprises; diversification in some of the engineering units into production of components; enterprises using non-agriculture based, newer raw materials such as PVC and plastic in response to demand for new consumer goods or producing new types of agro-based products such as ready made-clothing; diversification even within the food products into packed/processed items and the response to newer demands from the tertiary sector. Above all, the tremendous urge to improve their current status and graduate out of even the "primitive self-employed" are positive tendencies. However, there was no doubt that the nature of product (in favour of modern) and size,in terms of investment in machinery and use of hired labour, are more closely associated with a better performance. The dynamism of the middle size small units, employing 5–9 workers needs to be noted. Even while the units may not grow into large-scale enterprises, they have contributed in terms of mobilisation of capital and entreprenurial experience and attempts at inter-generational improvement of household incomes. It needs to be emphasised that even the large segment of the enterprises which appear to have a limited growth potential, do play a critical role in the process of development. They provide a vital source of employment and incomes to a large number of rural households.

While the larger small-scale units in the industrial development area certainly displayed a growth potential, a large proportion having already expanded, their spread effect on the rural sector appeared to be weak. Their sourcing of raw materials and sale of output had virtually no links with the local-rural sector; even in terms of employment, there was a greater tendency to use non-local labour. However, this issue has to be examined in greater detail and as a separate study in itself.

8.4 Some Emerging Policy Suggestions

It is not intended here to review critically, the elaborate small-scale industry policy in India which has had a fairly long history of protection and promotion, nor the increasingly independent individual state policies for promoting regional industrialisation. There are several other organisations too, involved in supporting small-scale or micro enterprises with the growing relevance of informal sector activities in generating employment and incomes. We would like to point out certain aspects for intervention which derive their rationale from our findings:

- The policy on rural diversification in general and rural industry in particular has to be two pronged, involving larger agriculutral investment as also non-agricultural expenditures. In large parts of Kerala in which land based factors still dominate economic activity, there is need to raise agricultural productivity, primarily through enhanced irrigation facilities. This was brought out from the situation prevailing in Kollengode, where intensity of cropping could increase with increased availability of irrigation, which is still problematic in certain parts, despite the existence of a large dam in the area. The positive impact on rural incomes would in turn generate the "downstream" effects for further employment and income creation.

- That non-agricultural allocation expenditures should include a fair share in favour of development of infrastructure, was revealed by the growing industrial environment of rural areas on either side of the National Highway in Malampuzha. A very severe problem of infrastructure in the area is the shortage of power which has drawn considerable attention and warrants immediate action. While the growth of transportation also tends to reduce the spread effect of local-rural industrial activity, it nevertheless helps to build a base and familiarise potential entrepreneurs with possible options.

- This has to be linked to a policy of promoting indigenous entrepreneurship in which the local banks have to play a greater facilitating role. Almost all the entrepreneurs, from the tiny to those operating the larger SSEs had expressed the need for a less rigid policy on banking finance, particularly working capital loans.

- This could be done through evolving newer organisational forms which are in any case warranted to overcome the constraints on growth of the small-scale sector in Kerala: a proliferation of tiny units with simple, low capital using technologies, over-crowding in similar activities and depressing individual earnings. There is an obvious need to bring together the very scattered small capital into a more coordinated framework of rural industrialisation. Perhaps this could be done through the intermediation of local-level planning. This would involve local participation and planning on the nature of manufacturing activity to be undertaken at each level from the panchayat to the district and even higher which could then be undertaken on a larger scale.

- However, these are not simple issues even in the context of a decentralised planning framework, given the conflict in objectives between income and employment of rural industrialistion strategies. In terms of employment, rural industrialisation should generate new jobs for the unemployed and under employed rural labour force. In order to improve the standard of living, new jobs should guarantee higher earnings. However, it is feared that higher earnings would mean the use of more capital intensive techniques and therefore lower employment. It is argued that this may be so in a static sense (assuming a diminishing marginal productivity of labour). However, in a more dynamic sense with changes in productivity, aid or trade it may be possible to increase employment and income, provided an appropriate choice is made in terms of long-run growth prospects - the familiar larger investment today ensures higher growth and incomes in the future. However empirical evidence has not substantiated the argument for capital intensive techniques as being more efficient for economic growth, incomes and savings. That the latter are channelled into investment is challenged. There is no doubt that a policy of proliferation of very small enterprises using very little capital is not very useful nor is a policy which gives too much emphasis to the small-scale enterprises at the upper end of the investment limit which itself is flexible due to pressures from vested interests. The choice of course depends on the perspective of the policy makers. While it is not argued here that a commitment to maximise employment can be made without any consideration of income level, and hence the need to increase the use of capital, the preference of policy makers at present for industrial/technology parks favouring a more capital-centered strategy of small-scale industrial development, needs to be corrected. These parks meet the employment/earnings needs of a section of the work force; development policy has to keep in view the requirements of the much larger numbers constituting the rural work force.

8.4.1 Limitations of the Study

A major limitation of our study is the enterprise approach we followed to understand the nature of linkages and their market orientaion. There is need to supplement it with a household survey to examine consumption linkages in greater depth and their local-non-local character. Goods which are not being produced locally but consumed by the households would have very high non-local linkages, not captured by our study at all.

With the growing relative importance of industrial development areas and technology parks for the promotion of high-tech small and medium scale enterprises, an indepth study of the IDA in Malampuzha needs to be undertaken. However, this was not possible at the time we had undertaken the survey, since very few small-scale units had started to function. This could he taken up as a future area of research.

There is a close link between local level planning and the growth of indigenous entrepreneurship, which has been emphasised in our study. The process of such planning in Kerala, has been in operation for the last two years. It would have been very illuminating to study this linkage and its positive impact on rural industrialisation at the panchayat or block level. This also appears to be a critical area which needs to be examined in greater depth. Of particular interest is the planning and coordination between the three tiers of the decentralised administrative set-up.

Appendix A

Distribution of Total Increase in Persons Employed between 1971–91 by Industry Groups and Spatial Categories

Industry group	Rural		Small Towns		Cities/Big Med. Towns		Total	
	Absolute increase	As % of increase	Absolute increase	As % of increase	Absolute increase	As % of increase	Absolute increase	As % of increase
I. Total workers (Main)	1728665	100	143346	100	384485	100	2256496	100
1. Cultivators	−97622	−5.6	14251	9.9	1961	0.5	−81410	−3.6
2. Agricultural Labourers	182165	10.5	30611	21.4	16488	4.3	229264	10.2
3. Livestock, Fishing etc	307684	17.8	35450	24.7	28907	7.5	372041	16.5
4. Mining and Quarrying	50792	2.9	1034	0.7	1288	0.3	53114	2.4
5. All Manufacturing	175920	10.2	13169	9.1	37122	9.6	226211	10.0
i. Household	−44917	−2.6	−56	−0.04	−5702	−1.5	−50675	−2.2
ii. Non household	220837	12.8	13225	9.2	42824	11.1	276886	12.3
6. Construction	173144	10.0	7162	5.0	48417	12.7	228723	10.1
7. Trade & Commerce	370112	21.4	18083	12.6	124077	32.3	512272	22.7
8. Transport & Communication	205859	11.9	8587	6.0	54388	14.3	268834	11.9
9. Other Services	360602	20.8	15053	10.5	70837	18.4	446492	19.8

Source: Same as Table 4.1

Appendix B

Table B.1: Palakkad: Economy and Population in a Comparative Perspective

	Characteristics		Region		
			Palakkad	Kerala	Relative share
1.	Population	P	2,382,235	29,098,518	8.2
		F	1,226,413	14,809,253	8.3
	Rural Population	P	2,007,658	21,418,224	9.4
			84.3 @	73.6@@	9.5
		F	1,034893	10,905436	
			84.4@	73.6@@	
2.	Total area (hectare)'91–92		438,980	3,885,497	11.3
	Gross cropped area '91-92		343,372	3,021,116	11.4
	GCA as% of Total area		78.2	77.8	
	% of GCA irrigated		37.7	13.2	
	Forest as % of Total area		31.0	27.8	12.6
3.	Area under paddy (hectare) '89-92		146497	566990	25.8
4.	Paddy production (tonnes) ('89–92)		332,819	1,095,670	30.4
5.	Total work force 1991		786,363	8,301,087	9.5
	Agriclture %		59.9	46,9	
	Manufacturing %		10.8	14.2	
	Construction %		2.3	4.0	
	Service %[1]		26.5	33.8	
6.	Registered factories ('91)		3883	55427	7.0
7.	Small-Scale Units$ (87-88) No.		2066	25717	8.0
	Employment		12,396	169,309	7.3
	Rural (%)		78.2	70.4	
8.	Literacy rate	P	81.3	89.2	
		F	75.7	85.8	
9.	Share of Agriculture in SDP** ('91)		40.0	36.2	
10.	Per Capita SDP (Rs) ('91) (at 80-1 prices)		1750	2023	

Source: 1. Statistics for Planning, State Planning Board, 1995; Statistics of Rural Development in Kerala, Commisionerate of Rural Development, Thiruvananthapuram 1995.

Notes: 1. Includes trade & commerce, transport and communication and other services.

2. $ These figures are taken from the 1987–88 Census on Small-scale Industries and exclude the closed units; @ As percent of district population. @@ as per cent of state population. ** State Domestic Product.

Table B.2: Basic Data on the Two Selected Blocks

Characteristics		Block	
		Kollengode	Malampuzha
Population		119886	200281
Workers		62337	74641
Total area (hectare) '89-92		18225	39203
Total cropped area (hectare)'89-92		11412	8013 @
Paddy output as % of district total		18.6	#
% of workers in*			
Agriculture		60.2	52.1
Manufacturing		10.1	17.1
Construction		2.1	2.8
Trade, commerce, transport and communication		14.4	14.9
Other services		9.4	10.2
Literacy rate	P	64.0	67.9
	F	57.7	61.5
No. of panchayats		5	8
Average population size of a panchayat		23977	25035

Source: 1. Statistics of Rural Development in Kerala, Commissionerate of Rural Development, Thiruvananthapuram, Kerala 1995; Kerala Economic Review, State Planning Board, Government of Kerala 1996; Block Level Agricultural Statistics, Department of Economics and Statistics, Thiruvananthapuram, 1995.

Notes: @ The proportion of area under forests is much higher in Malampuzha.

* Percentages do not add upto 100 since only major industry groups are given.

\# No separate figures are available on paddy production for Malampuzha. However that it would be much lower is suggested by the low percentage of cropped area. The relative share of Kollengode block is the highest in the district.

P - persons; F - females

Appendix C

CENTRE FOR DEVELOPMENT STUDIES

TRIVANDRUM 695 011

SURVEY ON RURAL SMALL SCALE INDUSTRIES

I. General Information

1. Name of Unit and Address					
2. Village		Panchayat		Block	
3. When set up			4. Ownership Type (1–5)		

1. Proprietorship 2. Partnership 3. Cooperative 4. Compand 5. Any other

5. Name of Owner		M/F	6. Age	
7. Is the unit located in/next to the house			Yes/No	
8. If no, where is it located				
9. Product(s) produced				
10. Nature of activity	☐ Manufacturing ☐ Assembling ☐ Service ☐ Repair ☐ Job-work			
11. Main source of energy	☐ No power Reqd ☐ Electricity ☐ Firewood ☐ Others			

II. Socio Economic Characteristics of the Entrepreneur

1. Did you start this enterprise	Yes/No	2. If No, who did	
3. Prior occupation of entrepreneur		4. Father's occupation	
5. Reasons for starting this enterprise	☐ Continuing father's work ☐ Unable to get desired/any job ☐ Do not want agricultural work ☐ Hope to earn higher income ☐ Want to set up own enterprise ☐ Need to earn supplementary income		
6. If supplementary, state main source of income (occupation code)			
7. Reasons for choosing this product line	☐ Good demand exists ☐ Have some skill ☐ Needs very little skill ☐ Low capital requirement ☐ Local raw material available		
8. Reasons for choosing this location	☐ It is your own home ☐ Land is relatively cheap ☐ Labour is cheap ☐ Has necessary infrastructure		
9. If not your Birth place, reasons for the choice	☐ Land is relatively cheap ☐ Labour is cheap ☐ Has necessary infrastructure		
10. Educational level of owner (general)		Technical	

Occupation Code
1. Unemployed 2. Agricultural Labourer 3. Farmer
4. Construction worker 5. Working in Traditional Industry 6. Employed in s/med/l industry
7. Owner of small unit/shop 8. Transport 9. Other services.

Education Code
General: 1. No education 2. Upto primary level 3. Upto middle level
4. Upto matric 5. Higher education (specify)
Technical: 1. Formal like ITI etc 2. As an apprentice 3. Attended training programme
4. Experience in similar industry

III. Linkages

A. Financial linkages

1. Total capital employed (Rs)

			Initial amount	As of now
i.	Fixed capital	a. Land & Building		
		b. Machinery & Equipment		
ii.	Working capital			

2.	Major items of capital equipment	i	
	(specify)	ii	
		iii	
3.	Are they new or were bought second hand		
4.	If second hand, reasons		
5.	Where did you procure this equipment		(L.C)
6.	How did you procure the equipment		☐ Directly from producer (small/large industry) ☐ Small/big shops in market ☐ Through a trader
7.	Any upgradation of capital equipment		

8. Source of capital

i.	Own savings	Rs.	☐ From agriculture	☐ Past Job (specify what/where)
ii.	Relations (same village/outside)	Rs.	☐ From agriculture	☐ Other Occupation (what/where)
iii.	Banks	Rs.	☐ (location)	
iv.	Government	Rs.	(specify scheme)	
v.	Big units	Rs.	☐ (location)	
vi.	Wholesalers/Traders/Middlemen	Rs.	☐ (location)	
vii.	NGOs	Rs.	☐ (location)	
viii.	Any other	Rs.	☐ (location)	

9. In case of expansion, how were funds generated? ☐ Internal savings ☐ Borrowings (specify)

-Location code (L.C.)
1-Location village 2-Other of panchayat 3-Within block 4-Nearest town/any other town/city
5-Within district 6-Other parts of state 7-Outside state

		Proprietor & Family		Hired		Apprentice		Any other	
1. Number	M	Now	Initially	Now	Initially	Now	Initially	Now	Initially
	F								
	T								
2. Regular	M								
	F								
Casual	M								
	F								
2a. Production	M								
	F								
Administration	M								
	F								
3. Not paid	F								
	F								
Paid	M								
	F								
4. Payment mode (code)	M								
	F								
5. Educn. level (code)	M								
	F								
6. Place of origin (LC)	M								
	F								
7. Prior occupation (cd)	M								
	F								

-Payment mode 1-Piece rate 2-Daily 3-Weekly 4-Monthly
-Prior occupation 1-Unemployed 2-Engaged in agriculture 3-Engaged in non-agriculture

8. If all/some workers are non local reasons there of ☐ Technically More qualified ☐ It is cheaper ☐ More Docile
9. What is the Average wage/day ☐
   Highest wage/day ☐
   Local casual wage/day ☐
   Local agricultural wage/day ☐

10. Can the earnings of a male worker in your unit support a family? ☐ Yes ☐ No

III. C. Raw materials (and other inputs) linkages

1. Raw materials used ☐ Agricultural
   ☐ Others
2. Other inputs (specify) ☐ i
   ☐ ii
   ☐ iii
3. Where are these raw materials procured from? (location code) ☐
4. Where are the other inputs procured from? (location code) ☐

5.	Do you procure the raw mats/other inputs	☐ Directly from producer (farmer, SS/LS inds) ☐ Wholesale/retail shops ☐ Trader/middleman
6.	If latter, state the reasons	☐ Has knowledgde of the sources ☐ Provides credit
7.	Did you try to procure materials yourself since	☐ Trader adds to your cost ☐ He controls the price
8.	If raw material/other inputs available locally, reasons for procuring from outside	☐ It is cheaper ☐ Can be bought on credit ☐ is a decision of the trader
9.	If an ancillary how do you procure raw mats/other inputs?	☐ From parent unit ☐ Yourself (how? see Q5)
10.	If doing subcontracting/job work, how do you procure materials?	☐ From parent unit ☐ Yourself (how? see Q.5)
11.	Is raw material available	☐ Through the year ☐ Only for some months (no.) ☐ Price fluctuates too much

III. D. Consumption Linkages (Consumer goods)

1.	Demand for your goods comes from (location code)	☐
2.	Do you export?	☐ Yes ☐ No
3.	If yes, destination, quantity and market channel	
4.	Locally who are your consumers?	☐ Rich farm households ☐ Poor farm households ☐ Rich non farm households ☐ Poor non farm households
5.	Do you make things on order	☐ Yes ☐ No
6.	If yes, is it with	☐ Local wholesalers/traders ☐ Non local Wholesalers/traders (specify) ☐ Others-local ☐ Non local (specify)
7.	Do you market your product yourself?	☐ Yes ☐ No
8.	If yes is it	☐ Directly to consumers ☐ To local wholesalers/retailers ☐ To non local wholesalers/retailers (specify)
9.	If No, do you depend on	☐ A trader (local/non loc) ☐ Middleman (local/non loc)
10.	Would you prefer to market on your own because	☐ Trader cuts into your profit ☐ Does not pay you on time
11.	What prevents you from marketing on your own?	☐ Lack of money ☐ Insufficient market knowledge ☐ Difficult to compete with trader
12.	Does your product face competition?	☐ Yes ☐ No
13.	If Yes is it from	☐ Other local small units ☐ Med/large local units ☐ Non local small units ☐ Non local med/large units

III. E. Forward production linkages (producer goods)

1. Who uses your product ? ☐ Agricultural sector ☐ Industry ☐ Construction ☐ Other sectors

2. Within agriculture is it ☐ Local small farmers ☐ Local med/large farmers ☐ Non local small farmers ☐ Non local med/large farmers

3. Within industry is it ☐ Other local small units ☐ Local medium/large units ☐ Non local small units ☐ Non-local medium/large units

4. Within construction is it purchased ☐ Locally ☐ By non local users

5. Do you have a subcontracting arrangement with ☐ Local med/large units ☐ Non local med/large unis

6. Describe the nature of this agreement

IV. Performance data

1.	Production capacity (units or value)	In a month	Qty	Value Rs
		Last year	Qty	Value Rs.
2.	Working days in a year			
3.	Total output (actual)	In a month	Qty	Value Rs.
		Last year	Qty	Value Rs.
4.	Total costs (Rs)	a. Raw material	In a month	Last year
		b. Power		
		c. Packing materials		
		d. Other costs (incl. sales ex)		
		e. Interest		
		f. Capital service cost		
5.	How much are you able to make after meeting all costs			
6.	What would remain after deducting cost of hired labour			

7. Do you think demand for your product ☐ Has grown in the past year (why) ☐ Has remained steady (why) ☐ Has declined (why)

8. Market location of increased demand (location code)

9. What are your future plans
   - ☐ To expand production
     (a) with existing cap and lab
     (b) increase both
   - ☐ To diversify into new products
   - ☐ To start another units
   - ☐ Happy with present business

10. What are the main problems in expanding/maintaining your business?
   - ☐ Difficulty of raising finance
   - ☐ Uncertainty of raw materials
   - ☐ Problems of marketing
   - ☐ Not enough training available
   - ☐ Rural infrastructure inadequate

11. Are you aware of govt policies for SSI? ☐ Yes ☐ No

12. Have you availed of the concessions?

13. What should be done to make them more effective?

References

Acs, Z. J., Carlsson, B. and Thurik, R. (1996): *Small Business in the Modern Economy*, Cambridge, Massachusetts: Blackwell Publishers.

Ahammed, C. S. and Herdt, R. W. (1984): Measuring the Impact of Consumption Linkages on the Employment Effects of Mechanisation in Philippine Rice Production, *Journal of Development Studies*, 20 (2).

Ahluwalia, M. S. (1978): Rural Poverty and Agricultural Performance in India, *Journal of Development Studies*, 14 (3).

Aiya, V. Nagam (1906): *The Trvancore State Manual*, Vol. 111, Government Press, Thiruvananthapuram.

A. K. G. Centre for Research and Studies (1994): *International Congress on Kerala Studies, Abstracts*, Volumes 1 to 4 and Supplementary Volumes, Thiruvananthapuram.

Alice Albin (1988): Manufacturing Sector in Kerala: A Study of Scale, Structure and Growth, *M.Phil Thesis*, Jawaharlal Nehru University, New Delhi.

Anderson, L. and Leiserson, M. W. (1980): Rural Non-farm Employment in Developing Countries, *Economic Development and Cultural Change*, 28 (2).

Anderson, D. (1982): Small Scale Industry in Developing Countries: A Discussion of Issues, *World Development*, 10 (11).

Bagachwa M. D. and Stewart, F. (1990): Rural Industries and Rural Linkages in Sub- Saharan Africa: A Survey, *Development Studies Working Paper No. 23*, Queen Elizabeth House: Oxford.

Baker, Thomas N. (1994): First Movers and the Growth of Small Industry in North eastern Italy, *Comparative Studies in Society and History*, 36 (4).

Bandyopadhyay, D. (1997): People's Participation in Planning, Kerala Experiment, *Economic and Political Weekly*, 32 (39).

Banerjee, D. and Ghosh, A. (1988): Indian Planning and Regional Disparity in Growth, in Bagchi, A.K. (ed), *Economy, Polity and Society: Essays in Political Economy of Indian Planning, In Honour of Prof. B. Datta*, Oxford University Press, Calcutta.

Banerjee, N. (1988): The Unorganised Sector and the Planner, in Bagchi, A. K. (ed) *Economy, Polity and Society: Essays in Political Economy of Indian Planning, in Honour of Prof. B.*

Datta, Oxford University Press, Calcutta.

Bar-el, R. (1984): Rural Industrialisation Objectives: The Income-Employment Conflict, *World Development*, 12 (2)

Bar-el, R. and Felsenstein, D. (1990): Entrepreneurship and Rural Industrialisation: Comparing Urban and Rural Patterns of Locational Choice in Israel, *World Development*, 18 (2).

Basant, R. and Kumar, B. L. (1988): Rural Non-agricultural Activities in India: A Review of Available Evidence: *Working Paper* No. 20, Gujarat Institute of Development Research.

Bell, C., Hazell, P. and Slade, R. (1982): *Project Evaluation in Regional Perspective: A Study of an Irrigation Project in Northwest Malaysia*, John Hopkins University Press, World Bank, Baltimore and London.

Berry, A. (1987): The Limited Role of Rural Small-Scale Manufacturing for Late-comers: Some Hypotheses on the Colombian Experience, *Journal of Latin American Studies*, 19 (2).

Berry, A., Cortes, M. and Ishaq, A. (1990): On the Dynamism of Small and Medium Industry in Colombia: Some Possible Lessons, in Stewart, F., *et al.* (ed.), *The Other Policy*, IT Publications, London.

Bhaduri, A. (1992): Alternative Development Strategies and the Rural Sector, in Singh, A. and Tabatabai, H. (eds), *The World Economic Crisis and Agriculture in the Third World in the Eighties: The Changing Role of Agriculture in Economic Development*, Geneva: International Labour Organisation: 149-178.

Bhalla, S. (1985): Work Force Structure 1981: The Turning of the Tide, in Mishra, G. P. (ed) *Regional Structure of Development and Growth in India*, Vol. 1.

Bharadwaj, K. (1982): Regional Differentiation in India: A Note, *Economic and Political Weekly*, Annual Number, 17 (14–16).

_________ (1987): Analytics of Agriculture-Industry Relation, *Economic and Political Weekly*, 22 (19,20,21).

_________ (1989): The Formation of Rural Labour Markets: An Analysis with Special Reference to Asia, *Working Paper* ILO/ARTEP: Geneva.

Bhat, P. N. Mari and Rajan,S. Irudaya (1990): Demographic Transition in Kerala Revisited, *Economic and Political Weekly*, 25 (35–36).

Bhattacharya, B. B. and Mitra, A. (1993): Employment and Structural Adjustment, A Look at 1991 Census Data, *Economic and Political Weekly*, 28 (38).

Boomgard, J. J. et al (1992): A Subsector Approach to Small Enterprise Development, *World Development*, 20 (2)

Breman, J. (1985): *Of Peasants, Migrants and Paupers:Rural Labour Circulation and Capitalist Production in West India*, Delhi: Oxford University Press.

Bryceson, D. F. (1996): Deagrarianisation and Rural Employment in Sub Saharan Africa: A

Sectoral Perspective, *World Development*, 24 (1)

Byrd, W. A. and Qingsong, L. (1990): China's Rural Industry: An Introduction, in (eds) Byrd, W. A. and Qingsong, L. *China's Rural Industry, Structure, Development and Reform*, Washington D.C: World Bank.

Byres, T (1991): The Agrarian Question and the Differing Forms of Capitalist Agrarian Transformation: An Essay with reference to Asia, Paper in Bremen and Mundle (eds). *Rural Transformation in Asia*, Delhi: Oxford University Press.

Cagatay, N (1997): Macro Economic Policy and Poverty Reduction, paper prepared for the UNRISD/UNDP/CDS *Workshop on Gender, Poverty and Well-Beging*, Thiruvananthapuram, 24–27 November.

Cartillier, M. (1975): Role of Small-scale Industries in Economic Development, Irrigation Pumpsets in Coimbatore, *Economic and Political Weekly*, November 1.

Casinader, R. (1994): Enigma of Kerala Spatial Formations: Gragara as an Invalidation/Recovery of the Desakota Hypothesis, AKG Centre for Research and Studies, International Congress on Kerala Studies, *Abstracts*, Vol 2.

Centre for Development Studies (1975): *Poverty, Unemployment and Development Policy: A Case Study of Selected Issues with Reference to Kerala*, New York, United Nations. .

Census of India, 1991 (1996): *Availability of Infrastructural Facilities in Rural Areas of Kerala - An Analysis of Village Directory Data*, Office of the Registrar General, New Delhi.

Centre for Monitoring Indian Economy (1993): *Performance of Agriculture by Major States, 1967-68 to 1991-92*, August, Bombay.

Chadha, G. K. (1986): Agricultural Growth and Rural Non Farm Activities: An Analysis of Indian Experience, in (eds) *Rural Industrialisation And Non Farm Activities of Asian Farmers*, Korea Rural Economics Institute: Asian and Pacific Development Centre.

Chakravarty, S. (1977): Reflections on the Growth Process in the Indian Economy, in Wadhwa, C. D. (ed)., *Some Problems of India's Economic Policy*, Bombay.

__________ (1987): *Development Planning: The Indian Experience*, Oxford: Clarendon Press.

Chandavarkar, R. (1985): Industrialisation in India before 1947: Conventional Approaches and Alternative Perspectives,*Modern Asian Studies*, Vol. 19 (3).

Chandrasekhar, C. P. (1993): Agrarian Change and Occupational Diversification: Non Agricultural Employment and Rural Development In West Bengal, *Journal of Peasant Studies*, 20 (2) January.

Chuta, E. and Liedholm, C. (1985): *Employment and Growth in Small Scale Industries: Empirical Evidence and Policy Assessment for Sierra Leone*, London: Macmillan Press Ltd.

Clarkson, L. A. (1985): *Proto-Industrialisation: the First Phase of Industrialisation?* London: Macmillan Publishers.

Davies, S. P., Mead, D. C., Seale, J. L. (1992): Small Manufacturing Enterprises in Egypt,

Economic Development and Cultural Change, 40 (2).

Deb, N. C. and Hossain, M. (1984): Demand for Rural Industries Products in Bangladesh, *The Bangladesh Development Studies*, XII (189).

Delgado, C., Hazell, P., Hopkins, J. and Kelly, V. (1994): Promoting Intersectoral Growth Linkages in Rural Africa through Agricultural Technology and Policy Reform, *American Journal of Agricultural Economics*, 76.

Development Commissioner, Small-Scale Industries, Ministry of Industry (1992): *Report on the Second All-India Census of Small-scale Industrial Units (Regd. upto 31st March, 1988)*, Kerala, Directorate of Industries, Thiruvananthapuram.

Government of Kerala (1958): *Second Five Year Plan: 1956-61*, Kerala.

———— (1969): *Fourth Five Year Plan, 1969-74*, Government Press, Thiruvananthapuram.

———— (1976): Kerala District Gazetteer, *Palghat*.

———— State Planning Board (1988): Formulation of Eighth Five Year Plan (1990-95), *Task Force on Agriculture*, Agriculture Division,Thiruvananthapuram.

———— (1989): *State Gazetteer* (Vol.III).

———— State Planning Board (1993; 1995; 1996; 1998): *Economic Review*, 1992, 1994, 1995 and 1997, Thiruvananthapuram.

———— Department of Economics and Statistics (1995): *Block Level Agricultural Statistics, Kerala*, Thiruvananthapuram.

———— Commissionerate for Rural Development (1995): *Statistics of Rural Development in Kerala*, Thiruvananthapuram.

Dunham, D. (1991): Agricultural Growth and Rural Industry: Some Reflections on the Rural Growth Linkages Debate, *Working Paper Series No. 14*, The Hague: Institute of Social Studies.

Eapen, M. (1994): Non Farm Employment in Kerala: A Study in Rural Transformation, Report (unpublished) submitted to IDPAD (3rd phase) New Delhi and The Hague.

———— (1994a): Employment and Unemployment in Kerala, Some Recent Trends, Paper presented at *One Day Workshop on Employment and Unemployment Trends in Kerala with Special Reference to the Eighth Five Year Plan*, January 17.

———— (1994b): Rural Non Agricultural Employment in Kerala: Some Emerging Tendencies, *Economic and Political Weekly*, 29 (21).

———— (1995): Rural Non Agricultural Employment in Kerala: Inter District Variations, *Economic and Political Weekly*, 30 (12).

Fei, J. C. H. and Ranis, R. (1964): *Development of the Labour Surplus Economy, Theory and Policy*, Illinois: Homewood.

Franke, R. W. and Chassin, B. H. (1991): Kerala State, India: Radical Reform as Development,

Monthly Review, 42 (8).

________ (1993): *Life is a Little Better: Redistribution as a Development Strategy in Nadur Village, Kerala*, Conflict and Social Change Series, Boulder and Oxford: Westview Press.

Gadgil, V. N. (1964): Notes on Rural Industrialisation, *Artha Vijnana*, 6 (1).

George, K. K. (1993): *Limits to Kerala Model of Development*, Centre for Development Studies, Thiruvananthapuram.

George, T. and Joseph T. (1992): Rubber Based Industrialisation in Kerala: An Assessment of Missed Linkages, *Economic and Political Weekly*, 27 (1–2).

George, T. and Kumar M. (1996): Rubber Products Manufacturing Sector in Kerala: A Note on Priorities and Strategies, Paper presented at a *Seminar on Industrialisation in Kerala*, Centre for Development Studies, Thiruvananthapuram.

Grosh, B. and Somolekae, G. (1996): Mighty Oaks from Little Acorns:Can Microenterprise Serve as the Seedbed of Industrialisation? *World Development*, 24 (12).

Goldar, B. (1988): Relative Efficiency of Modern Small-Scale Industries in India, in Suri, K. B. (ed) *op cit.*

Gulati, I. S. and Mody, A. (1983): Remittances of Indian Migrants to the Middle East: An Assessment with Special Reference to Migrants from Kerala, *Working Paper No. 182*, Centre for Development Studies, Thiruvananthapuram.

Gulati, I. S. and Narayanan, N. K. (1994): Financial Constraints to Kerala's Economic Development, in AKG Centre for Research and Studies, *Abstracts*, Vol. 2.

Habib, I. (1995): Capitalism in History, *Social Scientist*, 23 (7–9).

Haggblade, S., Hazell, P. and Brown, J. (1989): Farm-Nonfarm Linkages in Rural Sub- Saharan Africa, *World Development*, 17 (8).

Harris, B. (1987a): Regional Growth Linkages from Agriculture and Resource Flows in Non Farm Economy, *Economic and Political Weekly*, 22 (1 & 2).

________ (1987b): Regional Growth Linkages from Agriculture, *Journal of Development Studies*, 23 (2).

Harriss, B and Harriss, J. (1984): "Generative" or "Parasitic" Urbanism?Some Observations from the Recent History of a South Indian Market Town, *Journal of Development Studies*, 20 (3).

Harriss-White, B. (1996): Diversity and Diversification in Rural Northern Tamil Nadu, paper presented at Dissemination Workshop on *Adjustment and Development: Agrarian Change, Markets and Social Welfare in South India*, held in MIDS, March 27-29.

Harriss-White, B. and Janakrajan, S. (1997): From Green Revolution to Rural Industrial Revolution in South India, *Economic and Political Weekly*, 32 (30).

Harris, J. (1991): Agriculture/Non Agriculture Linkages and the Diversification of Rural Economic Activity, in (eds) Breman, J.and Mundle, S., *Rural Transformation in Asia*, Delhi: OUP.

Hart, G. (1989): The Growth Linkages Controversy: Some Lessons from the Muda Case, *Journal of Development Studies*, 25 (4).

Hazell, Peter B.R. and Roell, A. (1983): Rural Growth Linkages: Household Expenditure Patterns in Malaysia and Nigeria, *Research Report No. 41, International Food Policy Research Institute*: Washington, D.C.

Hazell, Peter B. R. and Slade, R. (1987): Regional Growth Linkages from Agriculture: A Reply, *Journal of Development Studies*, 23 (2).

Hazell, Peter B. R. and Hojjati, B. (1995): Farm/Non Farm Growth Linkages in Zambia, *Journal of African Economies*, 4 (3).

Hirschman, A. O. (1958): *The Strategy of Economic Development*, New Haven: Yale University Press.

Ho, S. P. S. (1979): Decentralised Industrialisation and Rural Development: Evidence from Taiwan, *Economic Development and Cultural Change*, 28 (1).

———— (1980): Small Scale Enterprises in Korea and Taiwan, *World Bank Staff Working Paper No. 384*, Washington D.C.: World Bank.

Hoselitz, B. F. (1959): Small Industry in Underdeveloped Countries, *Journal of Economic History*, 19 (4).

Hossain, M., Rahman, M., Bayes, A. (1994): *Rural Non-farm Economy in Bangladesh: A Dynamic Sector or a Sponge for Absorbing Surplus Labour?*, SAAT, New Delhi: ILO

Hudson, P. (1986): *The Genesis of Industrial Capital*, Cambridge University Press, Cambridge.

Innes, C. A. (Evans, F. B. ed) (1951): *Malabar*, Madras.

Ishikawa, S. (1962): A Comparison of Size Structure of Indian and Japanese Manufacturing Industrie, *The Historical Journal of Economics*, 2 (2).

Islam, R. (ed) (1987): *Rural Industrialisation and Employment in Asia*, New Delhi: ILO/ARTEP.

Issac, T. M., Thomas and Tharakan, P. K. M. (1986): An Enquiry into the Historical Roots of Industrial Backwardness of Kerala- A Study of the Travancore Region, *Working Paper No. 215*, Centre for Development Studies, Thiruvananthapuram.

Issac, T. M. Thomas, Reddy, R. M. and Duvvry, N. (1992): Regional Terms of Trade for the State of Kerala, *Working Paper No. 247*, Centre for Development Studies, Thiruvananthapuram.

Issac, T. M. Thomas (1993): Economic Consequences of the Gulf Crisis: A Study of India with Special Reference to Kerala, in Wickramasekara, P. (ed) *The Gulf Crisis and South Asia, Studies on the Economic Impact*, UNDP and ARTEP, New Delhi.

_________ (1997): Economic Consequences of Gulf Migration, in Zachariah and Rajan, S. Irudaya (ed) *Kerala's Demographic Transition: Its Determinants and Consequences*, Sage, New Delhi.

Jacob, P. (1986): Concept of Work and Estimates of the Workforce, *Sarvekshana*, 9 (4).

Jayaraj, D. (1996): Structural Transformation of the Rural Work Force in Tamil Nadu: An Analysis of the Impact of Sociological Factors, paper presented in *Workshop* on Adjustment and Development: Agrarian Change, Markets and Social Welfare in South India, 1973-93, March 27-29 1996: Madras Institute of Development Studies.

Johnston, Bruce F. and Kilby, P. (1975): *Agriculture and Structural Transformation, Economic Strategies in Late- Developing Countries*, New York: Oxford University Press.

Jose, A. V. (1980): Agricultural Labour in Kerala: A Historical cum Statistical Analysis, *Ph.D Thesis*, University of Kerala, Thiruvananthapuram.

_________ (1994): Social Policy towards Wage Determination: Some Lessons from the Indian States, AKG Centre for Research and Studies, International Congress on Kerala Studies, *Abstracts*, Vol.2.

Jose, S. (1991): Group Farming in Kerala , An Illustrative Study, *M.Phil Thesis*, Jawaharlal Nehru University, New Delhi.

Kabir, M. and Krishnan, T. N. (1991): Social Intermediation and Health Transition: Lessons from Kerala, paper prepared for a seminar on "*Health and Development in India*" jointly sponsored by the National Council of Applied Economic Research and Harvard University Centre for Population and Development Studies, held in New Delhi from 2 to 4 January 1992.

Kaldor, K. (1960): *Essays on Economic Growth and Stability*, London: Duckworth.

Kalecki, M. (1972): Problems of Financing Economic Development in a Mixed Economy, in *Selected Essays on the Economic Growth of the Socialist and the Mixed Economy*, Cambridge: CUP.

Kannan, K. P. and Pushpangadan, K. (1988): Agricultural Stagnation and Economic Growth in Kerala: An Exploratory Analysis, *Working Paper No. 227*, Centre for Development Studies.

Karshenas, M. (1992): Intersectoral Resource Flows and Development: Lessons of Past Experience, in Singh and Tabatabai (eds) *op cit*.

Kashyap, S. P. (1988): Growth of Small Enterprises in India: Its Nature and Content, *World Development*, 16 (6).

(KITCO) Kerala Industrial and Technology Consultancy Organisation (1994): *Industrial Potential of Palakkad District*, study prepared for the Government of Kerala.

(KRP), Centre for Development Studies, (1997): Kerala Research Programme on Local Level Development, *Annual Report 1995-96*, Thiruvananthapuram.

Krishnaji, N. (1979): Agrarian Relations and the Left Movement in Kerala, A Note on Recent

Trends, *Working Paper No. 80*, Centre for Development Studies, Thiruvananthapuram.

———— (1993): Widening Distances: State Domestic Product Variations, 1961-81, in Bardhan, P., Datta-Chaudhari, M and Krishnan, T. N. (eds), *Development and Change: Essays in Honour of Dr. K. N. Raj*, Oxford University Press, Bombay.

———— (1994): Food Security, AKG Centre for Research and Studies, *Abstracts*, Vol. 1.

Krishnamurty, J. (1971): The Industrial Distribution of the Working Force in India: 1901-61: A Study of Selected Aspects, *Ph.D Thesis*, University of Delhi.

———— (1984): Changes in the Indian Work Force, *Economic and Political Weekly*, 19 (50), December 15.

Krishnan, T. N. (1991): Wages, Employment and Output in Interrelated Labour Markets in an Agrarian Economy, A Study of Kerala, *Economic and Political Weekly*, 26 (26).

———— (1994): *Social Intermediation and Human Development, Kerala State, India; A Retrospective Study*, 1960–1993, Study Prepated for the World Summit on Social Development, UNICEF.

Kundu, A. and Raza, M. (1982): *Indian Economy - The Regional Dimension*, Centre for Study of Regional Development, Jawaharlal Nehru University (JNU), New Delhi.

Kurien, C. T. (1994): Kerala's Development Experience: Random Comments About the Past and Some Considerations for the Future, in AKG Centre for Research and Studies, International Congress on Kerala Studies, *Abstracts*, Vol. 1, Thiruvananthapuram.

———— Kurien, J. (1994): The Kerala Model: The Central Tendency and the Outlier, AKG Centre for Research and Studies, International Congres on Kerala Studies, *Abstracts*, Vol.2.

Lewis, W. A. (1954): Economic Development with Unlimited Supplies of Labour, *The Manchester School of Economic and Social Studies*, 22 (2): 131-91.

———— (1978): *The Evolution of the International Economic Order*, Princeton: Princeton University Press.

Liedholm, D. and Mead, C. (1987): Small Scale Industries in Developing Countries: Empirical Evidence and Policy Implications, *MSU International Development Paper No. 9*, East Lansing: Michigan State University.

Lindert, P. van and Verkoren, O. (eds) (1997): *Small Towns and Beyond: Rural Transformation and Small Urban Centres in Latin America*, Amsterdam: Thela Publishers.

Lipton, M. (1968): Strategy for Agriculture: Urban Bias and Rural Planning, in Streeten, P. and Lipton, M. (eds): *The Crisis of Indian Planning*, London: Oxford University Press.

———— (1984): Family, Fungibility, and Formality: Rural Advantages of Informal Non-farm Enterprises versus the Urban-formal State, in Amin, S. (ed). *Human Resources, Employment and Development, Vol.5, Developing Countries*: Macmillan.

Little, I. M. D., Mazumdar, D., Page, Jr., J. M. (1987): *Small Manufacturing Enterprises, A Comparative Analysis of India and Other Economies*, World Bank: Oxford University

Press.

Logan, W. (1906): *Manual of the Malabar District*, Vol. 1.

Lokanathan, P. S. (1961): Industrialisation: Kerala's Need Greater, in Pillai (ed), *Planning for Prosperity in Kerala*, Malayali Association, Delhi.

Mahadevan, R. (1988): Some Aspects of Pattern of Industrial Investment and Entrepreneurhip in Travancore During the 1930's and 1940's, in Rao, G.N. *et al.* (ed) *The South Indian Economy*, Oxford University Press.

Mahalanobis, P. C. (1953): Some Observations on the Process of Growth of National Income, *Sankhya: The Indian Journal of Statistics*, 12 ( ):307-312.

Marx, K (1961): *Capital*, Vol. 1, Moore-Aveling tr., Progress Publishers, Moscow.

Mathew, V. (1996) :Kerala's New Investment Destination-Palakad, Business Line, March 19.

Mead, D. C. (1991): Small Enterprises and Development, *Economic Development and Cultural Change*

Mellor, J. W. (1976): *The New Economics of Growth: A Strategy for India and the Developing Countries*, Ithaca: Cornell University Press.

Mendels, Franklin F. (1972): Proto-Industrialisation: The First Phase of the Industrialisation Process, *Journal of Economic History*, 32 (1): 241-261.

Menon, Dilip, M. (1994): *Caste, Nationalism and Communism in South India: Malabar 1900–48*, Cambridge University Press.

Menon, S. (1967): *A Survey of Kerala History*, National Book Stall, Kottayam, Kerala.

Mohan, Ram, K. T. and Raman, R. (1992): Of Cochin Stock Exchange and What it Means, *Economic and Political Weekly*, 25 (1).

Mukhopadhyaya, S.and Lim, C. P. (1985): *Development and Diversification of Rural Industries in Asia*, Kuala Lampur: Asian and Pacific Development Centre.

Mundle, S. (1985): The Agrarian Barrier to Industrial Growth, *Journal of Development Studies*, 22 (1).

Nagaraj, R. (1985a): Trends in Factory Size in Indian Industry, 1950-80, Some Tentative Inferences, *Economic and Political Weekly*, 20 (8).

_________ (1985b): Some Aspects of Small Scale Industries in India, Findings Based on Two all-India Sample Surveys, Parts 1 and 2, *Economic and Political Weekly*, 20 (41 & 42).

Nair, P. R. G. (1986): *Asian Migration to the Arab World, Migration from Kerala, India*, Centre for Development Studies, Thiruvananthapuram.

_________ (1989): Incidence, Impact and Implications of Migration to the Middle East from Kerala, in Ahmed, R. (ed) *To the Gulf and Back*, ILO-ARTEP, New Delhi.

———— (1994): Broad Trends in Migration to the Middle East: A Note, in AKG Centre for Research and Studies, *Abstracts*, Vol. 2.

Nair, Shyamsundaran K. N. (1994): Constraints to Kerala's Agricultural Development, or What Ails Kerala's Agriculture, AKG Centre for Research and Studies, International Congress on Kerala Studies, *Abstracts*, Vol 2.

Namboodiripad, E. M. S. (1961): Third Plan for Kerala, in Pillai (ed), *Planning for Prosperity in Kerala*, Malayali Association, Delhi.

Nanjudan, S. (1994): Changing Role of Small Scale Industry, International Influences, Country Experiences and Lessons for India, *Economic and Political Weekly*, 29 (22).

Narayána, D. (1990): Agricultural Economy of Keralain the Post-Seventies: Stagnation or Cycles, *Working Paper No. 235*, Centre for Development Studies.

National Bank for Agriculture and Rural Development (NABARD) (1995): *Potential Linked Credit Plan, Palakkad District, 1996-7 Update*, Thiruvananthapuram.

National Sample Survey Organisation (1983): 32nd Round, *Second Quinquennial Survey on Employment*, Report No. 298/10, July.

———— (1990): *Key Results of Employment and Unemployment Survey:All-India*, NSS 43rd Round (July 1987-June 1988), New Delhi.

———— (1996): *Key Results of Employment and Unemployment Survey*, 50th Round (July 1993-June 1994), New Delhi.

Nurkse, R. (1953): *Problems of Capital Formation in Underdeveloped Countries*, London: Basil Blackwell.

Odaka, K. (1980): A Theory of Ancillary Firm Development, *Discussion Paper*, School of Economics, University of Philippines.

Oommen, M. A. (1981): Mobility of Small-scale Entrepreneurs, Kerala's Experience, *Indian Journal of Industrial Relations*, XVII (1).

———— (1993): *Essays on Keralá Economy*, Oxford and IBH, New Delhi.

Padhi, S. P. and Nair, K. N. (1992): Dynamics of LAnd Distribution: An Alternative Approach and Analysis with Rference to Kerala, *Working Paper No. 245*, Centre for Development Studies, Thiruvananthapuram.

Panikar, P. G. K. and Soman, C. R. (1985): *Health Status Of Kerala: Paradox of Social Development and Economic Backwardness*, Centre for Development Studies, Thiruvananthapuram.

Panikar, P. G. K., Krishnan, T. N. and Krishnaji, N. (1977): *Population Growth and Agricultural Development, A Case Study of Kerala*, Centre for Development Studies, Thiruvananthapuram.

Papola, T. S. (1987): Rural Industrialisation and Agricultural Growth: A Case Study of India, in R. Islam (ed) *op cit.*

_________ (1992): Rural Non-Farm Employment: An Assessment of Recent Trends, paper presented at *All-India Workshop* On Rural Non-Farm Employment, Institute for Social and Economic Change, Bagalore.

Park, A. and Johnston, B. (1995): Rural Development and Dynamic Externalities in Taiwan's Structural Transformation, *Economic Development and Cultural Change*,

Perlin, F. (1983): Proto-Industrialisation and Pre-Colonial South Asia, *Past and Present*, number 98.

Pillai, N. N. O. (ed). (1961): *Planning for Prosperity in Kerala*, Delhi Malayali Association.

Piore,M.and Sabel, C. (1984): *The Second Industrial Divide: Possibilities for Prosperity*, New York: Basic Books.

Preobrazhensky, E. (1965): *The New Economics*, Oxford: Oxford University Press.

Pyatt, G. (1996): *Poverty versus the Poor*, Dies Natalis Address on October 10, Institute of Social Studies, The Hague.

Radhakrishnan, P. (1989): *Peasant Struggles, Land Reforms and Social Change: Malabar 1836-1982*, Sage Publications, New Delhi.

Raghaviah, J. (1990): *Basel Mission Industries in Malabar and South Canara, 1834-1914: A Study of its Social and Economic Impact*, New Delhi : Gian Publications.

Raj, K. N. (1956): Small-scale Industries, Problem of Technological Change, *Economic Weekly*, April.

_________ (1961): Approach to the Planning of Kerala's Economy, in Pillai (ed). *Planning for Prosperity in Kerala*, Delhi Malayali Association.

_________ (1994): Has There Been a "Kerala Model", in AKG Centre for Research and Studies, *Abstracts*, Vol. 1.

Raj, K. N. and Tharakan, P. K. M. (1983): Agrarian Reform in Kerala and its Impact on the Rural Economy-A Preliminary Assessment in Ghose, A. K. (ed), *Agrarian Reform in Contemporary Developing Countries*, Croom Helm and St. Martin's Press, London and New York.

Raj, K. N. (1992): Land Reforms and Complementary Measures in Kerala, *IASSI Quarterly*, 19 (3).

Rakowski, C. A. (1994): Convergence and Divergence in Informal Sector Debate, *World Development*, 22 (4).

Ramachandran, V. K. (1996): On Kerala's Development Achievements, in Dreze, J. and Sen A. K. (ed) *Indian Development: Selected Regional Perspectives*, Oxford University Press, Delhi.

Rangarajan, C. (1982): Agricultural Growth and Industrial Performance in India, *Research Report No. 33*, Washington D.C.: The International Food Policy Research Institute.

Ranis, G. (1990): Rural Linkages and Choice of Technology, in Stewart, F. et al. (ed.), *The Other Policy*, London: IT Publications.

Rao, V. K. R. V. (1961): Industrialisation: Crux of Kerala's Economic Salvation, in Pillai (ed), *Planning for Prosperity in Kerala*, Malayali Association, Delhi.

Ratcliffe, J. (1978): Social Justice and the Demographic Transition: Lessons from India's Kerala State, *International Journal of Health Services*, 8 (1).

Reddy, R. M. (1988): The Incidence of Agricultural Labour in India: Variations over Time and Space, 1881-1981 with a Study of Vidarbha in Maharashtra, *Ph.D Thesis*, Jawaharlal Nehru University, New Delhi.

Roy, T. (1984): *Interstate Variations in Industrial Growth in India, 1960- 1979-80*, M.Phil Thesis, Centre for Development Studies, Thiruvananthapuram.

Rudra, A. (1961): Industrialisation of Kerala, in Pillai (ed), *Planning for Prosperity in Kerala*, Malayali Association, Delhi.

Rutten, Mario A. F. (1991): Capitalist Entrepreneurs and Economic Diversification: Social Profile of Large Farmers and Rural Industrialists in Central Gujarat, India, *Ph.D Thesis* Amsterdam: University of Amsterdam.

Saith, A. (1989): Location, Linkage and Leakage: Malaysian Rural Industrialisation in National Perspective, *Working Paper Series No. 56*, The Hague: Institute of Social Studies Advisory Service.

_________ (1990): Development Strategies and the Rural Poor, *The Journal of Peasant Studies*, 17 (2).

_________ (1992): *The Rural Non Farm Economy; Processes and Policies*, Geneva: International Labour Organisation.

Saluja, M. R. (1988): Data Base of the Unorganised Manufacturing Industry: An appraisal, in Suri, K. B. (ed) *op cit*.

Sandesara, J. C. (1981): *Small Industries in India: Evidence and Interpretation*, Indian Planning and Economic Policies, Ahmedabad: Gujarat Economic Association.

_________ (1988): Small Industry Development Programmes in India- Efficacy, Explanations and Lessons: Some Field Studies, in Suri, K. B. (ed) *Small Scale Enterprises in Industrial Development, The Indian Experience*, New Delhi: Sage Publications.

_________ (1991): Small Scale Industrialisation: the Indian Experience, in Thomas, H. et al (ed.), Small Scale Production, Strategies for Industrial Restructuring, London: IT publications.

Sathian, L. (1994): Analysis of Agricultural Growth in Kerala, in AKG Centre for Research and Studies, *Abstracts*, Vol. 2.

Schmitz, H. (1982): Growth Constraints on Small Scale Manufacturing in Developing Countries: A Critical Review, *World Development*, 10 (6).

_________ (1990): Small Firms and Flexible Specialisation in Developing Countries, *Labour and Society*, 15 (3).

Shaji, K. F. (1990): Dynamics of Rural Labour Markets: An Analysis of Emerging Agricultural Labour Shortage in a Kerala Region, *M.Phil Thesis*, Jawaharlal Nehru University, New Delhi.

Shand, R. T. (ed) (1986): *Off Farm Employment in the Development of Rural Asia*, Canberra, ANU.

Shea Jr., Thomas W. (1959): Barriers to Economic Development in Traditional Societies: Malabar, A Case Study, *Journal of Economic History*, 19 (4), December.

Sigurdson, J. (1978): Rural Industrialisation: A Comparison of Development Planning in China and India, *World Development*, 6.

Simmons, C. P. and Kalantaridis, C. (1994): Flexible Specialisation in the Southern European Periphery: The Growth of Garment Manufacturing in Peonia County, Greece, *Comparative Studies in Society and History*,

Singh, A. and H. Tabatabai (eds) (1992): *The World Economic Crisis and Agriculture in the Third World in the Eighties: The Changing Role of Agriculture in Economic Development*, Geneva: ILO.

Sreekumar, T. T. (1993): *Urban Process in Kerala, 1900-1981, Centre for Development Studies*, Thiruvananthapuram.

Staley, E. and Morse, R. (1965): *Modern Small Industry for Developing Economies*, New York: McGraw Hill Book Company.

Stewart, F. and Ranis, G. (1990): Macropolicies for Appropriate Technology: A Synthesis of Findings, in Stewart, F, Thomas, H and De Wilde, T. (ed), *The Other Policy*, IT Publications, London.

Storm, S. (1992): *Macroeconomic Considerations in the Choice of an Agricultural Policy, A Study into Sectoral Interdependence with Reference to India*, Amsterdam: Thesis Publishers: 23–55.

Streefkerk, H. (1985): *Industrial Transition in Rural India: Artisans, Traders and Tribals in South Gujarat*, Bombay.

Subramanian, K. K. (1990): Development Paradox in Kerala: Analysis of Industrial Stagnation, *Economic and Political Weekly*, 25 (37).

Subramanian, K. K. and Mohanan Pillai (1986): Kerala's Industrial Backwardness: Exploration of Alternative Hypotheses, *Economic and Political Weekly*, April 5.

_________ (1994): Modern Small Industry in Kerala- A Review of Structural Change and Growth Performance, *Working Paper No. 254*, Centre for Development Studies, Thiruvananthapuram.

Sundaram, K. and Tendulkar, S. D. (1988): An Approximation to the Size Structure of Indian Manufacturing Industry, in Suri, K. B. (ed) *op cit*.

Sunny, K. P. (1988): Consumption Behaviour in Kerala-A Study of National Sample Survey Data, 1965-66 to 1983, *M.Phil Thesis*, Centre for Development Studies, Thiruvananthapuram.

Suri, K. B. (1968): Towns: Size, Economic Structure and Growth, *Economic and Political Weekly*, 3 (32).

Syrquin, M (1988): Patterns of Structural Change, in Chenery, H and Srinivasan, T. N. (eds),*Handbook of Development Economics*, North Holland, Vol. 1.

Tambunan, T. (1994): *The Role of Small Scale Industries in Rural Economic Development,A Case Study in Ciomas Subdistrict, Bogor district, West Java, Indonesia*, Ph.D.Thesis, Erasmus Univesity, Rotterdam.

Thampy, M. M. (1990): Wage Cost and Kerala's Industrial Stagnation, Study of Organised Small Scale Sector, *Economic and Political Weekly*, 25 (37).

Tharakan, P. K. M. (1976): Migration of Farmers from Travancore to Malabar from 1930 to 1960: An Analysis of its Economic Causes, *M.Phil Dissertation*, Jawaharlal Nehru University, Centre for Development Studies, Thiruvananthapuram.

_________ (1996): Socio Religious Reform Movements, Process of Democratisation and Human Development - The Case of Kerala, South-West India in Rudebeck, L. et al (ed) *Democratisation in the Third World*, Sweden: Uppsala University.

Thirsk, J. (1961): Industries in the Countryside, in Fisher, F. J. (ed) *Essays in the Economic and Social History of Tudor and Stuart England,* Cambridge: Cambridge University Press

Thomas, H. et al (1991): *Small-scale Production, Strategies for Industrial Restructuring*, London: IT Publications.

UNDP, UNIDO, ILO and Govt. of Netherlands (1988): *Development of Rural Small Industrial Enterprises: Lessons from Experience*, Vienna: UNIDO.

Unni, J. (1991): Regional Variations in Rural Non- agricultural Employment: An Exploratory Analysis, *Economic and Political Weekly*, 26 (3).

Uribe-Echevarria, F. (1991): Small Scale Manufacturing and Regional Industrialisation: The Urban and Regional Development Perspective, *Working Paper Series No. 116*, The Hague: Institute of Social Studies.

Vaidyanathan, A. and Eapen, M. (1984): Structure of Employment in Indian Industry: Some findings from Census Data, wp. 199; Centre for Development Studies.

Vaidyanathan, A. (1986): Labour Use in Rural India: A Study of Spatial and Temporal Variations, *Economic and Political Weekly*, 21 (52).

_________ (1996): Socio-economic Characteristics of Villages in North Arcot: An Exploratory Note, Madras Institute of Development Studies, Madras.

Varghese, T. C. (1970): *Agrarian Change and Economic Consequences, Land Tenures in Kerala, 1850-1960*, Allied Publishers, Bombay.

Velu Pillai, T. K. (1940): *Travancore State Manual*, (hereafer TSM) Government of Travancore, Thiruvananthapuram.

Watanabe, S. (1983): Inter-sectoral Linkages in Japanese Industries: A Historical Perspective, in Watanabe, S. (ed) *Technology, Marketing and Industrialisation: Linkages between Large and Small Enterprises*: Macmillan.

Weijland, H. (1989): Rural Industrialisation: Fact or Fiction, in S. Soemardjan et al (eds), *Indonesian Design of Industrialism, Collected Papers for the Indonesian-Dutch Symposium at the Roosevelt Study Centre*, Part 1 Middleburg.

Wickramanayake, B. W. E. (1988): *Rural Industries in Transition: A Case Study of Southern Sri Lanka*, Ph.D.Thesis, Erasmus University, Rotterdam.

Zachariah, K. C. (1992): *Demographic Transition in Kerala in the 1980's: Results of a Survey in Three Districts*, with contributions by S.Irudaya Rajan, K. Navaneetham, P. S. Sharma, U. S. Mishra and P. R. Gopinathan Nair, Centre for Development Studies, Thiruvananthapuram and Gujarat Institute of Area Planning, Ahmedabad, April.

Zachariah, K. C. and Rajan, S. Irudaya (ed) (1997): *Kerala's Demographic Transition: Determinants and Consequences*, Sage, New Delhi.

Index